D0214852

Reductions in U.S. Domestic Spending

Reductions in
U.S. Domestic Spending

How They Affect State and Local Governments

Edited by
JOHN WILLIAM ELLWOOD

Transaction Books
New Brunswick (U.S.A.) and London (U.K.)

Copyright © 1982 by Transaction, Inc.
New Brunswick, New Jersey 08903

Library of Congress Catalog Number: 82−10975
ISBN: 0−87855−472−6 (cloth), 0−87855−932−X (paper)
Printed in the United States of America

Library of Congress Cataloging in Publication Data
Main entry under title:
Reductions in U.S. domestic spending.
    1. United States—Appropriations and expenditures.
2. Intergovernmental fiscal relations—United States.
I. Ellwood, John William.
HJ2051.R43   1982   353.0072'5   82−10975
ISBN 0−87855−472−6
ISBN 0−87855−932−X (pbk.)

To Barbara L. Ellwood

Contents

Part 2
Descriptions of Forty Major Budget Reductions
Affecting State and Local Governments

Part 3
Initial Assessment of Effects

List of Tables

Foreword

By Samuel H. Beer
Professor of American Politics, Boston College

Periodically the election of a president has brought to power a distinctive public philosophy drawing support from various parts of the country and giving direction to public policy. We think of the unionism of Daniel Webster and Abraham Lincoln, the progressivism of Theodore Roosevelt and Woodrow Wilson, the liberalism of Franklin Roosevelt and Lyndon Johnson. Each of these outlooks on public affairs also shaped a different balance of power in our federal system. No ideal blueprint of American federalism can be found in the past. Our federal system has never been static, but has changed radically over the generations in response to deep tides of national development.

In 1980 the presidential election installed in Washington a champion of the conservative attitudes that had been gathering force throughout the country for a generation. President Reagan articulated these attitudes in a distinctive vision of American society at home and abroad and a set of strategies for realizing it. As in the past, a new public philosophy implied a new federalism. This book is the first fruit of a major effort to understand President Reagan's new federalism. A necessary first step is to have some grasp of his emerging public philosophy. This foreword is a preliminary attempt to sketch its outlines. A definitive account would take far more than these few pages. This sketch will stay close to the financial history and analysis presented in this book, seeking to supply some of the political and intellectual history that can help explain the trends revealed by these data.

Ronald Reagan's conception of the function of government in general has deep roots in the American political tradition. It is the old and familiar vision of rugged individualism, at once a theory of economic progress and a social ethic. As economic theory, American individualism puts its faith primarily in the free market as the means by which material wants will be most effectively satisfied and the capacity to satisfy them most rapidly increased. As ethical theory, it finds in a free society the setting most likely to promote the virtues of individual autonomy and of the self-reliant, self-disciplined, self-made man. Appropriately, the main thematic term used in President Reagan's inaugural address was "freedom."

Individualism in these senses, however, is so deeply rooted in our culture as to be common to all the main currents of American political thought. Socialist doctrines have been preached in this country from its early days, but they have never caught on and the United States is the only industrialized nation without a major socialist party. Similarly, when the case for equality has been urged in the field of social policy, the object has normally been not equality of condition, but equality of opportunity. Our shared individualism, however, while excluding socialist and social democratic values, allows for sharp and significant differences over the role of government. Parties and presidents have fought major battles over how far government should intervene in order to sustain, perfect, supplement, or supplant the free market. That issue has been with us since Thomas Jefferson, the great individualist, and Alexander Hamilton, the great nationalist, divided the first administration of George Washington. To call these differences merely matters of degree masks crucial conflicts of interest and value. Franklin Roosevelt, as he often said, was trying to save capitalism, not destroy it; his view of the role of government and especially of the federal government, however, aroused the profound and reasoned opposition of Herbert Hoover.

In order to characterize a public philosophy in American politics, we need to identify the rationale that defines the balance sought between individualism and interventionism. In contrast with the pattern of government activity when he took office, Ronald Reagan seeks to shift the balance toward individualism. Or, to put the proposition in economic language, we may say he seeks to shift social choice away from public choice and toward market choice. That observation, while helpful, leaves crucial questions unanswered. One way of getting at these questions is to put them historically. The historical approach is fully justified by the authentic conservative note of President Reagan's rhetoric. In his inaugural address, for instance, he promised not innovation but restoration, proposing not some bold new initiative, but rather to "reverse the growth of government" and to restore "the balance between the levels of government." We may legitimately ask: restoration to what date?

As a self-declared American conservative, Ronald Reagan could reasonably be expected to share the views of other recent Republican presidents, such as Richard Nixon and Gerald Ford. One could push the search for contrast back in time, hypothesizing, as is often alleged, that the Reagan admin-istration seeks to repeal the New Deal and to restore the conservatism of Herbert Hoover—or even William McKinley. A middle position would find the rationale of the Reagan public philosophy in the pattern of government that prevailed not in 1932 and surely not in 1976, but rather in 1960, at the end of the Eisenhower administration. All these comparisons have some-thing to be said for them. In my judgment the historical approach strongly suggests that the main object of attack of the Reagan administration during its first year in office was the Great Society.

The data presented in this book are essential to any serious testing of these hypotheses. The study of which the book is a first report—an analysis of the effects on state and local governments of the reductions in domestic spending made in 1981—has two aspects. One is to discover and describe what the federal government has done—the outputs. The other aspect, and the main purpose of the study, is to characterize and explain the intergo-vernmental effects—the outcomes. The present volume concludes with a preliminary assessment of the outcomes, which will be more definitively presented and analyzed in a later publication when more complete data are in. This comprehensive analysis, conducted according to the method of pro-gram evaluation pioneered by Richard Nathan and conducted by his network of observers in the field, will enable us to assess the Reagan public philoso-phy in a major area of its impact on the country. These outcomes will, of course, be determined by conditions in the state and local communities and by the reactions of their governments, as well as by the policy changes embodied in federal action. The study of the outputs in the present volume, therefore, takes us much closer to the intentions of the administration. The bulk of the book consists of an exact quantitative description of what hap-pened to forty major federal programs, thirty-eight of which were grants to state and local governments. The president did not get everything he wanted, but, as these detailed studies show, his defeats pale into insignifi-cance compared with his overwhelming success. In these outputs we see the main achievements in domestic policy of Reagan's first year and the priori-ties of that achievement.

These outputs are changes in federal spending. The administration had other goals: tax cuts, which were won in a bill making the largest reductions in history, and regulatory reforms, which, like the tax cuts, were intended to lift burdens on enterprise. Yet the cuts in spending merit being called the main achievement of the first year since they were an indispensable condition for the tax cuts and, more important, virtually halted the rising trend in fed-eral domestic spending that had extended over decades. The president's statements of policy also reflected this priority for the spending cuts. As he explained his economic strategy, its thrust was to cut spending in order to reduce inflationary pressure and ease the burden of taxes. That was the stress of the opening paragraphs of his inaugural address; in his message laying out his economic recovery program a few weeks later, the proposed spending reductions were first in emphasis and their exposition accounted for more than half the text. On signing the budget and tax bills, Reagan proclaimed that "they represent a turn-around of almost half a century of a course this country has been on and mark an end to the excessive growth of government bureaucracy and government spending."

Judging by these words, the president seeks to return to a pre-New Deal conservative model. But is that actually the *status quo ante* to which the priorities of his spending cuts point?

First, a question of long-run perspective. If President Reagan is seeking to return to a time when government spending was not on the rise, he will have to go back a very long way. In the nineteenth century, when theories of laissez-faire were popular, it was widely believed that human progress would diminish the sphere of government action. As Adolph Wagner pointed out almost a century ago, however, an increase in public expenditure seems to be a natural consequence of economic growth. In the United States as in other industrialized countries, the ratio of public expenditures at all levels—federal, state and local—to gross national product (the PE/GNP ratio) has been increasing for generations. In this century the ratio for public domestic expenditures alone (the PDE/GNP ratio) rose from 5.1 percent in 1906 to 8.9 percent in 1927. If the "course" the president wishes to reverse is the increase in the PDE/GNP ratio, then we must return at least to the nineteenth century. But the comparison with William McKinley is surely not relevant and the president's preferred model must be found in some more recent time.

The upward trend may seem inexorable, but it has not been steady. Table F.1 enables us to break out the trend in domestic spending into periods, distinguishing the federal role.

Clearly, the New Deal led to a massive increase in the federal role. As a result the PDE/GNP ratio rose sharply between 1929 and 1949, even though state and local governments took a slightly smaller share of national resources. In the 1950s, however, there was a marked pause. The federal ratio hardly changed and a slight recovery in state-local spending was largely responsible for the modest increase in the rate of total public expenditure. The sixties and early seventies brought a new surge as marked as that of the New Deal and involving both levels of government, although the federal contribution, in a prodigious leap, took the lead.

TABLE F.1

Government Domestic Expenditure
From Own Funds as Percentages of GNP, Selected Years

Year	Federal	State and local	Total
1929	1.5	7.3	8.8
1949	7.5	6.9	14.4
1959	7.7	8.2	15.9
1969	9.9	10.4	20.3
1975	15.7	11.4	27.1

Source: Advisory Commission on Intergovernmental Relations, *Significant Features of Fiscal Federalism,* 1980–81 ed. (Washington, D.C.: Advisory Commission on Intergovernmental Relations, 1981), table 1.

The political and intellectual history of the half century fits fairly neatly into this profile of financial history. In spite of his campaign promise to balance the budget, Franklin Roosevelt presided over vast increases in federal spending. Much of this, however, was justified as for the "emergency" only. When, for instance, federal aid to state and local governments rose from $193 million in 1933 to $2.9 billion in 1939, almost all the increase consisted of emergency spending. In harmony with this view, when public assistance for the elderly and for "deserving widows" with dependent children was added to the Social Security Act of 1935, it was felt that this sort of government support would be phased out as the provisions for old age and survivors insurance took hold. As employment and the economy recovered during and after the war, the emergency spending of the earlier years indeed was radically scaled down. Apart from social insurance (and arguably farm price supports), the principal innovations of the New Deal did not take the form of spending, but consisted of great structural reforms, such as the Wagner Act, the Wage-Hour Act, the Tennessee Valley Authority, and the Securities and Exchange Commission, whose object typically was not to redistribute income but to redistribute power in the economy.

If we are to get the present in perspective, we must not overlook the pause in reform and in spending that followed the years of New Deal activism and lasted into the 1960s. This conservative resurgence was reflected in a Republican recovery after the war and in Eisenhower's victories in 1952 and 1956. In Congress from the late 1930s the "conservative coalition" of southern Democrats and Republicans exercized a strong restraining influence. And although the election of 1960 put an activist into the White House, Kennedy during his thousand days was continually frustrated by congressional resistance to his many initiatives. Then came the sudden and massive breakthrough of the mid-1960s. The legislative outpouring of the Great Society led to the enormous growth of federal activity in the late 1960s and early 1970s.

Like the New Deal, the Great Society produced a wave of federal centralization. The differences, however, were fundamental. The New Deal was hammered out under the massive material blows of the Great Depression. The Great Society emerged from the unprecedented well-being of the age of affluence. The climate of opinion that presided over its innovations, accordingly, inspired a new brand of liberalism deriving from new sources of influence.

The most evident of these new influences and a principal reason for the emphasis on spending was the technocratic component in government. Reflecting the rapid advances in the natural and social sciences during and after World War II, professionally and technically trained people had gained a new role in policy making. Defense and space programs were the most striking illustrations. Social engineering based on the emerging policy sciences also won new prestige. In the 1960s and on into the 1970s, new federal programs drew heavily upon "professional specialisms" in the fields of health, housing, urban renewal, transportation, welfare, education, the environment, energy, and poverty.

Given this inspiration, the social programs typically followed a services strategy. Professionally trained persons provided specialized services to certain categories of beneficiaries. The services were not delivered directly by the federal government, but by agencies of state and local governments. This strategy meant that spending rather than structural reform would be the principal mode of federal government action. In what must be regarded as the triumph of the new technocracy in social science, the latest developments in economic theory revealed that the consequent increase in public spending was itself justified and indeed necessitated by the conditions for more rapid growth. "Gone is the countercyclical syndrome of the fifties," wrote the chairman of Johnson's Council of Economic Advisers in 1966. "Policy now centers on gap-closing and growth, on realizing and enlarging the economy's noninflationary potential."

Looking back, one might be tempted to call this attitude "hubristic Keynesianism." Yet those years really were a time when public spending soared, but prices were stable, national product increased, and the big tax cut of 1964 actually did lead to an increase in federal revenue. The social programs of those years were not measures of redistribution taken at the expense of production, but themselves served to promote economic growth.

The Great Society was launched on a wave of material progress. Yet it was greatly concerned with deprivation, its central thrust being directed toward the urban crisis. In consequence, the spending innovations of the Great Society were carried out in great part by a new federalism whose most urgent focus was an unprecedented expansion of direct federal-city relations. This urban crisis was not just a matter of physical decay. In human terms it was the problem of "the poor," which meant especially the poor blacks of the central cities. The quintessential effort of the Johnson years was the antipoverty program.

The New Deal also had addressed a problem of deprivation. Springing from industrialism and the business cycle, that problem was perceived as one that could be met largely by full employment supplemented by social insurance. The poverty problem identified by the Great Society, however, had cultural as well as economic roots, and called for measures seeking to impart skills and to reorient motivations as well as to enlarge opportunities. Because of this definition of the problem and its consequent stress on technocratic actors and solutions, the Great Society in contrast to the New Deal led to a far greater emphasis on public expenditure as the basic mode of government action.

The innovations proceeding from this approach were one major source of the upward bow in Wagner's curve that is registered in table F.1. Another major source, however, had a different rationale and derived from another and older origin. This latter type of federal spending consisted of direct payments to individuals, of which by far the larger part came from trust funds for unemployment compensation and above all social security. Table 1.1 in chapter 2 brings out the relative contribution of this type of spending to the surge of the 1960s and 1970s. Federal grants ("grant payments" and "other state and local grants") rose at a new and higher rate in the 1960s. "Direct payments," however, increasingly dominated federal domestic spending in the 1960s and 1970s.

In origin, social security, like unemployment compensation, went back to the New Deal and the Social Security Act of 1935. With its claim to be "insurance" and its use of an incomes rather than a services strategy, social security was sustained by a rationale quite different from the public assistance or the poverty programs and far more easily reconciled with the ethic of American individualism. Logically, the concept of social insurance had expanded step by step over the years to cover the needs of not only old age and widowhood, but also disability and finally medical and hospital care.

Distinct in origin and rationale, these two sources of the great surge in spending—social security and federal aid, the New Deal salient and the Great Society salient—met different fates at the hands of the Reagan budget cutters in 1981. Only the most gingerly advances were made toward reducing social security spending, and these were immediately thrown back by fierce bipartisan opposition in Congress. The brunt of the conservative attack was borne by programs deriving from the Great Society initiatives.

Indrawing this distinction, the Reagan strategy departed radically from the conservatism of Presidents Nixon and Ford. Like all conservatives from Hoover to Reagan, they strongly favored decentralization. Unlike the Reaganites, however, they agreed that many of the social and economic problems identified by the Great Society programs did demand government intervention and, moreover, that, although the federal government should radically relax its control over attempts to deal with these problems, it should continue to extend substantial aid to the state-local efforts. In brief, the new federalism introduced by President Nixon, while rejecting the centralized welfare state of Kennedy and Johnson, advocated a welfare state that would have been markedly decentralized, but only marginally diminished and still federally sustained.

In pursuing these goals, President Nixon acted on the economic premises that underlay the spending surge of the 1960s. As he once said, ''We are all Keynesians now.'' During Nixon's administration, social security benefits were repeatedly and substantially raised: in 1969 by 15 percent, in 1971 by 10 percent, in 1972 by 20 percent. During the 1970s, ''direct payments'' took the lead in rate of growth as compared with grants. Yet federal aid also continued to rise until 1978 when in constant (though not current) dollars it declined for the first time in decades.

The principal innovation of Nixon's new federalism was general revenue sharing. Other forms of less restrictive federal aid were also favored and by the end of the decade about a quarter of all federal aid was conveyed by broad-based grants. Conceived as a complement to these measures, Nixon's very expensive family assistance plan—a form of negative income tax (which was not enacted)—was intended to help the ''working poor'' become and remain self-supporting. In contrast, President Reagan has been outspoken in his opposition to general revenue sharing, has said that ideally block grants should be only a step toward ultimately ending all federal aid, has denounced any form of negative income tax, and in 1981 produced a set of budget reductions that, according to the concluding chapter of this volume, bear with special severity upon the working poor. As shown in the design of the new block grants, the Reagan administration has also sought greatly to reduce direct federal-city relations, which President Nixon after initial hesitation had accepted and developed.

The main point of this brief sketch of financial history has been to bring out the distinction between the New Deal and the Great Society in both public philosophy and government action. This sketch has also suggested that, judging by the outputs of 1981, the pattern of policy toward which the

Reagan administration is tending is to be found in the pause under Eisenhower that separated the two great periods of liberal advance. A closer look at the priorities expressed in the budgetary cuts of 1981 will elaborate this conclusion.

Table 1.4 of chapter 2 gives a broad overview. The last column in its lower half lists the annual growth rates in constant dollar outlays for fiscal 1982 in comparison with the previous year and against the background of previous patterns since 1951. The new priority for defense, of course, stands out. These figures also display the contrast between the treatment of what I have called the New Deal and the Great Society salients of federal spending. The rate of growth for direct payments actually rose slightly, while the rate for grants declined. The largest proportionate reduction among all six types of spending was made in the discretionary grants to state and local governments.

The detailed analyses refine these broad inferences. Tables 1.11 and 1.12 in chapter 4 set out the changes in the 232 accounts which bore virtually the whole of the reduction in budget authority and outlays. As explained in that chapter, budget authority calculations are a better measurement of the policy preferences being expressed, except for trust fund spending where outlays are a more accurate indicator. In terms of budget authority, the discretionary direct grants to state and local governments were reduced by 37.7 percent, while entitlement grants were cut by 23.5 percent, the grant reductions together totaling $35.4 billion. This was more than half the total budget authority reduction. When social insurance entitlements are separated from other direct payments they show a reduction, but of only 3.4 percent—in dollar terms, $8.6 billion. To pause over the big reductions in these 232 accounts and to follow the detailed analysis of the changes in the forty major programs set out in part 2 is to call the roll of the major social and economic legislative enactments of the 1960s and 1970s.

"Most of the money saved by the fiscal 1982 budget cuts," observe the authors of the concluding chapter of this volume, "was saved in programs administered by state and local governments." In this sense, President Reagan's new federalism was the main field within which his preferences in domestic policy were expressed during his first year in office. Accordingly, the assessment of the impact of these new policies on the country is primarily focused on their effects on state and local governments and the services they provide their citizens. The outputs leading to these outcomes are not a mere miscellany. They reflect the logic of ideas as well as the pressures of politics. Congressional action largely embodied the priorities of the public philosophy that shaped the president's submissions.

Judged by the outputs of the first year, that public philosophy does not aim at repealing the New Deal. The major effort of the first year was not directed at reversing the great structural reforms of the New Deal. And that characteristic innovation of Rooseveltian liberalism, social security, even with its later expensive additions, was barely touched. The reader may object that to judge only by one year's record is to leave out the president's further intentions. The objection is well taken. The public philosophy of any president takes time to reveal itself. My hypothesis is tentative. Ronald Reagan's admiring references to President Roosevelt and his advocacy of a "social safety net" may or may not prove to be bogus. Still, the thought that Ronald Reagan may go down in history as a "New Deal conservative" cannot be suppressed. I am reminded of a definition an older colleague once offered: "A conservative," he said, "is a person who was a liberal when young and has not changed his mind."

Acknowledgments

This volume is the first publication resulting from a study of the effects of cuts in federal domestic spending and related policy changes undertaken during the first two years of the Reagan administration. The study is being conducted by the Princeton Urban and Regional Research Center of the Woodrow Wilson School, Princeton University.

The study was supported by a grant from the Ford Foundation. The study team would like to express its appreciation to Susan V. Berresford, vice president, Program Division, and to Shepard Forman, program officer in charge, for having taken personal interest in this work and providing useful suggestions.

The analysis in parts 1 and 2 of this volume could not have been undertaken without cost estimates and other budget data provided by the Congressional Budget Office. We thank Alice Rivlin, the director of CBO, and James Blum, assistant director of the Budget Analysis Division. Most of all we thank the many CBO staff members who patiently explained what Congress had done when it enacted the Omnibus Reconciliation Act of 1981. To the extent that we failed to understand what had occurred, the error is ours.

In addition to the authors of the various chapters, the following individuals provided valuable assistance. Thomas Calhoun, Gary Ferrell, and Gilbert Gutierrez of the University of California, Riverside, researched the regulatory changes associated with the implementation of the budget reductions. Jacqueline V. Crawford, an M.P.A. student at the Woodrow Wilson School, provided research assistance to Robert F. Cook for the material on the effects of the tax reductions. Assistance in the preparation of part 3 was provided by Mitchell H. Wolfe and John R. Lago, research assistants at the Urban and Regional Research Center, and by Charles M. Cameron, a Ph.D.

student at the Woodrow Wilson School, and Amy R. White, a 1982 M.P.A. graduate of the School.

Hannah Kaufman of the Princeton University Computer Center helped prepare the computer program used in the photocomposition system by which this book was typeset. Photocomposition was performed by J. Schiller, Inc., of Edison, N.J.

The various versions of the manuscript were typed by Lori L. Davison, Michele Pollak, and Kathy Shillaber. The manuscript was edited by David L. Aiken and Mary Capouya. The authors, however, are responsible for what they have written.

Finally, we should like to express our appreciation to Donald E. Stokes, dean of the Woodrow Wilson School, for his steady support of the Princeton Urban and Regional Research Center and of this study.

Contributors

Robert F. Cook is a senior research associate for the Manpower Demonstration Research Corporation and a research economist at the Woodrow Wilson School, Princeton University. He has co-authored numerous books and reports on manpower issues. His most recent publication is *Public Service Employment: A Field Evaluation* (The Brookings Institution, 1981).

Philip M. Dearborn is vice president of the Greater Washington Research Center and a lecturer in public administration at Howard University. He participated in this research as a senior associate at the Princeton Urban and Regional Research Center. Mr. Dearborn is the author of "Financing Washington Area Local Governments in the 1980s," in *Greater Washington in 1980* (Greater Washington Research Center, 1980) and has consulted extensively on urban financial issues.

John W. Ellwood is an associate professor of public policy and management at the Amos Tuck School of Business Administration, Dartmouth College. While this book was in preparation, he was a researcher in public policy at the Woodrow Wilson School, Princeton University. He was previously on the staff of the Congressional Budget Office. He has published widely on budgeting and the U.S. Congress; his most recent article is "Making and Enforcing Federal Spending Limitations: Issues and Options" *(Public Budgeting and Finance,* spring 1981).

Clifford A. Goldman is a visiting senior researcher and a visiting lecturer at the Woodrow Wilson School, Princeton University. He was treasurer of New Jersey from 1977 until 1982.

Catherine H. Lovell is a professor of administration at the Graduate School of Administration, University of California at Riverside. She has written extensively on intergovernmental relations. Her most recent article is "Some Thoughts on Hyperintergovernmentalization" *(Annals of Public Administration,* scheduled for winter 1982).

Richard P. Nathan is the director of the Princeton Urban and Regional Research Center and a professor of public affairs at the Woodrow Wilson School, Princeton University. Before going to Princeton, he was a senior fellow at The Brookings Institution where he directed field network evaluation studies of several federal programs. His publications include *Revenue Sharing: The Second Round* (The Brookings Institution, 1977).

Advisory Committee
for Field Network Evaluation Study

Samuel H. Beer, Thomas P. O'Neill, Jr., professor of American politics, Boston College

George F. Break, professor of economics, University of California at Berkeley

Martha Derthick, director of governmental studies, The Brookings Institution

Mitchell I. Ginsberg, New York City; former dean, School of Social Work, Columbia University; former administrator of Human Resources Administration, New York City

Edward M. Gramlich, professor of economics, University of Michigan

T. Norman Hurd, Albany, New York; former budget director, New York State

Maynard H. Jackson, former mayor of Atlanta

Francine F. Rabinovitz, professor of public administration, University of Southern California; vice president, Hamilton, Rabinovitz & Szanton, Inc.

Robert D. Reischauer, vice president, The Urban Institute; former deputy director, Congressional Budget Office

Allen Schick, professor of public affairs, University of Maryland; former senior specialist, Congressional Research Service

Elmer B. Staats, Washington, D.C.; former comptroller general of the United Staes

Richard H. Ullman, professor of international affairs, Woodrow Wilson School, Princeton University

Robert C. Weaver, emeritus professor at Hunter College, City University of New York; former secretary, U.S. Department of Housing and Urban Development

Aaron Wildavsky, professor of political science, University of California at Berkeley

PART 1

The Federal Budget
and the 1981 Policy Changes

1

Introduction

By John W. Ellwood

During the first year of his presidency, Ronald Reagan scored a series of congressional victories that culminated with the passage of the Omnibus Reconciliation Act of 1981 (P.L. 97-35). At the signing ceremony, the president stated his belief that its enactment represented "a turn-around of almost half a century" of federal expansion and marked "an end to the excessive growth in government bureaucracy and government spending" that had characterized this period.[1] Almost immediately, however, a debate began over the size of the budget reductions and their potential effects on different classes of citizens and on the finances, services, and politics of state and local governments.

The debate became more diffuse because of confusion as to exactly what had been accomplished. Some of this confusion resulted from the use of different sets of economic assumptions by different actors in the budget process. The Congressional Budget Office (CBO) forecast 2.9 percent real growth (that is, growth even after taking inflation into account) in the gross national product (GNP) for calendar year 1982, while the administration more optimistically forecast 4.2 percent real growth for the same period. Because federal spending is highly sensitive to the state of the economy, CBO's estimates of total budget outlays for fiscal year 1982 were $13.5 billion higher than those of the administration. Yet CBO and the administration were but two of many actors in the process. At various times during the budget debate, differing sets of economic assumptions were put forth by House Democrats, House Republicans, Senate Republicans, Senate Democrats, and the Office of Management and Budget (OMB).

---

1. *New York Times,* August 14, 1981, p. A−10.

Confusion was widespread also because of the complexity of the changes that were advocated by the administration and enacted by Congress in the reconciliation act. In order to bring about lower levels of domestic spending, Congress modified programs in 232 budget accounts, some of them significantly. Some of the changes were made under such time pressure—as when the House of Representatives adopted the version of the reconciliation act that came to be known as Gramm-Latta II—that many members of Congress confessed that they were not sure what they were voting for or against.

During and after the budget debates of 1981, it appeared to be in everybody's interest to magnify the extent of the changes and reductions. Those who were in favor of the changes wanted to show that their political efforts had been successfully realized. Those who opposed the new policies sought to magnify the potentially harmful effects of these policies so as to mobilize opposition groups. For example, those who had supported the establishment of nine new block grants, which were intended to return decision making over many programs to the states, tended to inflate the size and importance of the grants in order to justify the political capital that had been used in their creation and to build momentum for the enactment of more block grants. Those who opposed these programs, on the other hand, exaggerated their impact so as to mobilize groups to oppose future action.

But doubts about claims of a massive change began to be heard. David Stockman, the director of the Office of Management and Budget, said of the Omnibus Reconciliation Act of 1981, "There's less there than meets the eye."[2] Six months later, when a declining economy caused federal outlays to rise and receipts to fall, the administration asked for even larger budget reductions and more significant shifts in federal responsibilities in its fiscal year 1983 budget.

Just how significant were the domestic policy changes made in 1981? What effects will they have? This book provides background material and analysis related to these questions. Because the largest domestic reductions were made in programs administered by state and local governments, the book concentrates on federal changes affecting the services, finances, and politics of these governments.

The book is the first product of a multiyear study by the Princeton Urban and Regional Research Center of how these new domestic priorities have affected American states and localities. The study employs teams of field evaluators to assess how these changes affect the governments and people of fourteen states and fourteen major cities, thirteen suburban jurisdictions, and thirteen rural towns within these states. Much of the material in this volume

---

2. William Greider, "The Education of David Stockman," *The Atlantic Monthly,* December 1981, p. 51.

was initially assembled to inform the field evaluators of the exact nature of the federal changes that could be expected to affect their jurisdictions. It quickly became evident that the political conflict over the adoption of the budget reductions had created such general confusion that this material could be of use to a much wider audience. Government agencies such as the Office of Management and Budget and the Congressional Budget Office, which had the capability to summarize the programmatic and budgetary effects of the 1981 changes, were so overwhelmed with the requirements of supporting further rounds of changes that they lacked the time to undertake a close and widely accessible analysis of past events.

The aim of this book is to provide perspective on the size, nature, and impacts of the budget reductions enacted in 1981. It does so by providing a consistent set of budget data that can be used to determine the magnitude and distribution of the budget changes and by analyzing the major changes that are expected to affect state and local governments and the people they serve.

The volume is divided into three parts. Part 1 provides an overview of the changes and the processes that were employed to bring them about. In addition to this introduction, it consists of five chapters. Chapter 2 contains a survey of the growth of federal domestic spending, an analysis of the causes of that growth, and a discussion of possible reasons these factors had so much less effect in calendar 1981 than in previous attempts to control the growth in spending. Chapter 3 explains how Congress controls the level of federal spending and how it legislated the domestic reductions of 1981. Chapter 4 analyzes the size and distribution of the budget reductions.

Chapter 5, written by Robert F. Cook, sets out the effects of the Economic Recovery Tax Act of 1981. This legislation will not only bring about the largest reduction of federal revenue in American history, but, because of the structure of the tax codes of many states and localities, it could also cause significant loss of revenue in these jurisdictions. Because the operating budgets of all but two states and almost all local governments cannot be in deficit, such a loss of revenue would require these jurisdictions either to separate their tax provisions from those of the federal government, to raise their taxes, to reduce their spending, or to do all three.

The last chapter in part 1 discusses a frequently overlooked topic—the implementation of changes in budget policy through regulations. The actual effects of the domestic policy changes that were enacted in 1981 will in large part depend on how they are implemented through the regulatory process. In this chapter Catherine Lovell summarizes the federal regulatory process and analyzes the approaches that have been employed by the Carter and Reagan administrations to "reform" that process.

Part 2 of the volume describes the programmatic and budgetary changes in forty budget accounts affecting state and local governments. The accounts were selected either because the reconciliation act reduced their fiscal year 1982 funding by a minimum of $100 million or, in the case of the new block grants, because they fund programs reflecting an important change in governmental policy. Each section summarizes the programs in the account prior to the changes enacted in 1981, sets out the changes that were made by Congress, describes relevant changes in regulations, and assesses how the changes have affected the program's goals and nature. Each description is accompanied by a summary table that incorporates the Congressional Budget Office estimates of the budgetary effects of the changes for fiscal years 1982, 1983, and 1984.

Part 3 of the book contains the initial report of the field network evaluation study team on the effects of the 1981 changes in a sample of fourteen states and fourteen large cities within them. This report, written by Richard P. Nathan, Philip M. Dearborn, Clifford A. Goldman, and associates, analyzes data collected by field associates between October 1, 1981 and December 31, 1981.

Each of the field associates is a political scientist or an economist who lives in one of the states under study. After gathering data from interviews with government officials and others and from budget and program documents, the associates present their analytical findings, using a common reporting format. The authors of the preliminary report in this volume drew generalizations and conclusions from these field reports. Their report presents initial findings on the groups most affected by the domestic policy changes made by Congress in 1981; it includes separate sections on the effects of changes in entitlement programs, medicaid, employment and training programs, block grants, and capital grants.

2

Controlling the Growth
of Federal Domestic Spending

By John W. Ellwood

The Reagan administration's 1981 successes in persuading Congress to cut taxes and reduce domestic spending followed several decades of almost continuous spending increases. By 1981 many observers of the American political system had come to believe that the system had a bias toward ever greater levels of spending. For this reason, many commentators have called the Reagan administration's victories an historic reversal of this trend.

This chapter reviews the pattern of the growth in federal spending since fiscal year 1951, sets out a commonly held view of the causes of that growth, and suggests several reasons why the growth in federal domestic spending was curtailed during the first year of the Reagan administration.

THE GROWTH OF FEDERAL SPENDING

In fiscal year 1981, the federal government spent $657.2 billion for programs contained in its budget.[1]   Of this amount, $159.7 billion, or 24.3 percent, was spent for national defense programs. Another $68.7 billion (10.5 percent of total outlays) went to pay interest on the national debt. An additional $57.4 billion (8.7 percent of the total) was used for a wide variety of federally run domestic programs, such as the space program; energy research and development; agricultural research and extension support; federal security operations such as the Coast Guard, FBI, and Secret Service; air traffic controllers; and the support of the federal bureaucracy.

---

1. The term "program" has no legal meaning to the federal government. In this book it is used interchangeably with the term "budget account." The federal budget is made up of more than a thousand such budget accounts, which fund its various programs.

Of the rest of the budget, the largest amount—$316.6 billion, or 48.2 percent of all budget outlays—went for income assistance programs. These programs—labeled payments to individuals in most budget documents—are of two general types:

- *Payments made directly by the federal government.* Included in this category are the largest federal domestic programs—social security, railroad retirement, military and civil service retirement, unemployment assistance, veterans' benefits, student loans and grants for higher education, and medicare.[2]   In fiscal year 1981, they accounted for 42.1 percent of all budget outlays, or $276.7 billion.

- *Payments that are federally funded but administered by state and local governments.* In this subcategory are many of the programs that are frequently grouped under the label ''welfare''—medicaid, aid to families with dependent children (AFDC), housing assistance, and child nutrition programs. These grant programs spent $39.9 billion in fiscal year 1981, or 6.1 percent of all budget outlays. In most budget documents the programs included in this subcategory are also classified as grants to state and local governments.

A third type of federal grant goes not to individuals but to state and local governments for their operations or capital projects. In fiscal year 1981, the federal government spent $54.8 billion, or 8.3 percent of all budget outlays, for such grants. This category of spending includes three kinds of grants:

- *categorical grants,* which provide federal support for purposes that are specifically set out in statutes and regulations;

- *block grants,* which provide federal support with fewer restrictions, and

- *general revenue sharing,* which provides federal funds that can be spent as recipient jurisdictions see fit.

The total of federal grant support flowing through state and local governments is the sum of (1) grant payments to individuals and (2) other grants to state and local governments. In fiscal year 1981, this total was $94.7 billion in outlays, or 14.4 percent of all budget expenditures.

Table 1.1 shows the level of outlays for the various types of budget activity in four fiscal years—1951, 1961, 1971, and 1981. A second way of analyzing the growth of federal activity is needed, however: the annual rate of growth. This is shown in table 1.2 for the three decades separated by these

---

2. This category of direct payments to individuals is frequently further divided into (1) programs that are funded from trust funds drawn from an earmarked tax or contribution—such as social security, medicare, disability insurance, and the governmental employee retirement programs—and (2) programs whose funding comes from general revenue—such as supplemental security income (SSI), higher education assistance, trade assistance benefits, and veterans' benefits.

TABLE 1.1
Federal Budget Outlays Since Fiscal Year 1951

Type of spending	FY1951	FY1961	FY1971	FY1981
IN BILLIONS OF CURRENT DOLLARS				
National defense	21.8	46.6	75.8	159.7
Payments to individuals	10.0	27.4	78.7	316.6
Direct payments	(8.7)	(24.5)	(67.7)	(276.7)
Grant payments	(1.3)	(2.9)	(11.0)	(39.9)
Other state and local grants	1.0	4.2	17.1	54.8
Net interest	4.7	6.7	14.8	68.7
All other operations	8.0	12.9	23.8	57.4
Total outlays	45.5	97.8	210.2	657.2
IN BILLIONS OF 1972 CONSTANT DOLLARS				
National defense	48.7	74.8	81.5	76.6
Payments to individuals	16.6	37.2	81.8	163.6
Direct payments	(14.4)	(33.3)	(70.4)	(143.0)
Grant payments	(2.2)	(3.9)	(11.4)	(20.6)
Other state and local grants	2.3	7.4	18.1	27.1
Net interest	8.2	9.6	15.5	35.5
All other operations	17.9	20.6	25.6	27.8
Total outlays	93.7	149.6	222.5	330.6
AS A PERCENTAGE OF THE GROSS NATIONAL PRODUCT				
National defense	7.0	9.2	7.4	5.6
Payments to individuals	3.2	5.4	7.6	11.1
Direct payments	(2.8)	(4.8)	(6.5)	(9.7)
Grant payments	(0.4)	(0.6)	(1.1)	(1.4)
Other state and local grants	0.3	0.8	1.7	1.9
Net interest	1.5	1.3	1.4	2.4
All other operations	2.6	2.5	2.3	2.0
Total outlays	14.6	19.2	20.4	23.0

Source: Office of Management and Budget, *Federal Government Finances: 1983 Budget Data* (Washington: Office of Management and Budget, February 1982), tables 10, 11, and 12, pp. 59–78.

four fiscal years and for the entire period of 1951 to 1981.

Both ways of analyzing federal spending must be used because some types of spending grew at faster rates than others but still account for a relatively small portion of the federal budget. For example, the programs in the "other grants to state and local governments" category grew at an average

TABLE 1.2
Average Annual Growth Rates of Federal Outlays

Type of spending	Fiscal years			
	1951–1961	1961–1971	1971–1981	1951–1981
ANNUAL PERCENTAGE GROWTH IN CURRENT DOLLARS				
National defense	10.8	5.4	7.9	8.0
Payments to individuals	10.8	11.3	15.1	12.4
Direct payments	(11.1)	(10.9)	(15.3)	(12.4)
Grant payments	(8.2)	(14.6)	(14.1)	(12.3)
Other state and local grants	16.7	15.2	12.9	14.9
Net interest	3.9	8.3	16.8	9.7
All other operations	7.0	7.0	10.5	8.2
Total outlays	8.8	8.1	12.2	9.7
ANNUAL PERCENTAGE GROWTH IN 1972 CONSTANT DOLLARS				
National defense	6.6	1.3	0.5	2.4
Payments to individuals	8.6	8.3	7.3	8.1
Direct payments	(9.0)	(7.9)	(7.5)	(8.1)
Grant payments	(6.1)	(11.5)	(6.4)	(8.0)
Other state and local grants	13.2	9.6	4.7	9.1
Net interest	1.8	5.0	8.8	5.2
All other operations	3.6	3.0	1.9	2.8
Total outlays	4.2	4.2	4.1	4.1

Source: Average annual percentage growth rates calculated from outlay data contained in Office of Management and Budget, *Federal Government Finances: 1983 Budget Data* (Washington, D.C.: Office of Management and Budget, February 1982), tables 10 and 11, pp. 59–70.

annual rate of 14.9 percent between fiscal years 1951 and 1981, while national defense programs grew by only 8.0 percent per year. Nevertheless, national defense spending accounted for 22.5 percent of the increase in budget outlays between fiscal years 1951 and 1981 while the programs in the "other grants" category made up only 8.1 percent of the increase.

When measured in current dollars, the amount of money spent on federal programs listed in the budget (budget outlays) was thirteen and a half times greater in fiscal year 1981 than it was in 1951. Much of this increase, however, was due to increases in the price level. When inflation is taken into account by expressing outlays in 1972 constant dollars, budget expenditures grew a little less than fourfold during these thirty years (see table 1.1). Moreover, once the effect of inflation is taken into account, budget outlays appear to have grown fairly steadily, increasing at average annual rates of 4.2 percent during the 1950s, 4.2 percent during the 1960s, and 4.1 percent during the 1970s (see table 1.2).

Federal budget outlays as a percentage of the gross national product (GNP) grew at an even more modest pace during the three decades. In fiscal year 1951, budget outlays equaled 14.6 percent of GNP,[3] and reached a post-World War II high of 23.0 percent in fiscal year 1981 (see table 1.1).[4] Over the three decades the federal budget's share of GNP increased at an average annual rate of 1.8 percent.

PATTERNS OF EXPENDITURE GROWTH

What led to the growth of federal spending between 1951 and 1981? Three components of federal expenditures—national defense, payments to individuals, and grants to state and local governments—account for 81.4 percent of the growth in budget outlays.

Growth in defense expenditures accounted for 22.5 percent of the increase in all budget outlays between 1951 and 1981 (see table 1.1), but the impact of defense spending was not caused by high growth rates during this period: Once the effects of inflation are taken into account, the average annual increase in defense outlays was declining during the 1950s and 1960s, and dropped to a negative 0.5 percent during the 1970s (see table 1.2). Rather, defense spending had a large impact on total growth in federal outlays because of the high initial level of defense spending in the 1950s, when the United States built up its forces for the Korean War and the succeeding period of "cold war." Between fiscal years 1950 and 1954, defense outlays increased from 29.1 to 65.3 percent of all federal expenditures, while nondefense outlays actually declined by just over $5.5 billion. As a result of the steady decline in the growth rate of defense spending, coupled with increases in the rates of other types of spending, by fiscal year 1979 defense outlays accounted for the smallest percentage of the GNP since fiscal year 1950 and

---

3. The 1951 percentage is not characteristic of the ratio during the 1950s. During the entire decade, budget outlays averaged 18.2 percent of GNP. The fiscal year 1951 figure is the second lowest (after fiscal year 1948) since World War II.

4. Much of this increase has been due to the poor performance of the economy in recent years. While the GNP in 1972 constant dollars (real GNP) grew at an average annual rate of 4.0 percent during the 1950s and at a 4.2 percent rate during the 1960s, its growth performance declined to a 3.4 percent rate during the 1970s. Joseph Pechman and Robert Hartman have shown that when federal budget outlays are expressed in constant dollars under full-employment conditions, the federal share of full-employment GNP peaks during the Vietnam War years of the late 1960s, declines somewhat during the 1970s, and stabilizes at a level roughly equivalent to that of the early 1960s. See Joseph A. Pechman, ed., *Setting National Priorities: The 1980 Budget* (Washington, D.C.: The Brookings Institution, 1979), p. 26.

the smallest proportion of all budget outlays since fiscal year 1940.

By contrast, federal payments to individuals and grants to state and local governments have increased in their proportion to GNP and to total federal outlays. Between 1951 and 1981, grants to states and localities grew faster than any other type of federal activity—14.9 percent per year in current dollars and 9.1 percent per year in 1972 constant dollars. Those programs providing income-transfer payments to individuals grew almost as rapidly—12.4 percent per year in current dollars and 8.1 percent per year in constant dollars (see table 1.2). Because their growth rates were applied to a much larger base, direct federal payments to individuals accounted for 50.1 percent of the growth in all outlays over the thirty-year period, while the growth in grants to states and localities led to only 8.8 percent of the total increase in outlays.[5]

Funding for the major income-transfer programs providing payments to individuals—social security, railroad retirement, military and civil service retirement, veterans' benefits, medicare and medicaid, housing assistance, and the various types of public assistance—has come to dominate the federal budget over the past three decades. These programs accounted for 22.0 percent of all budget outlays in fiscal year 1951, but 48.2 percent thirty years later. Several developments contributed to this growth. New programs such as medicare and medicaid were established, and benefit levels and eligible populations were expanded for existing programs.

Although spending on these programs increased in current dollars over all three decades, the rate of growth in inflation-adjusted constant dollars was slower during the 1970s than it had been in the preceding decades. As table 1.2 shows, total payments to individuals grew by 7.3 percent in constant dollars in the 1970s, compared with 8.6 percent in the 1950s and 8.3 percent in the 1960s. The growth rates in table 1.2 show that grants to state and local governments grew most rapidly during the 1950s, increasing fourfold between fiscal years 1951 and 1961. Just under half of this growth (46.2 percent), however, was due to the expansion of one account—the interstate highway program, which caused outlays from the highway trust fund to rise from $396 million to $2.6 billion during this decade.

The 1960s saw a large expansion in the number and cost of grants to state and local governments, which included many of the income-transfer programs that were initiated or dramatically expanded during the war on poverty of the Johnson administration. Payments to individuals administered by state

---

5. If one shifts those payments to individuals that are administered by states and localities to the grants category, the growth in grants was responsible for 15.1 percent of the total growth in budget expenditures, while the remaining accounts funding direct payments to individuals led to 43.8 percent of the total outlay growth.

and local governments increased at an average annual rate of 14.6 percent between fiscal years 1961 and 1971, as medicaid was initiated and such programs as AFDC and child nutrition were expanded. Other grants to state and local governments also expanded during these years. These grant programs included model cities, urban renewal, community services, and aid to elementary and secondary education. Outlays for this type of activity grew at a faster rate than any other type of spending during the 1960s—15.2 percent per year in current dollars and 9.6 percent annually when adjusted for inflation.

Funding for grants continued to grow during the first seven years of the 1970s. Funding for transfer payment programs administered by states and localities rose at an annual rate of 14.1 percent during the decade of the 1970s as benefits of the medicaid, assisted housing, and child nutrition programs were expanded and the number of people eligible for these programs increased. Funding for other direct grants rose at a 12.9 percent yearly rate—4.7 percent in constant dollars—as new grant programs such as general revenue sharing, wastewater treatment, and public service employment were initiated, and existing programs such as federal aid to elementary and secondary education and higher education loans and grants were expanded.

The direct operations of the federal government have not been a major factor in the overall growth of budget outlays. Between fiscal years 1951 and 1981, funding for this type of activity increased at an average annual rate of 2.8 percent once inflation was taken into account. As a percentage of the GNP, funding for these programs fell from 2.6 percent in fiscal year 1951 to 2.0 percent in fiscal year 1981.

Finally, the increased cost of paying the interest on the public debt has affected the overall growth of federal outlays. In constant dollars, net interest on the public debt grew at an average annual rate of 1.8 percent during the 1950s. Its real rate of growth increased to 5.0 percent during the 1960s, and rose again to 8.8 percent during the 1970s. In fiscal year 1981, such interest payments made up 2.4 percent of GNP, compared with 1.5 percent in 1951.

OTHER TYPES OF FEDERAL ACTIVITY

Although the programs that make up the federal budget account for most of the federal government's efforts to allocate benefits to various groups, a growing amount of federal activity is carried on outside of the budget. This volume concentrates on changes in programs whose financing is included in the budget. It is well to remember, however, that, as indicated in table 1.3, the federal activities that are excluded by law from the budget's totals have in recent years been expanding faster than on-budget outlays.

TABLE 1.3

**Levels and Growth Rates of Six Types of Federal Activity
During the 1970s**

Type of activity	Level of activity (billions of dollars)			Percentage average annual growth rate FY1976–FY1981
	FY1971	FY1976	FY1981	
On-budget activity				
(outlays)	210.2	364.5	657.2	12.6
Off-budget activity				
Off-budget agencies (outlays)	0.0	7.3	21.0	24.1
Direct loans (new obligations)	0.0	6.7	16.3	19.8
Loan guarantees (new obligations)	16.1	11.2	76.5	54.5
Government-sponsored enterprises[a] (outlays)	0.0	4.6	33.4	59.8
Tax expenditures	51.7	97.4	228.6	18.7

Sources: On-budget outlays and off-budget outlays, direct loans, loan guarantees, and outlays of government-sponsored enterprises from *Budget of the United States Government: Fiscal Year 1983* (Washington, D.C.: Executive Office of the President, February 8, 1982). Tax expenditure data from Congressional Budget Office, *Tax Expenditures: Current Issues and Five-Year Budget Projections For Fiscal Years 1982–1986* (Washington, D.C.: Congressional Budget Office, September 1981), p. 35.

a. Less than $50 million in fiscal year 1971.

For example, between fiscal years 1976 and 1981, outlays for the programs that make up the budget increased at an average annual rate of 12.6 percent. But during this same period, outlays for a number of programs whose funding is excluded by law from the budget increased at a 24.1 percent annual rate. Similarly, new obligations for federal direct loans for programs that by law are not included in the budget increased at a 19.8 percent annual rate between fiscal years 1977 and 1981. The increase in new obligations for off-budget loan guarantees during this period was even more dramatic—an annual average rate of increase of 54.5 percent. Outlays for government-sponsored enterprises also grew faster than on-budget expenditures, rising at a 59.8 percent annual rate.

Tax expenditures are provisions in the tax code that grant a special privilege to groups or individuals. Because they have been established to foster certain types of activity—such as capital formation, private homeownership, or the support of a particular industry—many observers equate such tax subsidies with subsidies from programs in the budget. (Many conservatives, however, reject this concept on the ground that it implies that all revenue belongs to the government unless a special provision is granted.) Since fiscal year 1976, the loss in federal revenue from tax expenditures has increased at an annual rate of 18.7 percent, compared with the 12.6 percent annual rate of on-budget outlay growth.

Finally, there is general agreement that federal regulatory activity has grown in recent years. We do not have a good measure of such activity, because the number of pages or the number of regulations in the *Federal Register* is a poor if not misleading measure of the impact of such activity. All that can be said, therefore, is that the growth of federal regulations during the 1970s has been perceived by many in the private sector and some state and local governments to be more burdensome than the increase in taxation needed to pay for the programs funded through the budget.

REDIRECTING SPENDING PRIORITIES—THE CARTER YEARS

Although the Reagan victories of 1981 are generally seen as a major break with past spending patterns, many of the new priorities were anticipated during the last three years of the Carter presidency. Chapter 4 provides a full analysis of the overall effects of the budget redirection of 1981. Here we will simply outline President Reagan's basic budget goals and see to what extent President Carter had already started working toward the same or similar objectives. In its public statements, the Reagan administration included the following among its policy goals:

1. Reducing the overall rate of growth in federal spending.
2. Increasing the rate of growth in national defense spending.
3. Cutting federal domestic spending, except for those income-transfer programs that the administration included under the "safety net."
4. Reducing federal support for state and local governments, and allowing those jurisdictions greater freedom in allocating their federal grants.
5. Returning many direct federal operations—such as support for fossil energy research and production—to the private sector or to the states.

Table 1.4 compares the average annual growth rates during the last three fiscal years of Jimmy Carter's presidency with the equivalent measures for the fiscal years 1971 to 1978 and OMB's estimate of the effect of the actions of calendar year 1981 on fiscal year 1982 spending. The Reagan priorities are clearly evident in the last column of the table. But it is also clear that the reversal in priorities occurred around fiscal year 1978 rather than 1982.

TABLE 1.4

Growth Rates of Federal Outlays During the Carter Years

Type of spending	FY1971– FY1978	FY1978– FY1981	FY1981– FY1982 (estimate)
ANNUAL PERCENTAGE GROWTH IN CURRENT DOLLARS			
National defense	4.9	15.0	17.4
Payments to individuals	14.9	15.4	11.0
Direct payments	(15.2)	(15.4)	(12.1)
Grant payments	(13.5)	(15.5)	(3.9)
Other state and local grants	17.5	1.9	−9.3
Net interest	13.4	24.8	20.8
All other operations	12.6	5.7	−6.5
Total outlays	11.5	13.6	10.4
ANNUAL PERCENTAGE GROWTH IN 1972 CONSTANT DOLLARS			
National defense	−2.5	4.1	7.8
Payments to individuals	7.9	5.7	3.1
Direct payments	(8.2)	(5.7)	(4.0)
Grant payments	(6.7)	(5.6)	(−3.4)
Other state and local grants	9.3	−6.1	−16.6
Net interest	6.3	14.6	11.5
All other operations	4.1	−3.2	−11.2
Total outlays	4.1	4.0	2.3

Source: Average annual percentage growth rates calculated from outlay data contained in Office of Management and Budget, *Federal Government Finances: 1983 Budget Data* (Washington, D.C., February 1982), tables 10 and 11, pp. 59–70. Growth rate from fiscal year 1981 to fiscal year 1982 is based on the Feburary 1982 OMB estimate of fiscal year 1982 outlays.

Whether because of President Carter's own policies or because of the wishes of Congress, several significant shifts occurred in federal spending during Carter's administration. Defense outlays in constant dollars went from a negative growth rate of 2.5 percent to a positive one of 4.1 percent.[6]

---

6. The increase in the growth rate of defense outlays during the Carter years was partly the result of prior increases in authority for defense spending that had been granted during the Ford administration. From fiscal year 1970 through fiscal year 1975 the amount of authority (budget authority) for defense spending in constant dollars decreased every year, with the real growth rate declining at a yearly rate of 4.8 percent. Fiscal years 1976 and 1977 saw real increases in defense budget authority of 4.1 and 5.4 percent. After a real decrease in fiscal year 1977 of 1.5 percent, the last three Carter years saw constant dollar defense budget authority increasing at a 4.9

The real growth rate of grant expenditures switched from a positive 9.3 percent to a negative 6.1 percent, and the real growth rate of spending for other direct federal operations was reduced from a positive 4.1 percent to a negative 3.2 percent.[7] Only the rapid rise in the cost of interest on the public debt prevented a decline in the constant-dollar growth rate of budget outlays during the last three fiscal yearsof the Carter presidency. When net interest outlays are excluded, the average annual growth rate of budget expenditures in constant dollars declines from 4.0 percent for fiscal years 1971−78 to 3.0 percent for fiscal years 1978−81.[8]

THE REAGAN REDIRECTION OF SPENDING PRIORITIES

If many of the budget priorities sought by the Reagan administration had been set in motion around 1978, were the events of 1981 really a break from the past? On a number of grounds, the answer is clearly yes.

First, the actions of 1981 dramatically accelerated the pace of the shifts initiated during the Carter administration. Where defense spending was budgeted for increases of between 4 and 5 percent under Carter, the Reagan budget of 1981 implied real growth of between 8 and 14 percent.[9] While the Carter years saw real growth in the "other grants" category decline to a neg-

---

percent yearly rate.

7. Some might argue that the reduction of grant outlays between fiscal years 1978 and 1981 was simply the result of the phasing out of grants that had been enacted to counter the 1974−75 recession. These grants included the CETA title VI public service employment program; local public works supported by the Economic Development Administration; and the antirecession fiscal assistance program, which provided countercyclical revenue sharing for states and localities in fiscal need. Two points can be made against this argument. First, during past economic cycles, supposedly countercyclical programs tended to become or be replaced by structural efforts as the recession ended. What was unique about the 1978−81 period was that temporary programs turned out to be temporary. Second, even when the outlays for the three major stimulus grants are left out of the total, the Carter years saw a decline in the growth rate of outlays for other grants to state and local governments. For example, when we include the three stimulus programs the average annual growth rate in constant dollars for the programs in the "other grants" category was reduced from a positive 8.8 percent for fiscal years 1975−78 to a negative 6.1 percent for fiscal years 1978−81. When the three stimulus programs are left out of the calculation, a reduction still takes place: The annual growth rate declines from a positive 2.5 percent for 1975−78 to a negative 0.4 percent for 1978−81.

8. The decline in the growth rate of nondefense, noninterest outlays is more dramatic. Between fiscal years 1971 and 1978 these expenditures rose at an average annual rate of 7.2 percent when measured in constant dollars. Using the same measure, they only grew at a 2.6 percent annual rate from fiscal year 1978 to fiscal year 1981.

9. The 14 percent figure is implied by the acceleration of authority for defense spending. Such authority for the purchase of new weapons systems will cause defense outlays to increase dramatically during the 1980s.

ative 6.1 percent annual rate, the policies of 1981 sought to accelerate that decline to a negative 16.6 percent annual rate. And while other direct federal operations declined in constant dollars at a 3.2 percent annual rate between fiscal years 1978 and 1981, the spending priorities of 1981 caused them to decline by 11.2 percent in real terms between fiscal years 1981 and 1982.[10]

Second, during the Carter years few new programs for payments to individuals were created, and expansion of existing programs slowed. The 1981 budget changes went farther; they reduced the number of beneficiaries and the size of benefit payments of existing programs. This reduction is most clearly seen in grants to state and local governments for payments to individuals—that is, the medicaid, AFDC, housing assistance, and child nutrition programs. In current dollars, spending on these programs grew by 15.5 percent between fiscal years 1978 and 1981, while the growth rate in constant dollars was 5.6 percent; both of these figures were within a percentage point or two of the rate between fiscal years 1971 and 1981 (see table 1.4). By contrast, the 1981 budget actions called for reducing the growth rate in these programs to 3.9 percent in current dollars and a negative 3.4 percent in constant dollars.

This leads to the final and most significant difference between the budget strategies and priorities of the Carter years and the Reagan administration. Beginning around fiscal year 1978, the Carter administration adopted the goal of reducing federal expenditures as a percentage of the gross national product. The goal was to be accomplished, however, not by dramatically reducing current domestic spending—although this was done in individual programs—but by keeping the growth rate below the rate of the increase in the gross national product. As GNP rose, the ratio of outlays to GNP would fall.

The Reagan administration also sought to reduce federal outlays as a percentage of GNP. But it was not willing just to rely on increases in the GNP to achieve this goal; the rate of federal spending was to be cut in current dollars. Because defense spending was growing, meeting this goal required significant reductions in the rate of domestic outlay growth and rather dramatic current-dollar reductions in expenditures for those domestic programs that were not part of the "social safety net." As the economy declined during 1982, the Reagan administration was forced to seek further reductions to compen-

---

10. It could be argued that the unanticipated severity of the 1981−82 recession will undo these spending priorities as federal budget outlays rise for additional unemployment compensation benefits. The funding for programs in the defense, other grants, and other direct payments categories is not automatically responsive to economic change. Therefore, the OMB estimates of February 1982 in table 1.4 should be accurate for the programs in these categories unless further policy changes are enacted by Congress affecting outlays in fiscal year 1982.

sate for rising outlays in those programs—unemployment compensation, social security, food stamps—that are sensitive to changes in the economy. The number of programs making up the "social safety net" has shrunk. But the goal of the administration has remained the same—to gain control over what had become a politically uncontrollable rate of domestic spending.

THE REAGAN ACHIEVEMENT

In 1981 the Reagan administration overcame a series of formidable forces to achieve significant reductions in federal domestic spending. These forces consisted of the desire to placate special interests by adopting new spending programs. By the end of the 1970s, those seeking to control federal domestic spending had lost hope that these forces could be overcome.

The imbalance of power between those seeking to restrain domestic spending and those seeking to create new programs arose from a simple fact: The benefits of each federal program were concentrated on a small group, each member of which stood to gain substantially, while the costs were spread over a large number of taxpayers, each of whom paid only a few dollars per program. As government grew, it was in the interest of each special group and the government agency most closely connected with that group to ask for larger and larger governmental subsidies. Elected officials found themselves in a difficult position: If they voted against a program increase or championed a reduction, they would encounter well-organized opposition from the program's beneficiaries, but gain little praise from taxpayers in general. Moreover, as the power and sophistication of special-interest groups increased, the influence of those institutions that traditionally had acted as brakes on the pressures of special interests, such as the presidency, OMB, and political parties, declined.[11]

A detailed analysis of the forces that enabled the Reagan administration to overcome this traditional pattern is beyond the scope of this volume. It is obvious, however, that President Reagan and his staff and allies in Congress exploited a series of economic, political, and institutional factors to win the enactment of his 1981 legislative program. Economically, the president had the advantage of following an administration whose stewardship of the economy was perceived—rightly or wrongly—to be a failure. During the last half of the Carter administration, the real GNP increased at only 1.5 percent

---

11. A good brief summary of the theories of those social scientists who believe that modern representative democracy is institutionally biased in favor of ever greater levels of government spending is set out in Aaron Wildavsky, *How to Limit Government Spending* (Berkeley: University of California Press, 1980), pp. 58−70. For an international perspective on the same topic, see Daniel Tarschys, "The Growth of Public Expenditures: Nine Models of Explanation," *Scandinavian Political Studies,* vol. 10 (1975), pp. 9−31.

per year, less than half the 3.2 percent average rate of real GNP growth during the previous ten years. This sluggish economic performance did not result in a moderation of the rate of inflation, however. During calendar 1979 and 1980 the consumer price index, measured on a December-to-December basis, rose at an average rate of 12.9 percent.

If one considers a hypothetical family of four with one breadwinner working at a manufacturing job, one would have to go back to 1961 to find lower real spendable weekly earnings ($167.21 in 1977 dollars) than existed in December 1980 ($171.19 in 1977 dollars). In such an environment, the public desired a change in policy and wanted Congress to give the new administration a chance to bring about such a change.

The desire of the American public for change was enhanced by the perception that the Democratic party lacked new ideas. President Reagan was able to point out that his opponents offered no alternatives to his policies except those that had already been tried and found wanting. In this environment, Ronald Reagan reintroduced politics—in the best sense of that term—to the debate over budget priorities and reinvigorated the effectiveness of the presidency as a political office. Following a period when some were beginning to talk of a limited presidency, the president and his staff put on a textbook performance of how to use the powers of the office to mobilize public and interest-group support and to build and maintain political coalitions.

It is possible that President Reagan would not have won his 1981 victories if, in 1974, Congress had not made major changes in its budget procedures with the enactment of the Congressional Budget and Impoundment Control Act of 1974. Previously, budget accounts (programs) were reviewed and voted on one at a time; as a result, the imbalance between the desires of those benefiting from the programs and the will of the public at large continued to exist. But the 1974 act contained a set of procedures—called the reconciliation process—that allowed the Reagan administration in 1981 to shift the debate and voting on budget matters from the parts to the whole. In so doing it achieved its victory. To understand what happened in 1981, therefore, one has to understand what reconciliation is and how it works. That is the topic of the next chapter.

3

How Congress Controls Expenditures

By John W. Ellwood

This chapter explains how Congress controls federal spending and analyzes the procedures Congress used to achieve the budget reductions in 1981. It also assesses the implications of these procedures for the likelihood of achieving further reductions.

HOW CONGRESS CONTROLS FEDERAL EXPENDITURES

Congress does not directly control the level of federal spending that will occur in a particular year. Rather, it grants the executive branch authority (referred to as *budget authority*) to enter into *obligations,* which are legally binding agreements with suppliers of goods or services or with a beneficiary. When those obligations come due, the Treasury Department issues a payment. The amount of payments, called *outlays,* over an accounting period called the fiscal year (running from October 1 to September 30) equals federal expenditures for that fiscal year. Federal spending (outlays) in any given year, therefore, results from the spending authority (budget authority) granted by Congress in the current and in prior fiscal years.

Thus, the reader has to distinguish among three distinct aspects of the spending process: budget authority, obligations, and outlays. Congress provides (enacts) budget authority. Outlay figures that appear in congressional documents—and in this document—are estimates. They are estimates, moreover, that frequently are very sensitive to executive branch actions and changes in economic and demographic conditions.

Budget authority can be provided in three distinct ways, described in the following sections.

Model 1: Authorization Followed by Appropriation

Most federal programs are set up and funded in the following manner. First, the program is created through an authorization. This statute sets out the rules under which the program will work. The power to create authorizations is under the jurisdiction of the legislative committees of Congress.

The authorization process accomplishes two goals. It sets up a program (the *program authorization*), and it sets a limit on the amount of funds that can be appropriated for the program *(authorization of appropriations)*. The length of the program authorization and the authorization of appropriations limit can differ. A statute can authorize a program for several years, but set funding limits for only a year or two. In addition, some programs have specific authorization of appropriation limits for each year during which the program is authorized, while others have a single global appropriations limit for the entire multiyear period of the authorization, and some simply use the term "such sums as may be appropriated" as the limit for appropriations. In the past, authorization for appropriations limits frequently have been double the actual amount of budget authority that Congress eventually provided.

Once an authorization of appropriations has been passed, Congress funds the program by granting budget authority in appropriation acts. The budget authority is granted to an appropriation account rather than to a program or an authorization. At the beginning of the fiscal year 1982 budget cycle (in the spring of calendar 1981), there were 1,314 appropriation accounts. Some accounts funded a single large authorization, such as the account which funded medicare. Others either funded several authorizations or a single small program.

The appropriations acts fall under the jurisdiction of the appropriations committees. Each year Congress passes thirteen regular appropriations acts and one or more supplemental appropriations acts. If Congress fails to enact one or more appropriations acts before the beginning of a fiscal year, it must pass a *continuing resolution*. Such a resolution is an appropriations act that maintains a level of budget authority for an agency for a specified period until the Congress is able to pass the new budget authority levels.

Most federal grants to states and localities are funded by the process described by this model. It should be noted, however, that more than half of federal spending results from entitlement funding, which is described under models 2 and 3 below.

For many federal construction and procurement programs, and for federal housing subsidies, the budget authority that Congress provides this year will not result in federal outlays until the obligations come due one or more years in the future. This means that much of a particular year's outlays (16.5 percent in fiscal year 1981) results from budget authority granted in past years.

Because of this lag between budget authority and outlays, some of the federal budget cuts will not result in dramatic outlay reductions until several years from now. This is particularly true for capital (or project) grants to fund construction projects[1] and for housing subsidies.

Model 2: Entitlements

For several programs, authorization statutes contain unlimited grants of budget authority. These programs include social security, aid to families with dependent children (AFDC), medicare, child nutrition, unemployment insurance, and the various federal employee retirement accounts. They make up most of the payments to individuals category. They do not go through the yearly appropriations process. Their expenditures are listed in appropriations accounts, but the appropriations committees do not control the level of their funding.

Four factors control the amounts that are spent for these programs: (1) economic conditions, especially the cost of living and level of unemployment; (2) the number of people in groups eligible for program benefits; (3) the rules determining who is eligible, and (4) the rules specifying the levels of benefits. Anyone is entitled to benefits from these programs who meets certain criteria—an income level, an age level, a certain marital status, or having contributed to a trust fund. Most entitlements have tied the level of their benefits to a measure of inflation, most frequently the consumer price index (CPI).

Congress can attempt to control spending under these entitlement programs only indirectly, by rewriting eligibility rules or changing benefit levels. In congressional documents (and in this volume), the levels of budget authority and outlays for these programs are estimates until they become "actuals" at the end of the fiscal year. Changes in the economy can easily bring about spending levels that are far different from the estimates. For example, a one percentage point rise in the CPI will cause budget authority and outlays to rise by $200 million for social security and by $200 million for medicaid and medicare during the initial fiscal year. A one percentage point increase in the unemployment rate will lead to a $5.1 billion rise in spending for unemployment compensation and a $600 million rise in food stamps payments during the initial fiscal year.[2]

---

1. Capital grant programs include the wastewater treatment program, the community development block grant (CDBG) and urban development action grant (UDAG) programs, and the programs operated by the Economic Development Administration (EDA) of the Commerce Department.

2. A few programs, such as interest on the public debt, operate like entitlements in that they cannot be controlled by the annual appropriation process, although technically they are funded through a permanent appropriation.

Model 3: Appropriated Entitlements

Certain entitlement programs—most notably veterans' compensation, supplemental security income (SSI), food stamps, and medicaid—do go through the yearly appropriations process. For these programs, therefore, it is at least theoretically possible to control funding in three ways: (1) by making changes in the entitlement provisions contained in the program's authorization, (2) by "capping" the program through its authorization of appropriations limit, or (3) by limiting the amount of budget authority that is appropriated.

Previous attempts at controlling spending levels of mandated entitlements through appropriations "caps" or budget authority limits have not been successful. Typically a funding shortage arises halfway through the fiscal year, and Congress is told that unless it passes a supplemental appropriation, the food stamp program (or some other appropriated entitlement) will shut down during the last few months of the fiscal year.

HOW CONGRESS ACHIEVED THE CUTS

During the first session of the 97th Congress, budget reductions were achieved through three types of legislative procedures—rescissions, the reconciliation process, and annual appropriation acts.

After the Reagan administration on March 10, 1981, submitted its revisions of the Carter administration's fiscal year 1982 budget, Congress passed a supplemental appropriations act for fiscal year 1981 (P.L. 97-12) that rescinded (took back) $14.3 billion budget authority for fiscal year 1981. Because changes in budget authority sometimes lead to delayed changes in outlays, this action had the effect of reducing fiscal year 1982 outlays by $2.1 billion, according to Congressional Budget Office (CBO) estimates.

The most significant budget cuts of 1981 were achieved with the enactment of the Omnibus Reconciliation Act of 1981 (P.L. 97-35) on July 31, 1981. This act contained amendments to more than 250 authorizations that affected 232 budget accounts. According to CBO estimates—which will be used throughout this book—these changes reduced fiscal year 1982 budget authority by $53.2 billion and lowered fiscal year 1982 outlays by $35.2 billion below what they would have been if the budgetary policies of fiscal year 1981 had been continued into fiscal year 1982.

Because most federal programs—including most of those affected by the reconciliation act—are funded through models 1 and 3, the appropriations committees had a third opportunity to make budget reductions in individual accounts: by reducing the levels of fiscal year 1982 budget authority for programs funded through the thirteen annual appropriations acts. Congress took advantage of this opportunity.[3]

During the appropriations process, Congress granted the Reagan administration's request for significant increases in defense, increasing defense budget authority by $20.3 billion dollars above current levels or by 10.4 percent in real terms. In the nondefense areas of the budget, the appropriations process brought about further reductions. Nondefense budget authority for fiscal year 1982 was reduced by an additional $14.2 billion and nondefense outlays for the same fiscal year were cut by an additional $12.0 billion.

By December 1981, when the first session of the 97th Congress ended, the effects of rescissions, reconciliation, and appropriations actions could be totaled. All fiscal year 1982 budget authority had been reduced by $45.1 billion and all outlays by $44.1 billion below what they would have been if current policy had been continued. Nondefense budget authority had been reduced by $62.8 billion and nondefense outlays by $44.7 billion.

To understand how the rescission, reconciliation, and appropriations reductions were achieved, it is necessary to understand Congress's budget process.

The Congressional Budget Process

Congress each year must adopt at least two concurrent resolutions on the budget. These resolutions are not laws; they are mechanisms that allow Congress to coordinate its debate on appropriations for individual programs within the context of an overall fiscal policy and budgetary allocation.

The first concurrent resolution on the budget must be adopted in May of each year. It sets targets for five budgetary aggregates: (1) total budget authority, (2) total outlays, (3) total revenues, (4) the surplus or deficit (revenues minus outlays), and (5) the total public debt. The first resolution also sets targets for budget authority and outlays for nineteen federal budget functions such as national defense, agriculture, health, and income security.

Once it sets these targets, Congress proceeds to enact various spending and revenue bills. The spending bills either create budget authority or control entitlements.

In September, Congress must pass a second budget resolution. This resolution still sets targets for the nineteen functions, but it also sets ceilings for total budget authority and total outlays and a floor under total revenues. Once this resolution has been passed and once the new fiscal year begins on

---

3. All but three of the thirteen regular appropriations bills for fiscal year 1982 had been enacted by December 1981. On December 11, 1981, Congress passed a continuing appropriation bill to cover nonentitlement funding for the departments of Education, Health and Human Services, and Labor. In spring 1982, that continuing resolution was extended through the end of fiscal year 1982 (September 30, 1982).

October 1, a member of either the House or Senate can, by raising a point of order, prevent consideration of any bill that would cause total budget authority or CBO's estimate of total outlays to exceed the ceilings, or that would cause CBO's estimate of revenues to fall below the floor. Such a bill cannot be taken up until compensating budget actions are taken (cuts in other programs or raising other taxes) or until Congress passes a new concurrent resolution on the budget that makes room for the new action.

Reconciliation Process

What happens if, for example, Congress passes a budget resolution that calls for a balanced budget while the sum of various spending bills implies a large deficit? The reconciliation process was written into the Congressional Budget Act to provide a mechanism for Congress to reconcile these two types of actions.

The budget act's drafters assumed that Congress would reconcile the second budget resolution with the expenditure and revenue bills that were passed between the first and second budget resolutions. As the budget process developed after the budget act's passage in 1974, it became evident that for the reconciliation process to be effective, the process would have to be associated with the first budget resolution. This is what occurred in 1981.

The reconciliation process has two stages: the passage of reconciliation instructions and the passage of a reconciliation bill—a law—to fulfill those instructions.

Reconciliation Instructions

As part of the first concurrent resolution, the House and Senate have the option of mandating their committees to report out by a certain date legislation that will cause budget authority, outlays, and revenues (as estimated by CBO) to meet certain targets. (These mandates usually involve cuts in budget authority and outlays and increases in revenues, but the reverse can be the case under the budget act.)

Because the committees of the House and Senate are artificial creations of each body, the House and Senate have the power to order them to take certain actions. Reconciliation instructions are not a bill or a law. Rather, they are internal orders mandating that certain committees report out legislation.

In the spring of 1981, the congressional allies of the Reagan administration decided that the best way to pass the president's budget package was to use the reconciliation process. The Senate (in April) and the House (in May) instructed their committees to report out legislation by June 12, 1981, that would achieve $36 billion in outlay savings as measured against CBO's baseline. What has come to be called Gramm-Latta I was the administration version of such instructions, in the House.[4]

Once the various committees receive these instructions, they can achieve budget savings anywhere within the programs under their jurisdiction. Each committee sends its legislative changes to the budget committee of the appropriate house. The budget committee groups the changes, without changing their substance, into a reconciliation bill. This bill then goes through the normal legislative process: enactment by each chamber, a conference to iron out differences in the bills passed by the two chambers, agreement by each chamber to the conference report, and signing by the president.

On June 17, 1981, the House and Senate budget committees assembled the legislative changes that had been reported by the instructed committees into two reconciliation bills, H.R. 3982 and S. 1377. CBO estimated at the time that these two bills would lower outlays by $37.7 billion and $39.6 billion, respectively. The Senate easily approved its version on June 25 by an 80-to-15 vote. In the House a conservative substitute replaced the reconciliation bill that had been framed by the various instructed committees. The substitution (called Gramm-Latta II) carried by a roll call vote of 217 to 211.

Compromises on the differing versions were reached in a mammoth conference. Between July 15 and July 29, more than 250 legislators met in fifty-eight subconferences. The conference agreement was adopted by a voice vote in the House and by an 80-to-14 roll call vote in the Senate on July 31. President Reagan signed the act on August 13, 1981.

The reconciliation act of 1981 was not the first reconciliation act enacted by Congress. In 1980 Congress enacted the Omnibus Reconciliation Act of 1980 (P.L. 96-499), which reduced CBO's estimate of fiscal year 1981 budget authority by $3.1 billion and its estimate of outlays by $4.6 billion. The 1980 law also raised CBO's estimate of revenues by $3.6 billion.

Much of the debate that was reported in the press centered around the allocation of the cuts in the reconciliation bill. What came to be called Gramm-Latta II was the administration substitute that set out its preferred allocation of cuts. The debate over Gramm-Latta II also centered around the various ways of making cuts. The administration wanted to make permanent program changes that would guarantee that the cuts would be effective for several years into the future, while some committees sought to make short-term cuts that could be reversed should the political climate change.

---

4. The version of the instructions was named after Reps. Phil Gramm (D., Texas) and Delbert L. Latta (R., Ohio), its primary sponsors.

What Was Cut?

The reconciliation bill did not affect appropriations directly. To see how the cuts were achieved and what this implies for future cuts, it is best to return to the three models of funding that were set out at the beginning of this chapter.

Model 1. For programs that are set up with an authorization and then funded through yearly appropriations, the reconciliation act achieved savings by lowering the authorization of appropriations limit so that the appropriations committees would have to enact lower levels of budget authority. For these programs—which include most grants to state and local governments—the reconciliation act amended the authorization of each program to lower the authorization of appropriations limit. In doing so the act achieved a minimum cut. Further cuts are possible when each program receives its appropriation. Although the appropriations committees cannot appropriate above the authorization of appropriations limit, they can grant less budget authority than is specified in the limit.

Model 2. About 40 percent of the reduction in budget authority and 39 percent of the outlay savings in the reconciliation act was achieved from entitlement programs. These cuts were made by amending the authorization of each entitlement to change the eligibility rules and benefit formulas. Whether or not these changes achieved the required level of savings was determined by cost estimates produced by the CBO.

Because entitlements do not go through the appropriations process, the changes made by the reconciliation act are actual rather than minimal cuts. They are also permanent cuts; to undo them or to make more cuts, Congress would have to reamend the authorizations of the entitlements.

Model 3. Congress had two options for appropriated entitlements: either change the entitlement and benefit rules or place an appropriations cap on the programs by lowering the authorization of appropriations limit. The Reagan administration successfully fought for the first alternative as a permanent and more effective way to achieve savings.

Because these programs must go through the yearly appropriations process, however, the Reagan administration had an opportunity to achieve a second round of reductions. At its urging, Congress used the appropriations process to further reduce the fiscal year 1982 budget authority for several of the major appropriated entitlements—food stamps, assisted housing payments, and public housing subsidies.

ADVANTAGES OF THE RECONCILIATION PROCESS

Given the current structure of federal spending, it is unlikely that major reductions can be made in the rate of domestic spending growth in the future unless Congress continues to use its reconciliation process. Reconciliation has two unique advantages—it is primarily directed at changes in entitlement programs (described by model 2), and it allows those who seek to curb spending to shift the focus of debate from individual programs to the size of the entire budget.

As originally conceived, the reconciliation process was directed at controlling the levels of expenditures of those programs subject to the annual appropriations process (programs described by models 1 and 3). The authors of the Congressional Budget Act assumed that Congress might pass its first concurrent resolution in May, but then pass appropriations acts containing more budget authority than would be called for by the targets of the second budget resolution. But, in practice, when actual budget authority has exceeded the targets of the resolutions, the appropriations committees have not been the reason. The problem—if it is a problem—has been caused by the growth of spending in entitlement programs. The accounts for these programs are funded as described in models 2 and 3. The appropriations committees, therefore, have no legal way to limit spending entitlement programs (model 2), and no practical way to do so for appropriated entitlements (model 3).

When the reconciliation process was switched from the second to the first budget resolution, its focus shifted from controlling excess spending from accounts funded under model 1 to limiting excess expenditures from accounts funded under models 2 and 3. Because, under the Congressional Budget Act, appropriations bills cannot be enacted until the first concurrent resolution on the budget has been passed, reconciliation instructions contained in that first continuing resolution cannot require the appropriations committees to rescind budget authority that has yet to be granted. But the reconciliation instructions can require the legislative committees and the tax committees to change authorizations.

The reconciliation instructions of calendar 1981 led to the modification of many major entitlements, such as social security, unemployment compensation, AFDC, medicare, medicaid, and food stamps. By requiring authorizing committees to lower various authorization of appropriation limits, the reconciliation process also was used to limit the discretion of the appropriations committees to grant budget authority.

This second procedure caused great resentment among members of Congress. It violated the traditional congressional norm of separating programmatic decisions from funding actions. It attacked the rationale of the appropriations committees to the point that some members of Congress suggested eliminating the appropriations committees and shifting their power to grant budget authority to the various legislative committees. Should this resentment continue to build, it is unlikely that the reconciliation process will survive. A likely outcome, therefore, is that in the future reconciliation will only be directed against entitlements, appropriated entitlements, and tax legislation.

Congress has been unable or unwilling to control the growth of entitlement expenditures for two reasons: Many of the programs are very popular and the programs are shielded from movements to limit spending by their multiyear or permanent status. Their popularity is mostly due to their large number of beneficiaries. Overcoming such popularity is a political problem for those who want lower levels of federal spending. Obviously there is an alternative to reducing the outlay levels of these programs—raising taxes to cover the additional expenses.

The problem of the permanent or multiyear length of the authorizations of these entitlements does create an institutional bias toward more spending that can be modified through use of the reconciliation process. This bias results from a political fact: Those who seek to maintain spending levels for annually appropriated accounts must achieve a positive action to reach their goal, but those who want to maintain spending levels for the major entitlements must simply prevent others from taking positive action.

The reconciliation process provides a tool for the forces that seek to limit entitlement spending by requiring committees to amend entitlement authorizations that, under normal circumstances, would not be considered in a given year. Thus, even though such entitlements as social security, disability insurance, railroad retirement, military and civil service retirement, and medicare have permanent authorizations, the tax committees (which have had jurisdiction over their authorizations) can be forced to report out changes in their provisions that would cause their expenditures to be lower than would otherwise be the case.

The reconciliation process also reverses the bias in favor of more spending by shifting the argument from the parts to the whole. Over the past eight years the House of Representatives has had a difficult time passing budget resolutions. One reason is that when budget resolutions are taken up on the floor of the House, the members find it difficult to oppose line-item amendments giving more money to individual programs. It is not unusual to see the resolution that is reported by the House Budget Committee amended on the floor to raise veterans' benefits, increase funding for health research, or expand the number of summer jobs for young people. Although all these actions reflect worthy goals—goals that appear to be difficult to oppose on the floor of the House—they also have the effect of increasing the size of the budget deficit. On several occasions the House has increased the funding for a budget resolution by passing a series of amendments, only to vote down the final resolution because its total spending level was too high. This is a classic example of the war between the parts and the whole that characterizes most budgeting decisions.

The major advantage of the reconciliation process as implemented in 1981 was that it overcame this dilemma by grouping a series of reductions into a single package and then required members to vote on substitutes to the entire package. Those who opposed the budget reductions sought a voting procedure (a House rule) that would have allowed individual amendments to specific programs. The Reagan administration and its congressional allies successfully opposed this strategy. In doing so they focused the reconciliation debate on the virtues of the whole rather than the goodness of the parts.

4

The Size and Distribution
of Budget Reductions

By John W. Ellwood

It is clear that the budget reductions enacted in calendar year 1981 represented an historic change in direction in national policy, and that they stemmed from a combination of factors related to politics, the economy, and the internal procedures of Congress. But just how big were they?

The simple answer is that, as noted in the previous chapter, by the end of calendar year 1981 total fiscal year 1982 budget authority had been reduced by $45.1 billion, causing an estimated total outlay reduction of $44.1 billion from the level they would have reached if Congress had continued the previous year's policy. These are valid and useful figures, but they are based on certain political and economic assumptions and on certain methods of calculating the baseline against which comparisons are made. Different assumptions and methods yield different results. For example, the magnitude of the reductions in the 232 accounts that were affected by the reconciliation act can range from a high of $51.2 billion in fiscal year 1982 budget authority and $33.2 billion in outlays to a low of $36.9 billion in budget authority and $14.6 billion in outlays.

This chapter describes the alternative ways of calculating the baseline, sets out the varying assumptions that affect calculations of the size of the reductions, and shows how different baselines and different assumptions affect the resulting estimates. Finally, it shows how the reductions were distributed among different types of programs.

ALTERNATIVE WAYS OF MEASURING REDUCTIONS

As explained in the previous chapter, Congress has only the option of cutting budget authority; it does not directly control outlays. Because outlays

33

along with revenues determine the size of the deficit, however, the media, Congress, and the administration tend to focus on changes in budget outlays.

Most press accounts have stressed that the reconciliation act cut $35.2 billion in outlays, but have seldom noted that it did so by cutting $53.2 billion in budget authority. The budget authority reductions are more important, because they will cause outlays to drop even faster in the future as construction projects are not undertaken and housing subsides are ended.

The budget authority cut is also significant for those studying the effect of cuts on grants to states and localities. State and local officials plan their budgets in anticipation of federal obligations rather than outlays, and budget authority is a better indicator of obligations (it used to be called obligational authority) than are outlays.

Alternative Baselines

Throughout 1981, reports of the size of the reductions enacted by Congress differed. The major reason for this was that different reports used different baselines against which to measure the reductions. The various baselines reflected different sets of economic assumptions and varying methodological approaches. For example, at separate times the reductions were measured from:

1. the fiscal year 1981 budget authority and outlay levels for each program,

2. the Carter administration's recommendations for the fiscal year 1982 budget authority and outlay levels for each program, and

3. current policy—that is, the fiscal year 1982 budget authority and outlay levels for each program that would result if the federal government's fiscal year 1981 policies were continued into the future.

The first baseline is unsatisfactory because it does not take into account economic changes. Almost half of federal expenditures are either formally or informally indexed to inflation, so holding expenditures constant from year to year would mean a decline in services and the size of the governmental sector.

The second baseline is unsatisfactory because it incorporates policy changes advocated by the Carter administration. Eliminating a Carter initiative might not imply a cut from actual spending levels.

The third baseline, though far from perfect, was the one used by Congress, and is the alternative adopted for this volume. This baseline is a measure of *current policy* constructed by the Congressional Budget Office. CBO describes its baseline as follows:

Federal spending can be divided essentially into two categories. About half of total net federal spending is mandated by existing law. This includes spending for Social Security benefits and other entitlement programs, for permanent appropriations such as interest on the public debt, and for most trust funds and other special funds. The baseline spending projections for these programs are comparable to the baseline revenue projections. The projections assume that existing law at the close of the 96th Congress will continue unchanged, and that future spending will respond to assumed economic and population changes in essentially the same way that they have responded to such changes in the past.

The remainder of the federal spending budget is discretionary under existing law and is subject to annual review through the appropriation process. The baseline projections for these programs are generally based on fiscal year 1981 appropriation funding levels as enacted by the Congress through December 1980, with increases in the projection period to keep pace with inflation. For some discretionary spending, such as defense programs, the baseline projections also include future programmatic changes that can be associated with specific congressional decisions through the end of the 96th Congress.[1]

During the first session of the 97th Congress, CBO used a baseline that had been produced in the spring of 1981. At that time CBO estimated that federal spending for fiscal year 1981 (the base year) would be $723.8 billion in budget authority and $659.8 billion in outlays. From this baseline it projected budget authority and outlays for subsequent fiscal years as follows (with dollar figures in billions):

Fiscal year	Budget authority	Outlays
1982	$795.6	$738.7
1983	$859.3	$792.5
1984	$916.8	$843.3

By the summer of 1981, two factors had caused the baseline to be out of date. First, in March 1981 Congress rescinded $14,258 million in fiscal year 1981 unobligated budget authority. This action—which was not reflected in the various measurements of the size of the reconciliation cuts—lowered the outlay estimate for fiscal year 1981 by $1,382 million and the outlay estimate for fiscal year 1982 by $2,143 million. Some of the cutbacks reflected in these rescissions, such as the curtailment of the public service employment sections of CETA, were reinforced by the later budget cuts in the reconciliation act. Others reflected separate cuts. The estimates in this book attempt to take into account the major rescissions passed in June 1981.

The second problem with the baseline is that, as with all federal expenditures, its estimates of federal spending are highly sensitive to economic change. Table 1.5 shows the economic assumptions that CBO used to produce its current policy projections in 1981 and 1982, which were the basis for congressional debate on the budget for fiscal years 1982 and 1983. For

---

1. Congressional Budget Office, *Baseline Budget Projections: Fiscal Years 1982–1986* (Washington, D.C.: Government Printing Office, July 1981), pp. 2–3.

the first time since it began to produce multiyear budget projections in 1975, CBO in calendar 1981 was required to adopt the multiyear forecast and assumptions from the first concurrent resolution on the budget (for fiscal year 1982) for its baseline rather than its own forecast and assumptions. Because they are part of a political process, the economic forecasts and assumptions in budget resolutions have historically been more optimistic than those of CBO and major private forecasters.[2]

The extremely optimistic nature of the assumptions used in calendar 1981 is apparent in table 1.5. As of spring 1981, Congress and the CBO were assuming that during calendar 1982 the gross national product would rise by 4.1 percent after taking account of rising prices. A year later, when calendar 1982 was already a few months old and economic trends had turned downward, it appeared that real GNP would actually decline by 0.1 percent during the year. Similarly, in spring 1981 the unemployment rate for calendar 1982 was projected to average about 7.2 percent; a year later CBO's forecast called for an 8.9 percent average unemployment rate in calendar 1982. The 1981 forecast also was overly optimistic on interest rates of ninety-one-day Treasury bills, which it assumed would average 10.5 percent for calendar 1982; a year later CBO's forecast was based on a 12.0 interest rate during this period.

On the other side, the forecast that was used in 1981 was overly pessimistic on the rate of inflation. It assumed that the measure of price changes known as the GNP deflator would increase during calendar year 1982 by 8.6 percent, while a year later it appeared that this measure would rise by only 7.5 percent. The pattern for the consumer price index (CPI) was the same; the 1981 forecast assumed that it would increase by 8.3 percent in calendar 1982 while a year later CBO forecast that it would rise by only 7.5 percent.

The effects of these overly optimistic economic assumptions are set out in table 1.6. For each percentage point that real growth in the GNP was overestimated, the projection of outlays would be underestimated by $3 billion in fiscal year 1982, $5 billion in fiscal year 1983, and $13 billion in fiscal year 1984. For each percentage point that the unemployment rate was underforecast, projected outlays would be underestimated by $7 billion in fiscal year 1982, $11 billion in fiscal year 1983, and $12 billion in fiscal year 1984. For each percentage point that the interest rates of ninety-one-day Treasury bills were underestimated, outlays for interest on the public debt would increase by $2 billion in fiscal year 1982, $5 billion in fiscal year 1983, and $6 billion

---

2. It should be noted that only the first two years of economic variables in table 1.5 reflect a forecast of economic performance; that is, in calendar 1981, the forecast covered calendar years 1981 and 1982. The numbers for years beyond are assumptions.

TABLE 1.5
Economic Assumptions Used by CBO to Produce Current Policy Baselines for FY 1982 and FY 1983 Budget Cycles

Economic measure and time at which estimate was made	Calendar year to which estimate applies				
	1981	1982	1983	1984	1985

GROSS NATIONAL PRODUCT (GNP) (percentage change, year to year)					
Current dollar GNP					
As est. in spring 1981	12.0	13.0	12.4	10.8	9.8
As est. in spring 1982	11.4[a]	7.5	11.9	10.4	9.7
Constant dollar GNP					
As est. in spring 1981	2.0	4.1	5.0	4.5	4.2
As est. in spring 1982	2.0[a]	−0.1	4.4	3.6	3.5
PRICES (percentage change, year to year)					
GNP deflator					
As est. in spring 1981	9.7	8.6	7.0	.6.0	5.4
As est. in spring 1982	9.2[a]	7.5	7.3	6.6	6.0
Consumer price index					
As est. in spring 1981	11.0	8.3	6.2	5.5	4.7
As est. in spring 1982	10.3[a]	7.5	6.9	6.9	6.4
UNEMPLOYMENT RATE (percentage, annual average)					
As est. in spring 1981	7.5	7.2	6.6	6.4	5.9
As est. in spring 1982	7.6[a]	8.9	8.0	7.4	7.2
INTEREST RATE (91-day Treasury bills, annual average)					
As est. in spring 1981	13.5	10.5	9.4	8.2	7.0
As est. in spring 1982	14.0[a]	12.0	13.2	11.3	9.4

Sources: Congressional Budget Office, *Baseline Budget Projections: Fiscal Years 1982−1986* (July 1981), p. 8, and *An Analysis of the President's Budgetary Proposals for Fiscal Year 1983* (February 1982), p. 38.

a. Actual figure; other figures are estimates and projections.

TABLE 1.6

Effect on Baseline Projections
of Changes in Economic Assumptions
(by fiscal year in billions of dollars)

Economic change	FY1982	FY1983	FY1984
Real growth: Effect of one percentage point lower annual rate beginning January 1982	+3	+5	+13
Unemployment: Effect of one percentage point higher annual rate beginning January 1982	+7	+11	+12
Interest rates: Effect of one percentage point higher annual rate beginning January 1982	+2	+5	+6
Inflation: Effect of one percentage point higher annual rate beginning January 1982	+1	+5	+11

Source: Congressional Budget Office, *Baseline Budget Projections: Fiscal Years 1982–1986* (Washington, D.C.: Government Printing Office, July 1981), p.19.

Note: The one percentage point change is assumed to occur each year from the economic assumptions shown in table 1.5 for calendar years 1982–86.

in fiscal year 1983. On the other hand, for each percentage point that the GNP deflator measure of inflation was overestimated, outlays would drop by $1 billion in fiscal year 1982, $5 billion in fiscal year 1983, and $11 billion in fiscal year 1984.

The Current Law Alternative

The current policy methodology that was employed in producing CBO's baseline makes adjustments to reflect inflation in all programs except such programs as general revenue sharing and programs whose appropriations levels are at their authorization of appropriations limits. (By law, the policy baseline for these programs is not adjusted for inflation.)

Before 1981, however, Congress required CBO to produce a *current law* baseline. This projection only makes adjustments for inflation in those programs that must be adjusted under law. In a current law baseline, the expenditure levels of those programs not indexed to a measure of inflation would be held constant over the entire period of the projection. If such a baseline had been employed in calendar 1981, therefore, the fiscal year 1982 funding levels of the accounts in the "other grants to state and local governments" and "direct federal operations" categories would have been the same as CBO's estimate of their fiscal year 1981 funding levels.

Because Congress wanted to make its reductions look as big as possible, it did not request a current law projection from CBO for the fiscal year 1982 budget cycle. For this chapter we have attempted to create a fiscal year 1982 current law projection for the 232 accounts that were modified by the enactment of the reconciliation act of 1981. The projection was created by combining CBO's fiscal year 1982 current policy estimates for those accounts that CBO in the past inflated under both current law and current policy methods, and CBO's fiscal year 1981 estimates for those accounts that in the past were not inflated under current law.[3] For the 232 accounts, this measure results in a fiscal year 1982 current law projection of $574.9 billion, a reduction of 3.3 percent from CBO's current policy projection. Fiscal year 1982 current law outlays under this projection for the 232 accounts are $532.9 billion, a 4.5 percent reduction from CBO's current policy figures.[4]

MAGNITUDE OF REDUCTIONS

During calendar year 1981, Congress cut $45.1 billion from the fiscal year 1982 current policy baseline of $795.6 billion in budget authority, and cut $44.1 billion from the baseline of $738.7 billion in outlays. These overall figures, however, mask a large increase in defense spending. As shown in tables 1.7 and 1.8, for all budget functions other than defense, Congress in 1981 cut fiscal year 1982 budget authority by $62.8 billion and outlays by $44.1 billion below their current policy levels.

From the entire fiscal year 1982 current policy budget, Congress's actions reduced budget authority by 5.7 percent and outlays by 6.0 percent. When defense expenditures and interest on the public debt are excluded, the relative size of the cuts increases to 12.3 percent in budget authority and 9.4 percent in outlays.

Some people—including Budget Director David Stockman—have charged that these apparent reductions are overstated. They believe that

---

3. The CBO figure we used for the accounts that were not inflated under current law are estimates that CBO produced in spring 1981. Actual figures were available to us, but we did not use them because they would be based on different economic data.

4. In 1979 CBO produced both a current law and a current policy baseline. At that time, CBO estimated that estimates of outlays under current policy would exceed estimates under current law by 2.5 percent in the first year of the projection, by 5.5 percent in the second year, and by 8.3 percent in the third.

TABLE 1.7

Changes in Total Fiscal Year 1982 Budget Authority, by Budget Function

Function	FY 1982 CBO current policy baseline (millions of dollars)	Change in millions of dollars			Percentage change		
		Reduction due to reconciliation	Reduction due to appropriations	Total reduction	Percent cut by reconciliation	Percent cut by appropriations	Total reduction
050 National defense	198,073	-2,580	+20,336	+17,756	-1.3	+10.4	+9.0
150 International affairs	17,143	-1,001	-432	-1,433	-5.8	-2.7	-8.4
250 General science, space and technology	7,191	-54	-136	-190	-0.8	-1.9	-2.6
270 Energy	9,418	-5,540	+818	-4,722	-58.8	-21.1	-50.1
300 Natural resources and environment	14,006	-5,042	-1,267	-6,309	-36.0	-14.1	-45.0
350 Agriculture	5,567	-194	-480	-674	-3.5	-8.9	-12.1
370 Commerce and housing credit	8,068	-1,617	+2,018	+401	-20.0	+31.3	+5.0
400 Transportation	23,671	-2,962	-1,748	-4,710	-12.5	-8.4	-19.9
450 Community and regional development	9,510	-2,062	-584	-2,646	-21.7	-7.8	-27.8
500 Education, training, employment, and social services	36,937	-9,377	-3,321	-12,698	-25.4	-12.1	-34.4
550 Health	85,719	-2,320	-631	-2,951	-2.7	-0.8	-3.4
600 Income security	283,671	-19,430	-3,910	-23,340	-6.8	-1.5	-8.2

Table 1.7, continued

Function	FY 1982 CBO current policy baseline (millions of dollars)	Change in millions of dollars			Percentage change		
		Reduction due to reconciliation	Reduction due to appropriations	Total reduction	Percent cut by reconciliation	Percent cut by appropriations	Total reduction
700 Veterans benefits	25,546	−456	−272	−728	−1.8	−1.1	−2.8
750 Administration of justice	4,916	−267	−159	−426	−5.4	−3.4	−8.7
800 General government	5,486	−242	−542	−784	−4.4	−10.3	−14.3
850 General-purpose fiscal assistance	6,436	−39	+135	+96	−0.6	+2.1	+1.5
900 Interest	87,968	−26	−2,268	−2,294	−0.0	−2.6	−2.6
920 Allowances	0	0	+668	+668	—	—	—
950 Undistributed offsetting receipts	33,675	0	−100	−100	0.0	+0.3	−0.3
Total budget authority	795,649	−53,209	+8,125	−45,084	−6.7	+1.1	−5.7

TABLE 1.8

Changes in Total Fiscal Year 1982 Outlays by Function

Function	FY 1982 CBO current policy baseline (millions of dollars)	Change in millions of dollars			Percentage change		
		Reduction due to reconciliation	Reduction due to appropriations	Total reduction	Percent cut by reconciliation	Percent cut by appropriations	Total reduction
050 National defense	183,756	-2,583	+3,196	+613	-1.4	+1.8	+0.3
150 International Affairs	11,355	-369	+91	-278	-3.2	+0.8	-2.4
250 General science, space and technology	6,992	-52	-61	-113	-0.7	-0.9	-1.6
270 Energy	11,422	-4,671	-977	-5,648	-40.9	-14.5	-49.4
300 Natural resources and environment	14,290	-1,156	-630	-1,786	-8.1	-4.8	-12.5
350 Agriculture	6,542	-1,308	-796	-2,104	-20.0	-15.2	-32.2
370 Commerce and housing credit	6,404	-1,321	-665	-1,986	-20.6	-13.1	-31.0
400 Transportation	22,572	-1,920	-463	-2,383	-8.5	-2.2	-10.6
450 Community and regional development	11,055	-1,059	-446	-1,505	-9.6	-4.5	-13.6
500 Education, training, employment, and social services	35,870	-6,417	-2,836	-9,253	-17.9	-9.6	-25.8
550 Health	76,581	-2,791	-704	-3,495	-3.6	-1.0	-4.6
600 Income security	255,736	-10,647	-1,647	-12,294	-4.2	-0.7	-4.8
700 Veterans benefits	25,054	-448	-589	-1,037	-1.8	-2.4	-4.1

Table 1.8, continued

Function	FY 1982 CBO current policy baseline (millions of dollars)	Change in millions of dollars			Percentage change		
		Reduction due to reconciliation	Reduction due to appropriations	Total reduction	Percent cut by reconciliation	Percent cut by appropriations	Total reduction
750 Administration of justice	4,961	−223	−165	−388	−4.5	−3.5	−7.8
800 General government	5,354	−218	−525	−743	−4.1	−10.2	−13.9
850 General-purpose fiscal assistance	6,438	−40	+124	+84	−0.6	+1.9	+1.3
900 Interest	87,968	−26	−2,268	−2,294	−0.6	−2.6	−2.6
920 Allowances	0	0	+644	+644	0.0		
950 Undistributed offsetting receipts	33,675	0	−100	−100	0.0	+0.3	+0.3
Total budget outlays	738,677	−35,249	−8,817	−44,066	−4.8	−1.3	−6.0

"there is less there than meets the eye."[5] To give perspective on the actual magnitude of the reductions, this chapter uses several varying sets of budgetary assumptions to analyze changes in the 232 budget accounts whose funding levels were affected by the reconciliation act of 1981. Funding for these accounts made up 95.8 percent of all nondefense current policy budget authority and 96.6 percent of all nondefense current policy outlays in fiscal year 1982.

The objective of the analysis is to give the reader sets of numbers that can be viewed as a range. Which point on the range a reader adopts will depend on whether one looks at current or constant dollars. That is, if a program received $100 million in fiscal year 1981 and Congress chose to appropriate $105 million for fiscal year 1982, one could say that the program has been increased by 5 percent in current dollars. Alternatively, one could say that, given a 10 percent inflation rate for the type of spending engaged in by the program, spending for the program in constant dollars was reduced by 4.5 percent.

Have Reductions Been Overestimated?

Although it is difficult to generalize about the nature and magnitude of the reductions enacted during 1981, it can be argued that their total size has been either over- or understated in the public discussion of these changes.

Those who believe that the magnitude of the reductions has been overstated point to the inflated nature of the CBO baseline against which the cuts were measured; the fact that some of the cuts are "paper reductions"; the likelihood that some of the changes would have been made even without the Reagan program; and the tendency for some individual aid recipients who are cut from one program to be transferred to another program. It can also be argued that several of the cuts will not affect spending beyond fiscal year 1982. Such one-shot reductions will have a minor effect on curbing the long-term upward trend in public-sector growth.

Effects of Baselines

Since most of the reductions were achieved by lowering the various authorization of appropriations limits, the use of current law rather than current policy as a baseline would have reduced the estimate of the size of the reductions in most programs that are not entitlement payments to individuals. This is because the size of the cuts was determined by calculating the difference between the baseline and the new authorization of appropriations limits

---

5. William Greider, "The Education of David Stockman," *The Atlantic Monthly,* December 1981, p. 51.

TABLE 1.9
Fiscal Year 1982 Changes in 232 Accounts
Affected by Reconciliation Act
(millions of dollars)

Change	Budget authority		Outlays	
	Current policy	Current law	Current policy	Current law
RECONCILIATION REDUCTIONS CLAIMED BY CONGRESS				
In 232 budget accounts	−53,209	−33,316	−35,249	−9,889
ADDING BACK QUESTIONABLE REDUCTIONS				
Shifting to off-budget status				
SPRO	+3,833	+2,831	+3,666	+2,378
Commitment to reauthorization				
Wastewater treatment	+2,360	+2,360	—	—
Paper savings				
Medicare	—	—	+685	+685
Disaster loans	—	—	+500	—
Would have occurred anyway				
Cut in pay comparability	+3,781	—	+3,694	—
CETA−PSE titles	+3,800	+2,965	+3,675	+2,378
Subtotal, after adding back questionable cuts	−39,435	−25,160	−23,029	−4,448
ADDITIONAL REDUCTIONS CLAIMED BY CONGRESS				
Appropriations reductions	−11,753	−11,753	−10,192	−10,192
TOTAL REDUCTIONS IN CALENDAR 1981				
In 232 accounts	−51,188	−36,921	−33,221	−14,640

established by the act. If a baseline with lower spending levels, such as the current law baseline, is adopted, these differences are made smaller.

Using a current law baseline instead of one based on current policy causes a large drop in the size of the budget reductions. Budget authority savings from the reconciliation act drop by 37.4 percent while the estimate of outlay savings declines by 71.9 percent (see table 1.9). Just over a third of the decline in budget authority and just over half of the drop in outlays is attributable to holding direct federal operations to current dollar levels. An additional 34.6 percent of the decline in budget authority and 26.9 percent of the drop in outlays results from holding three defense accounts to current-dollar fiscal year 1981 levels in fiscal year 1982.

The major accounts affecting both these categories of spending are those that fund pay comparability increases for military and civilian workers. To maintain comparability with pay levels in the private sector, the federal government would have been required to boost its salaries and wages by 13 percent; instead, it raised them by 5 percent. Granting a pay comparability increase is a discretionary action; it is not assumed under current law. As a result, an analyst using current policy as a baseline would count this action as a reduction; with current law as a baseline, it is considered a $6.4 billion increase to fiscal year 1982 budget authority and outlays.

Finally, the shift from current policy to current law for the forty-five reconciliation act accounts funding grants to state and local governments is responsible for 18.5 percent of the total falloff in budget authority and 10.5 percent of the total decline in outlays. During the last three years of the Carter presidency, funding for these programs remained fairly constant, so some might advocate adopting the lower current law figures. Because such a choice would fail to adjust for the effects of inflation, however, it would imply a decline in the real level of the goods and servces that are funded through these accounts.

It should be remembered that a current law projection is a bottom-line base, because it assumes no federal pay increases and holds most grants to state and local governments and direct federal operations at a constant-dollar level throughout the projection period. It thus implies a declining federal sector in an economy experiencing real growth or inflation.

Paper Cuts

It can be argued that some of the cuts made by Congress in the reconciliation act are fictitious. Because some of these artificial reductions are quite large, their exclusion from the list of "real" cuts significantly reduces the magnitude of the cuts.

For example, as part of the reconciliation act Congress shifted the strategic petroleum reserve (SPRO) to an off-budget account. On a current policy basis, this lowered on-budget fiscal year 1982 budget authority by $3,833 million and on-budget outlays by $3,666 million, but the program is still financed by the federal government.

The authorization for appropriations limit for the wastewater treatment grant program was lowered to $40 million by the reconciliation act pending congressional consideration of a series of legislative changes in the program. At the time of the reconciliation act, however, the administration had agreed to support a reauthorization of the program with a $2.4 billion authorization of appropriations limit. That reauthorization has been enacted, although the Congress has yet to grant fiscal year 1982 budget authority. The real savings attributable to the reconciliation act for this program is $1,120 million in budget authority rather than the $3,560 million that was claimed when the reconciliation act was passed.

Both the $500 million outlay savings in the disaster loan program and the $685 million outlay savings in the medicare program were artificial. The first came about because Congress required the CBO to assume that a $780 million supplemental appropriation would be made to the program's budget authority for fiscal year 1981, leading to an additional $500 million in outlays in fiscal year 1982. When the Small Business Administration (SBA) did not request a supplemental appropriation, which it had been expected to do in March 1981, Congress took credit for saving the $500 million.

Paper savings in medicare took place when the reconciliation act shifted $685 million of medicare payments from the first month of fiscal year 1982 to the last month of fiscal year 1981. One year earlier, Congress had made the reverse change—shifting the same amount from fiscal year 1981 to fiscal year 1982. These moves allowed Congress to take credit for savings that did not exist.

If one views all of these changes as artificial, the size of the total current policy budget cut package is reduced by $6,193 million in fiscal year 1982 budget authority and by $4,851 million in outlays.

Cuts That Would Have Occurred Anyway

It can also be argued that certain savings would have occurred in the normal course of events, even if the Reagan administration had never taken office. Under current policy, for example, fiscal year 1982 savings of $3,781 million in budget authority and $3,694 million in outlays are attributable to the adoption in the reconciliation act of lower comparability pay raises for the federal military and civilian work force. But similar savings had been adopted through congressional action in each of the prior four years.

A similar, though more tentative, case can be made that, due to their unpopularity, the public service employment titles of the Comprehensive Employment and Training Act (CETA) were likely to be eliminated (or at least phased out) whether or not the Reagan administration had been elected. Such an assumption would lower the reconciliation act's fiscal year 1982 budget authority savings by $3,800 million and its outlay savings by $3,675 million.

A summary of the effects of adding back these questionable savings is contained in table 1.9. Adding back all the questionable reductions causes the budget authority savings in the reconciliation act, as compared with the current policy baseline, to decline by 25.9 percent to $39.4 billion while the outlay savings drop by 34.7 percent to $23.0 billion. A similar pattern occurs under current law assumptions, with the reconciliation's act savings in budget authority dropping by 24.5 percent to $25.2 billion and the estimate of outlay reductions falling by 55.0 percent to $4.4 billion.

It should be noted, however, that Congress further significantly reduced funding for these 232 accounts during the appropriations process, cutting an additional $11.8 billion in budget authority and an additional $10.2 billion in outlays.

Interaction of Programs

It is possible that the Congressional Budget Office's estimates of outlay savings for entitlement programs might be overstated because they fail to take into account the ability of persons excluded from receiving aid under reduced programs to qualify for other federally aided transfer payments. For example, some persons who lose their minimum social security benefits will be able to meet the eligibility standards for the supplemental security income program, some who have lost trade adjustment assistance benefits will qualify for welfare payments, and some of the working poor who would otherwise be excluded from the AFDC program might choose to drop or reduce their earnings in order to qualify for AFDC and medicaid. Of course, the degree to which these interactions will occur is a major issue in evaluating the effects of the Reagan domestic program. At this point it is only necessary to note that, to the extent these interactions occur, savings achieved by the reconciliation act will be lower than estimated.

The Case for Underestimated Reductions

Those who believe that the reductions brought about by the reconciliation act have been underestimated point to the public attention given to outlays rather than budget authority, the extremely optimistic economic assumptions underlying CBO's current policy baseline, and program interdependencies that may cause multiple reductions as a result of changes in entitlement programs.

The Need to Look at Budget Authority

As previously noted, most public officials and the press focus on outlays as the best indicator of changes in the expenditure side of the budget. Total outlays saved will eventually equal the total budget authority saved by the reconciliation act, but during the early years of the act's four-year accounting period, budget authority savings will be greater than outlay savings.

A concentration on outlay savings can cause a distortion, as shown by the programs that were eliminated in the reconciliation act. Programs such as state and community highway safety grants and the Department of Energy's construction program for fossil energy were terminated by eliminating their authorization for appropriations. Focusing on outlay reductions would lead an observer to conclude that these programs had been reduced by only 15 and 60 percent, respectively. Similar underestimates can occur for programs that have been reduced though not terminated. If one looked only at outlays, urban mass transit funding would appear to have been reduced by only 7 percent, whereas the level of commitment for new grants by the Urban Mass Transit Administration (UMTA) was cut 31 percent. Focusing on outlays would lead one to believe that Economic Development Administration (EDA) grants have only been reduced by 33 percent, while in actuality the level of commitments for new grants will decline by about 68 percent.

This lag between changes in budget authority and shifts in outlays is one reason for adopting a multiyear approach to budgeting. The reconciliation act adopted such an approach; its savings were costed out for three fisal years—1982, 1983, and 1984. Most of the changes enacted are permanent in the sense that modifications in the basic authorizing statutes of programs were enacted. In the case of entitlements and appropriated entitlements (programs described by models 2 and 3 of the previous chapter), changes in the eligibility and benefit formulas were enacted. In the case of those programs which must receive a yearly appropriation, the authorization of appropriations limit (contained in the authorization statute) was permanently lowered. Most of the dollar budget authority savings, therefore, reflects a new permanent lower level of activity. Over several years this new level will come to be reflected in lower outlay levels.

Although budget authority is the correct measure to focus on for most federal programs, outlays provide the best indicator for programs funded through trust funds, such as social security, medicare, unemployment compensation, federal worker retirement benefits, and the highway trust fund. This is because under federal accounting procedures the budget authority figures for trust funds measure revenues going into the funds during the fiscal year. Thus, following the reconciliation act's attempt to reduce basic social security expenditures by eliminating the minimum benefit and other welfare aspects of the program, the CBO estimate of budget authority for the old age and survivors' insurance (OASI) trust fund increased by $86 million for fiscal year 1982 while the estimate for the trust fund's outlays declined by $2,031 million.

One could argue, therefore, that the best measure of the reconciliation act's effects is a combination of the outlay reductions for trust funds and the

TABLE 1.10

Fiscal Year 1982 Budget Changes in 232 Accounts
(millions of dollars)

Change	Current policy	Current law
RECONCILIATION REDUCTIONS CLAIMED BY CONGRESS		
In 232 accounts	−58,696	−37,181
ADDING BACK QUESTIONABLE REDUCTIONS		
Shifting to off-budget status		
SPRO	+3,833	+2,831
Commitment to reauthorization		
Wastewater treatment	+2,360	+2,360
Paper savings		
Disaster loans	+500	+500
Would have occurred anyway		
Cut in pay comparability	+3,781	—
CETA−PSE titles	+3,800	+2,965
Subtotal, after adding back questionable reductions	−44,422	−28,525
ADDITIONAL REDUCTIONS CLAIMED BY CONGRESS		
Appropriations reductions	−15,113	−15,113
TOTAL REDUCTIONS IN CALENDAR 1981		
In 232 accounts	−59,535	−43,638

Note: Size of changes is determined by budget authority figures except for trust funds, for which outlay figures are used.

budget authority reductions for the rest of the budget. Table 1.10 sets out such a measure for the 232 reconciliation accounts.

The numbers in this table represent the upper boundary of the true size of the reductions in these 232 accounts. From a current policy baseline and using this measure, the fiscal year 1982 expenditure level for these accounts was reduced by 10.2 percent. The reconciliation act accomplished a 7.6 percent reduction while the appropriations process accounted for the other 2.6 percent. From a current law baseline the 232 accounts were reduced by 7.7 percent using this measure. Of this reduction, 5.1 percentage points are associated with reconciliation and 2.6 percentage points with the appropriations process.

Optimistic Baseline Assumptions

While most press coverage—including the *Atlantic Monthly* article on David Stockman—focused on the supposedly inflated nature of CBO's current policy baseline, a counter argument can be put forth to the effect that CBO was required (by the budget committees) to adopt optimistic economic assumptions that actually understated the magnitude of current policy spending.

As shown in table 1.5, the economic assumptions that CBO used to produce CBO's current policy baseline for fiscal years 1982 to 1984 were overly optimistic. Real growth in the economy has been slower and unemployment and interest rates higher than forecast. Under the original economic assumptions, CBO estimated that after all the congressional action of calendar year 1981 had occurred total budget outlays would be around $694.6 billion in fiscal year 1982. Under its new set of assumptions, however, fiscal year 1982 outlays are projected to be in the $735 to 740 billion range. This $40 to $50 billion increase is almost solely due to declining economic conditions.

It is possible, therefore, that CBO's current policy estimates were too low for those programs whose funding levels are sensitive to the unemployment rate—unemployment compensation, social security, and food stamps. If this is the case, the amount of savings in these programs could be underestimated.

Interdependencies

It is possible to reverse the previously stated argument that the interdependencies of federal programs will lead to overestimates of the savings brought about by the reconciliation act. Tightening eligibility for one federal program frequently leads to the loss of eligibility for others, because those who are eligible for programs such as AFDC are automatically eligible for other programs such as medicaid. When CBO produced its cost estimates for the various programs affected by the reconciliation act, it made every effort to take these interactions into account. But because the reconciliation act made extensive changes, it is possible that some unanticipated interactions will occur.

In producing its cost estimates, CBO relied whenever possible on data from program evaluations and microeconomic simulations of existing programs to determine what would happen if given programs were modified in certain ways. But given the pressures of time and the limitations of our understanding of how federal programs work and interact, some estimates were made "on the back of an envelope." Sometimes it was assumed that a decline in funding of a given percentage would lead to an equivalent program cut. But it is possible that thresholds exist that will cause state and local administrators of federally aided programs to drop out entirely. For example, some critics of the Reagan administration's child nutrition policy believe that the estimates of the reductions in the school breakfast and lunch programs are understated because higher prices for participants will lead to such low participation rates that many school districts will withdraw from the program. Should this occur, the savings from the reconciliation act's changes to these programs will have been underestimated.

The federal cuts could put states and localities under such great fiscal pressure that some could react not only by passing the cuts through to people but also by making additional reductions in their budget for programs whose funding is shared with the federal government. Because federal outlays for these programs are frequently tied to the degree of state matching, a decline in the state share could lead to additional reductions in federal spending. Should this occur, the estimates of the reconciliation act's savings will have been underestimated.

THE DISTRIBUTION OF THE REDUCTIONS

The initial Reagan budget cuts can be better understood by looking next at the distribution of the reductions by budget function and program type. The reconciliation act of 1981 affected spending levels in 232 out of the 1,314 accounts that made up the federal budget. Just as not all accounts were affected, not all accounts that were affected bore an equal share of the reductions. In seeking to achieve reductions, the president and Congress had to come to grips with the following three important constraints imposed by the structure of the federal budget and the nature of the budget process:

1. While there are many budget accounts and even greater numbers of authorizations (what we call "programs"), most federal spending is located in a few large accounts.

2. As shown in chapter 2, the largest accounts, which fund transfer programs making payments to individuals, are the most difficult to control because they fund entitlement programs whose funding levels are determined by the number of people who are eligible, rather than by the annual appropriations process.

3. As a consequence of the first two constraints, the easiest programs to control (and to reduce) are grants to state and local governments and direct federal operations. But because these programs are much smaller than the entitlement programs, it is necessary to make deep cuts affecting many accounts (and programs) to achieve appreciable savings.

It is useful, therefore, to employ two measures to describe and analyze the reductions: the dollar amount that was cut and the percentage by which an account (or a program) was reduced. The largest dollar savings tend to be associated with some of the smallest percentage reductions because they were achieved from a large entitlement base. Conversely, the reconciliation act terminated many relatively small grants to state and local governments with a resulting savings equal to a small fraction of the cuts in some of the entitlement programs. In sum, although the reconciliation act changed 232 budget accounts, most of the dollar savings occurred in a handful of accounts.[6]

Distribution by Type of Spending

Tables 1.11 and 1.12 set out the fiscal year 1982 budget authority and outlay reductions that were achieved during the first session of the 97th Congress for the 232 reconciliation accounts. The accounts have been grouped into the eight major categories of federal spending—expenditures for national defense, payments to individuals from trust funds, other payments to individuals directly administered by the federal government, payments to individuals from programs administered by state and local governments, other grants to states and localities, net interest on the public debt, and all other direct federal operations. The reductions in table 1.11 are measured from CBO's current policy baseline, while the cuts in table 1.12 are estimated from current law. The questionable reductions, which were removed from the totals in tables 1.9 and 1.10, have not been removed from these data.

Each table sets out the number of budget accounts in each category of spending, the fiscal year 1982 baseline, and (in millions of dollars and percentages) the amount reduced by the reconciliation act and the total amount saved by all actions during calendar year 1981. The last column of each table shows what percentage of all reductions made in these 232 accounts fell in each spending category.

Depending on which column is chosen, one can give different interpretations of which category bore the greatest burden of the reductions. For example, when measured against the current policy baseline in table 1.11, the three categories of payments to individuals, with their large entitlements—such as social security, military and civil service retirement, unemployment compensation, medicare, medicaid, food stamps, AFDC, housing assistance, and the nutrition programs—bore nearly a third of all the fiscal year 1982 budget authority reductions in these 232 accounts. But the average percentage reduction in the accounts in this category was relatively small:

---

6. For example, tables 1.13 and 1.14 set out the changes in sixty-five large accounts that made up 92.5 percent of the reconciliation act's fiscal year 1982 budget authority reductions and 96.1 percent of its outlay cuts for the same fiscal year.

TABLE 1.11

Fiscal Year 1982 Reductions in 232 Accounts Measured Against Current Policy Baseline

Type of spending	Number of budget accounts	Current policy baseline	Millions of dollars		Percentage reduction		As percentage of all reductions
			Due to reconciliation	Due to all 1981 actions	Due to reconciliation	Due to all 1981 actions	
BUDGET AUTHORITY							
National defense	4	22,469	−2,580	−2,305	−11.5	−10.3	−3.5
Payments to individuals	30	366,499	−21,059	−21,264	−5.7	−5.8	−32.7
Social insurance payments	(12)	(267,166)	(−2,891)	(−1,184)	(−1.1)	(−0.4)	(−1.8)
Other direct payments	(7)	(29,830)	(−2,679)	(−3,730)	(−9.0)	(−12.5)	(−5.7)
Grant payments	(11)	(69,503)	(−15,489)	(−16,350)	(−22.3)	(−23.5)	(−25.2)
Other state and local grants	45	50,626	−14,888	−19,075	−29.4	−37.7	−29.4
Net interest	2	104,268	−26	−2,190	0.0	−2.1	−3.4
All other operations	148	50,880	−14,648	−20,128	−28.8	−39.6	−31.0
Total in 232 accounts	232	594,742	−53,201	−64,962	−8.9	−10.9	−100.0
OUTLAYS							
National defense	4	22,405	−2,583	−2,619	−11.5	−11.7	−5.8
Payments to individuals	30	335,165	−13,345	−16,120	−4.0	−4.8	−35.5
Social insurance payments	(12)	(256,247)	(−7,384)	(−8,607)	(−2.9)	(−3.4)	(−19.0)
Other direct payments	(7)	(29,919)	(−2,033)	(−3,461)	(−6.8)	(−11.6)	(−7.6)
Grant payments	(11)	(48,919)	(−3,928)	(−4,052)	(−8.0)	(−8.3)	(−8.9)
Other state and local grants	45	50,099	−7,036	−8,910	−14.0	−17.8	−19.6
Net interest	2	104,268	−26	−2,190	0.0	−2.1	−4.8
All other operations	148	46,318	−12,260	−15,603	−26.5	−33.7	−34.3
Total in 232 accounts	232	558,255	−35,250	−45,442	−6.3	−8.1	−100.0

TABLE 1.12

Fiscal Year 1982 Reductions in 232 Accounts Measured Against Current Law Baseline

Type of spending	Number of budget accounts	Current law baseline	Millions of dollars		Percentage reduction		As percentage of all reductions
			Due to reconciliation	Due to all 1981 actions	Due to reconciliation	Due to all 1981 actions	
BUDGET AUTHORITY							
National defense	4	15,584	+4,305	+4,580	+27.6	+29.4	−10.2
Payments to individuals	30	365,609	+20,169	+20,374	−5.5	−5.6	−45.2
Social insurance payments	(12)	(267,166)	(2,891)	(1,184)	(1.1)	(0.4)	(2.6)
Other direct payments	(7)	(29,830)	(2,679)	(3,730)	(9.0)	(12.5)	(8.3)
Grant payments	(11)	(68,613)	(14,599)	(15,460)	(21.3)	(22.5)	(34.3)
Other state and local grants	45	45,947	−10,209	−14,396	−22.2	−31.3	−31.9
Net interest	2	104,268	−26	−2,190	0.0	−2.1	−4.9
All other operations	148	43,449	−7,217	−12,697	−16.6	−29.2	−28.2
Total in 232 accounts	232	574,857	−33,316	−45,077	−5.8	−7.8	−100.0
OUTLAYS							
National defense	4	15,577	+4,245	+4,209	+27.3	+27.0	−21.0
Payments to individuals	30	332,232	−10,412	−13,187	−3.1	−4.0	−65.7
Social insurance payments	(12)	(256,247)	(7,384)	(8,607)	(2.9)	(3.4)	(42.9)
Other direct payments	(7)	(29,919)	(2,033)	(3,461)	(6.8)	(11.6)	(17.2)
Grant payments	(11)	(46,066)	(995)	(1,119)	(2.2)	(2.4)	(5.6)
Other state and local grants	45	48,003	−4,940	−6,814	−10.3	−14.2	−33.9
Net interest	2	104,268	−26	−2,190	0.0	−2.1	−10.9
All other operations	148	32,814	+1,244	−2,099	−3.8	−6.4	−10.5
Total in 232 accounts	232	532,894	−9,889	−20,081	−1.9	−3.8	−100.0

5.8 percent in budget authority and 4.8 percent in outlays.

Four patterns stand out from the data in tables 1.11 and 1.12:

1. The largest reductions were made in those programs that went through the annual appropriations process.

2. Of the various types of spending, grants to state and local governments suffered the sharpest reductions.

3. Of the various accounts that funded programs making payments to individuals, those that were targeted on the poor and working poor received the deepest cuts while those that were not associated with a means test suffered the smallest reduction.

4. Using a current law baseline instead of a current policy baseline does not alter the distribution of the reductions among the different types of accounts, though it does make the overall size of the reductions smaller.

The largest dollar and spending reductions were achieved in those programs whose funding levels were easiest to control—the 148 accounts funding direct federal operations and the 45 accounts funding grants to state and local governments. On a current policy basis, the fiscal year 1982 budget authority in these categories was reduced by $20.1 billion and $19.1 billion respectively (see table 1.11). This meant that on average the 148 direct operations accounts had their fiscal year 1982 budget authority reduced by 39.6 percent while the 45 grant accounts had their funding lowered by 37.7 percent compared to what it would have been under current policy. Because all the accounts in these two categories must be funded through the annual appropriations process, very large additional cuts were made after the passage of the reconciliation act—an additional $5.5 billion in fiscal year 1982 budget authority in the case of the 148 direct operations accounts and an additional $4.2 billion in the case of the 45 direct grant accounts.

Second, the data in tables 1.11 and 1.12 show that the accounts that provide grants to state and local governments were among the most severely affected by the reductions of calendar year 1981. The budget authority of the direct grant accounts was reduced by more than a third. However, within the "payments to individuals" category, the accounts funding those income transfer programs administered by state and local governments bore the greatest burden. Of their fiscal year 1982 current policy budget authority, 23.5 percent was cut as compared with reductions of 0.4 percent (4.8 percent of outlays) for the accounts funding the social insurance entitlements and 12.5 percent for the other payments to individuals programs directly administered by the federal government. When the "direct grants" and "grant payments to individuals" categories are combined, it is evident that these fifty-six grant accounts bore 54.6 percent of the reduction in fiscal year 1982 budget authority, when measured from current policy. On average, each account had its budget authority reduced by 29.5 percent compared with its current policy level.

Third, within the large "payments to individuals" category, those accounts that fund programs benefiting the poor and working poor were cut the most while those funding programs benefiting the middle class were least affected. As previously stated, the "grant payments" category, which contains many welfare programs—medicaid, housing assistance, aid to families with dependent children (AFDC), and the child nutrition programs—was the most severely affected, with 23.5 percent of its current policy budget authority and 11.6 percent of its fiscal year 1982 current policy outlays being cut. The "direct payments to individuals" category, which includes many programs whose eligibility and benefits are linked to an income test—such as food stamps, supplemental security income, and trade assistance—was also significantly affected. The current policy budget authority and outlays for the seven accounts in this category were reduced by 12.5 percent and 11.6 percent, respectively. On the other hand, the twelve trust fund accounts funding the large social insurance entitlements whose eligibility and funding levels are not income-tested were hardly affected. Only 0.4 percent of their fiscal year 1982 current policy budget authority and 4.8 percent of their current policy outlays were cut by the actions of Congress during calendar year 1981.

The final pattern evident in tables 1.11 and 1.12 is that, while the substitution of current law for current policy as the baseline against which the reductions are measured lowers the magnitude of the reductions, the basic pattern of burden remains the same. Because most entitlement (and many appropriated entitlement) programs are indexed to a measure of inflation, their current law and current policy baselines are identical. This is particularly true for all the social insurance and direct payment to individuals accounts. It is also true for nine out of the eleven grant payments accounts. Thus the substitution of current law for current policy is most significant for those accounts that go through the annual appropriations process—the 4 national defense accounts, the 45 direct grant accounts, and the 148 direct federal operations accounts. The use of current law for these 197 accounts causes a 45.8 percent decline in the amount of their fiscal year 1982 budget authority that was cut in calendar 1981 and leads to an 82.7 percent drop in the size of the estimated fiscal year 1982 outlay savings. The substitution causes the average percentage reduction in each of the 197 accounts to decline from 33.5 percent to 21.4 percent in the case of budget authority and to drop from 22.8 percent to 4.9 percent in the case of outlays.

Yet even with the use of current law, the direct federal operations and direct grants to state and local governments accounts still bore a majority

(60.1 percent) of budget authority reductions and over two-fifths (44.4 percent) of the outlay cuts. These accounts still bore the largest percentage reduction in their fiscal year 1982 budget authority (30.3 percent) and the second largest decline in their outlays (11.0 percent).

In short, though the overall magnitude of cuts is affected by one's choice of a current policy or current law baseine, the distribution of cuts among categories of programs is not so affected.

TABLE 1.13

Major Fiscal Year 1982 Budget Authority Reductions Enacted in 1981
(dollars in millions)

Program	FY 1982 dollar level			Change in dollars			Percentage change		
	CBO current policy base	Level after reconciliation	Level after appropriations	Change from reconciliation	Change from appropriations	Total change	From reconciliation	From appropriations	Total change
PAYMENTS TO INDIVIDUALS (ENTITLEMENTS)									
Social insurance payments									
OASI (basic social security)	130,633	130,719	131,098	+86	+379	+465	0	0	0
Disability insurance	22,188	22,199	22,277	+11	+78	+89	0	0	0
Railroad retirement	5,164	5,167	5,679	+3	+512	+515	0	+10	+10
Military retirement	15,484	15,053	15,059	−431	+6	−425	−3	0	−3
Civil service retirement	30,624	30,085	30,085	−539	0	−539	−2	0	−2
Medicare	56,339	56,152	56,162	−187	+10	−177	0	0	0
Unemployment compensation (a)	24,089	23,889	21,257	−200	−2,632	−2,832	−1	−11	−12
Subtotal (insurance payments)	284,521	283,264	281,617	−1,257	−1,647	−2,904	0	−1	−1

Table 1.13, continued

Program	FY 1982 dollar level			Change in dollars			Percentage change		
	CBO current policy base	Level after reconciliation	Level after appropriations	Change from reconciliation	Change from appropriations	Total change	From reconciliation	From appropriations	Total change
Other direct payments (means-tested payments)									
Student financial assistance	4,483	3,933	3,352	-550	-581	-1,131	-12	-15	-25
Student loan programs	3,082	2,603	2,603	-479	0	-479	-16	0	-16
Trade assistance benefits	1,828	268	306	-1,560	+38	-1,522	-85	+14	-85
Food stamps (a)	12,304	10,596	10,280	-1,708	-316	-2,024	-14	-3	-16
Supplemental security income (a)	7,799	7,949	7,779	+150	-170	-20	+2	-2	0
Veterans burial benefits (a)	193	118	147	-75	+29	-46	-39	+25	-24
Subtotal (direct payments)	29,689	25,467	24,467	-4,222	-1,000	-5,222	-14	-4	-18
Grant payments (means-tested payments) (b)									
Medicaid (a)	18,515	17,343	17,624	-1,172	+281	-891	-6	+2	-5
Assisted housing, sect. 8 (a)	28,637	17,080	16,367	-11,557	-713	-12,270	-40	-4	-43
Public housing operating asst. (a)	1,240	1,500	1,156	+260	-344	-84	+21	-23	-7
Special milk	125	30	28	-95	-2	-97	-76	-1	-77
Child nutrition programs	4,110	2,712	2,847	-1,398	+135	-1,263	-34	+5	-31
AFDC (a)	6,568	5,410	5,461	-1,158	+51	-1,107	-18	+1	-17
Low-income energy assistance (a)	2,247	1,875	1,752	-372	-123	-495	-17	-7	-22
Subtotal (grant payments)	61,442	45,950	45,235	-15,492	-715	-16,207	-25	-2	-26
Subtotal: All payments to individuals	375,652	354,681	351,319	-20,971	-3,362	-24,333	-6	-1	-6

Table 1.13, continued

Program	FY 1982 dollar level			Change in dollars			Percentage change		
	CBO current policy base	Level after reconciliation	Level after appropriations	Change from reconciliation	Change from appropriations	Total change	From reconciliation	From appropriations	Total change
OTHER GRANTS TO STATE AND LOCAL GOVERNMENTS									
Energy conservation grants	775	485	234	-272	-251	-523	-36	-52	-69
Wastewater treatment grants	3,600	40	40	-3,560	0	-3,560	-99	0	-99
Payment to Postal Service	1,825	946	834	-879	-112	-991	-48	-12	-54
Highway trust fund	7,854	8,279	8,279	+425	0	+425	+5	0	+5
State highway safety	42	0	0	-42	0	-42	-100	0	-100
UMTA grants	5,090	3,792	3,495	-1,298	-297	-1,595	-26	-8	-31
Air transportation grants	789	600	0	-189	-600	-789	-24	-100	-100
CDBG	3,960	3,666	3,456	-294	-210	-504	-7	-6	-13
UDAG	675	500	440	-175	-60	-235	-26	-12	-35
EDA grants	623	265	199	-358	-66	-424	-57	-25	-68
Impact aid	866	475	437	-391	-38	-429	-45	-8	-50
Elementary and secondary education block grant	764	589	470	-175	-119	-294	-23	-20	-38
ESEA title I	3,961	3,531	2,914	-430	-617	-1,047	-11	-17	-26
CETA except title VI	8,354	3,906	3,037	-4,448	-869	-5,371	-53	-22	-64
CETA title VI	1,129	0	0	-1,129	0	-1,129	-100	0	-100
Social services block grant	3,099	2,400	2,400	-699	0	-699	-23	0	-23
Community services block grant	586	389	348	-197	-41	-238	-34	-11	-41
Primary care block grant	352	282	248	-70	-34	-104	-20	-12	-30
Maternal and child health services block grant	493	373	347	-120	-26	-146	-25	-7	-30

Table 1.13, continued

Program	FY 1982 dollar level			Change in dollars			Percentage change		
	CBO current policy base	Level after reconciliation	Level after appropriations	Change from reconciliation	Change from appropriations	Total change	From reconciliation	From appropriations	Total change
Alcohol, drug abuse, and mental health block grant	691	491	432	−200	−59	−259	−29	−12	−37
Preventive health and health services block grant	128	95	82	−33	−13	−46	−26	−14	−36
Refugee assistance	652	583	560	−69	−23	−92	−11	−4	−14
Capital loans to D.C.	194	155	155	−39	0	−39	−20	0	−20
Subtotal (other grants)	46,502	31,842	28,407	−14,660	−3,435	−18,095	−32	−11	−39
ALL OTHER DIRECT FEDERAL OPERATIONS									
Defense department pay comparability	6,876	5,251	5,582	−1,625	+331	−1,294	−24	+6	−19
Contributions to international organizations	554	454	398	−100	−56	−156	−18	−12	−28
Food for Peace (P.L. 480)	1,437	1,305	1,000	−132	−305	−437	−9	−23	−30
Farm price supports	2,296	2,296	2,092	0	−253	−253	0	−11	−11
Export-Import Bank	5,982	4,633	3,974	−1,349	−659	−2,008	−23	−14	−34
Fossil energy R & D	748	460	413	−288	−47	−335	−39	−10	−45
Fossil energy construction	482	18	4	−464	−14	−478	−96	−78	−99
Energy supply R & D	2,547	2,137	1,971	−410	−166	−576	−16	−8	−22
Uranium supply and enrichment	320	318	1	−2	−317	−319	−1	−100	−100
Strategic petroleum reserve	4,093	260	191	−3,833	−69	−3,902	−94	−27	−95

Table 1.13, continued

Program	FY 1982 dollar level			Change in dollars			Percentage change		
	CBO current policy base	Level after reconciliation	Level after appropriations	Change from reconciliation	Change from appropriations	Total change	From reconciliation	From appropriations	Total change
Department of Energy economic regulation	192	45	21	-147	-24	-171	-77	-53	-89
Dept. of Interior absorption	0	0	0	-586	0	-586	-100	0	-100
Army Corps of Engineers construction	1,725	1,547	1,417	-178	-130	-308	-10	-8	-18
Agriculture credit insurance fund	755	755	755	0	0	0	0	0	0
Business loan and investment fund	680	362	326	-318	-36	-354	-47	-10	-52
Grants to Amtrak	1,048	735	735	-313	0	-313	-30	0	-30
Youth Conservation Corps	60	0	0	-60	0	-60	-100	0	-100
Rehabilitation loan fund	137	0	0	-137	0	-137	-100	0	-100
Disaster loan fund	180	0	0	-180	0	-180	-100	0	-100
Conrail subsidy	560	455	0	-105	-455	-560	-19	-100	-100
Northeast corridor track improvement	386	200	170	-186	-30	-216	-48	-15	-56
Civilian pay comparability	3,345	1,189	689	-2,156	-500	-2,656	-65	-42	-79
Subtotal (direct operations)	34,403	22,420	19,739	-11,983	-2,681	-14,664	-35	-12	-43

Table 1.13, continued

Program	FY 1982 dollar level			Change in dollars			Percentage change		
	CBO current policy base	Level after reconciliation	Level after appropriations	Change from reconciliation	Change from appropriations	Total change	From reconciliation	From appropriations	Total change
OTHER REDUCTIONS TO ACCOUNTS AFFECTED BY RECONCILIATION									
167 other accounts	138,185	132,590	130,315	−5,595	−2,275	−7,870	−4	−2	−6
TOTAL FEDERAL BUDGET									
All 1,314 budget accounts	795,649	742,440	750,566	−53,209	+8,125	−45,804	−7	+1	−6

Note: All changes are measured from the Congressional Budget Office current policy baseline of December 1980. Estimates obtained from the Congressional Budget Office.

a. These programs are appropriated entitlements.

b. These programs are also classified as grants to state and local governments by the Office of Management and Budget.

TABLE 1.14

Major Fiscal Year 1982 Outlay Reductions Enacted in 1981
(dollars in millions)

Program	FY 1982 dollar level			Change in dollars			Percentage change		
	CBO current policy base	Level after recon- ciliation	Level after appropri- ations	Change from recon- ciliation	Change from appropri- ations	Total change	From recon- ciliation	From appropri- ations	Total change
PAYMENTS TO INDIVIDUALS (ENTITLEMENTS)									
Social insurance payments									
OASI (basic social security)	140,928	138,897	138,767	−2,031	−130	−2,161	−1	0	−2
Disability insurance	19,615	19,359	19,316	−256	−43	−299	−1	−0	−2
Railroad retirement	6,039	5,721	5,712	−318	−9	−327	−5	0	−5
Military retirement	15,477	15,046	14,786	−431	−260	−691	−3	−2	−5
Civil service retirement	20,073	19,529	19,527	−544	−2	−546	−3	−0	−3
Medicare	48,127	46,743	46,571	−1,384	−172	−1,556	−3	−0	−3
Unemployment compensation (a)	19,736	18,950	18,287	−786	−663	−1,449	−4	−3	−7
Subtotal (insurance programs)	269,995	264,245	262,966	−5,750	−1,279	−7,029	−2	−1	−3

Table 1.14, continued

Program	FY 1982 dollar level			Change in dollars			Percentage change		
	CBO current policy base	Level after reconciliation	Level after appropriations	Change from reconciliation	Change from appropriations	Total change	From reconciliation	From appropriations	Total change
Other direct payments (means-tested payments)									
Student financial assistance	4,600	4,546	3,518	−54	−1,028	−1,082	−1	−23	−24
Student loan programs	3,006	2,683	2,683	−323	0	−323	−11	0	−11
Trade assistance benefits	1,828	268	342	−1,560	+74	−1,486	−85	+28	−85
Food stamps (a)	12,298	10,590	10,407	−1,708	−183	−1,891	−14	−1	−15
Supplemental security income (a)	7,833	7,983	7,813	+150	−170	−20	+2	−2	−0
Veterans burial benefits (a)	193	118	135	−75	+17	−58	−39	+14	−30
Subtotal (direct payments)	29,758	26,188	24,898	−3,570	−1,290	−4,860	−12	−5	−16
Grant payments (means-tested payments) (b)									
Medicaid (a)	18,016	17,072	17,297	−9 4	+225	−719	−5	+1	−4
Assisted housing, sect. 8 (a)	6,981	6,865	6,860	−116	−5	−121	−2	0	−2
Public housing operating asst. (a)	1,071	1,206	1,206	+135	0	+135	+13	0	+13
Special milk	124	21	27	−103	+6	−97	−83	+29	−78
Child nutrition programs	4,032	2,662	2,662	−1,370	0	−1,370	−34	0	−34
AFDC (a)	8,588	7,430	7,483	−1,158	+53	−1,105	−13	+1	−13
Low-income energy asst. (a)	2,247	1,875	1,752	−372	−123	−495	−17	−7	−22
Subtotal (grant payments)	41,059	37,131	37,287	−3,928	+156	−3,772	−10	+1	−9
Subtotal: All payments to individuals	340,812	327,564	325,151	−13,248	−2,413	−15,661	−4	−1	−5

Table 1.14, continued

Program	FY 1982 dollar level			Change in dollars			Percentage change		
	CBO current policy base	Level after reconciliation	Level after appropriations	Change from reconciliation	Change from appropriations	Total change	From reconciliation	From appropriations	Total change
DIRECT GRANTS TO STATE AND LOCAL GOVERNMENTS									
Energy construction grants	778	745	660	-33	-85	-118	-5	-11	-15
Wastewater treatment grants	4,320	4,245	4,245	-75	0	-75	-2	0	-2
Payment to Postal Service	1,825	946	834	-879	-112	-991	-48	-12	-54
Highway trust fund	8,285	7,785	8,065	-500	+280	-220	-6	+4	-3
State highway safety grants	210	93	118	-117	+25	-92	-56	+91	-15
UMTA grants	4,090	3,892	3,792	-198	-100	-298	-5	-3	-7
Air transportation grants	674	522	485	-152	-37	-189	-23	-7	-28
CDBG	4,750	4,720	4,128	-30	-592	-622	-1	-13	-13
UDAG	744	727	500	-17	-227	-244	-2	-31	-33
EDA grants	548	537	515	-11	-22	-33	-2	-4	-6
Impact aid	837	524	488	-313	-36	-349	-37	-7	-42
Elementary and secondary education block grant (c)	NA	NA	NA	NA	NA	NA	NA	NA	NA
ESEA title I	3,475	3,437	3,358	-38	-79	-117	-1	-2	-3
CETA except title VI	8,338	4,931	4,276	-3,407	-655	-4,062	-41	-18	-51
CETA title VI	1,118	26	10	-1,092	-16	-1,108	-98	-61	-99
Social services block grant	3,086	2,387	2,952	-699	+565	-134	-23	+24	-4
Community Services block grant	569	451	264	-118	-187	-305	-21	-59	-54
Primary care block grant (c)	NA	NA	NA	NA	NA	NA	NA	NA	NA
Maternal and child health services block grant (c)	NA	NA	NA	NA	NA	NA	NA	NA	NA

Table 1.14, continued

Program	FY 1982 dollar level			Change in dollars			Percentage change		
	CBO current policy base	Level after reconciliation	Level after appropriations	Change from reconciliation	Change from appropriations	Total change	From reconciliation	From appropriations	Total change
Alcohol, drug abuse, and mental health block grant (c)	NA	NA	NA	NA	NA	NA	NA	NA	NA
Preventive health and health services block grant (c)	NA	NA	NA	NA	NA	NA	NA	NA	NA
Refugee assistance	675	583	560	-92	-23	-115	-11	-4	-14
Capital loans to D.C.	185	145	145	-40	0	-40	-22	0	-22
Subtotal (direct grants)	44,507	36,696	35,395	-7,811	-1,301	-9,122	-18	-4	-21
DIRECT FEDERAL OPERATIONS									
Defense department pay comparability	6,852	5,227	5,495	-1,625	+268	-1,357	-24	+5	-20
Contributions to international organizations	522	449	341	-73	-108	-181	-14	-24	-35
Food for Peace (P.L. 480)	1,404	1,276	983	-128	-293	-421	-9	-23	-30
Farm price supports	3,601	2,881	2,092	-720	-789	-1,509	-20	-27	-42
Export-Import Bank	2,267	2,156	2,135	-111	-21	-132	-5	-1	-6
Fossil energy R & D	742	506	441	-236	-65	-301	-32	-13	-41
Fossil energy construction	377	183	152	-194	-31	-225	-52	-17	-60
Energy supply R & D	2,481	2,345	2,098	-136	-247	-383	-6	-11	-15
Uranium supply enrichment	250	59	-4	-191	-63	-254	-76	-107	-102
Strategic petroleum reserve	3,906	240	225	-3,666	-15	-3,681	-94	-6	-94

Table 1.14, continued

Program	FY 1982 dollar level			Change in dollars			Percentage change		
	CBO current policy base	Level after reconciliation	Level after appropriations	Change from reconciliation	Change from appropriations	Total change	From reconciliation	From appropriations	Total change
Department of Energy economic regulation	181	93	84	−88	−9	−97	−49	−10	−54
Dept. of Interior absorption	0	0	0	−341	0	−341	−100	0	−100
Army Corps of Engineers construction	1,678	1,543	1,457	−135	−86	−221	−8	−6	−13
Agriculture credit insurance fund	848	444	450	−404	+6	−398	−48	+1	−47
Business loan and investment fund	668	461	619	−207	+158	−49	−31	+34	−7
Grants to Amtrak	930	659	659	−271	0	−271	−30	0	−30
Youth Conservation Corps	60	12	1	−48	−11	−59	−80	−97	−98
Rehabilitation loan fund	147	13	66	−160	−53	−213	−100	−307	−145
Disaster loan fund	767	160	64	−607	−96	−703	−40	−60	−92
Conrail subsidy	460	125	250	−355	+125	−210	−73	+100	−46
Northeast corridor track improvement	315	307	350	−8	+43	+35	−3	+14	+11
Civilian pay comparability	3,241	1,172	665	−2,069	−507	−2,576	−64	−43	−80
Subtotal (direct operations)	36,697	20,285	18,491	−16,412	−1,794	−18,206	−45	−9	−50
OTHER RECONCILIATION REDUCTIONS									
167 other accounts	136,239	138,461	133,776	+2,222	−4,685	−2,463	+2	−4	−2

Table 1.14, continued

Program	FY 1982 dollar level			Change in dollars			Percentage change		
	CBO current policy base	Level after reconciliation	Level after appropriation	Change from reconciliation	Change from appropriations	Total change	From reconciliation	From appropriations	Total change
TOTAL FEDERAL BUDGET									
All 1,314 budget accounts	738,677	703,428	694,611	−35,249	−8,817	−44,066	−5	−1	−6

Note: All changes are measured from the Congressional Budget Office current policy baseline produced in spring 1981. Estimates were obtained from the Congressional Budget Office.

a. These programs are appropriated entitlements.

b. These programs are also classified as grants to state and local governments by the Office of Management and Budget.

c. Outlay data not available for the five block grants that were created from more than one previously existing budget account.

5

The Economic Recovery Tax Act
and Its Effects
on State and Local Revenues

By Robert F. Cook
with the assistance of Jacqueline V. Crawford

On August 13, 1981, President Reagan signed the Economic Recovery Tax Act (ERTA), enacted as part of the administration's domestic program. The act made changes in federal taxes on corporate profits, personal income, and gifts and estates. Although most attention has been focused on the revenues that the federal government gave up, the act could also result in substantial revenue losses for state and local governments. Because most state constitutions and city charters prohibit deficits, such losses in revenues would translate into significant reductions in expenditures and services.

This chapter summarizes these tax law changes, indicates their magnitude at the federal level, provides information on state linkages to the federal tax system, and suggests how the tax law changes state and local revenues.

FEDERAL REVENUE LOSSES

The changes in the tax code are expected to cause total reductions of $481.1 billion between fiscal years 1981 and 1985. This loss and the administration's proposed increases in defense spending have resulted in projected deficits so large that Congress, including the Republican Senate, has resisted the administration's fiscal 1983 budget. The Congressional Budget Office (CBO), which uses less optimistic economic assumptions than those adopted by the administration, estimates lost revenues at $2 billion in 1981, $38 billion in 1982, $93 billion in 1983, $150 billion in 1984, and $199 billion in 1985.[1] The data used here are based on CBO figures developed for the Joint

1. Congressional Budget Office, *Baseline Budget Projections for Fiscal Years 1983-1987*, part 2 (Washington, D.C.: Government Printing Office, February 1982), summary table 3, p. xix.

Committee on Taxation. We use these estimates because they are consistent in their economic assumptions with those used for the outlay estimates presented in other parts of this book.

The major tax provisions are summarized in the following paragraphs; for details, see the appendix to this chapter.

Personal Income Taxes

The act reduces individual income tax rates by 5 percent in fiscal year 1981, 10 percent in 1982, and 10 percent in 1983, for a total reduction of 23 percent by 1984. Starting after fiscal year 1984, the income tax brackets as well as the zero tax bracket (the level of income under which no income tax is paid) will be indexed to the consumer price index (CPI), so that the tax rate on real income (income after adjusting for inflation) will remain constant. The act also provides for a special deduction for two-earner married couples, an increase in the deduction for child care expenses, a reduction in the tax rate on unearned income, and a new deduction of charitable contributions on tax returns that are not itemized.

Incentives for Individual Savings

The law attempts to increase individual savings through several provisions, including liberalizing provisions for the establishment of individual retirement accounts, raising the deductible amount for Keogh plans (pension plans for self-employed individuals), increasing the exclusions for interest and dividend income, and providing for tax-free "all-savers" certificates.

Corporate Income Tax Reductions

Corporate tax rates were also reduced. More importantly, depreciation schedules were simplified and reduced in number from thirty to four, and the period of time over which assets are depreciated was reduced for each category. This change, referred to as the accelerated cost recovery system (ACRS) is the largest part of the corporate changes. The act also liberalized the transfer of tax credits among firms through provisions for "leasing" credits and for the writing-off of research expenses. It also expanded the targeted-jobs tax credit by broadening the eligible populations.

Estate Tax Provisions

The amounts of gifts and estates that are exempt from taxation were increased and the tax rates on gifts and estates reduced. In addition, transfers between spouses were made exempt, and the provisions for generation-skipping transfers were extended.

Miscellaneous and Administrative Changes

Other provisions in the tax law made miscellaneous changes that, for example, extended the use of tax-free municipal bonds for transit vehicles and volunteer fire departments. In addition, administrative changes were made that limited the use of tax straddles (the purchase or sale of commodities contracts in both the long and short term for tax advantages).

Categories of Federal Revenue Loss

Of all the provisions of the 1981 tax act, the changes in the individual income tax code lead to the largest loss of federal revenues, at least after fiscal year 1981 (see table 1.15). The annual losses are expected to grow from $39 million in 1981 to $148.2 billion in fiscal 1985. The savings provisions cause an additional revenue loss of $247 million in fiscal year 1982; the loss is expected to increase to $5.6 billion in 1985. Finally, the revenues lost each year through the proposed individual estate and gift taxes changes start at $204 million in 1982 and rise to $4.2 billion in 1985.

Table 1.16 shows how reductions in income taxes affect each income category. Included in the estimates are the effects of the tax rate reductions, the deduction for two-earner married couples, and, in 1985, the effect of indexation of the tax brackets and the zero tax amount. In general, the percentage reductions rise over time and by income category.

Although the largest absolute amounts of tax reduction occur in individual income taxes, as a proportion of the total package shown in table 1.15, some of the other percentage reductions are larger. Individual income tax reductions start at 7.9 percent in 1982 and rise to 27.6 percent in 1985. The business income tax reductions, by contrast, start at 15.4 percent in 1982 and rise to 37.6 percent in 1985. The estate and gift tax reductions are also larger by comparison. They start at a 2.7 percent reduction in 1982 and rise to 24.9 percent in 1983, 34.2 percent in 1984, and 40.8 percent in 1985.[2]

Because of the immediate effects of the depreciation provisions, business taxes will be reduced by an estimated $1.6 billion in 1981 and by $39.4 billion in 1985. The "other" category in the table includes tax straddles, energy tax provisions, and administrative and miscellaneous provisions.

All told, the act is expected to lead to the largest tax reduction in United States history. At the same time, it must be noted that the changes in the personal income tax only remove the increases that would have taken place between fiscal year 1980 and fiscal year 1984 due to inflation and bracket creep, in which inflation pushes individuals with the same "real" income

---

2. Percentage reductions are estimated using the estimated revenue effects of ERTA in fiscal years 1981−85 and the CBO baseline revenue projections based on the economic assumptions of the 1982 budget resolution.

TABLE 1.15
Summary of Estimated Federal Revenue Effects,
Fiscal Years 1981–85
(dollars in millions)

Type of Provision	1981	1982	Percent of 1982 loss	Total, 1981–85
Individual income tax provisions	$ −39	$−26,947	71.6	$−361,052
Business incentives	−1,563	−10,727	28.5	−98,920
Savings provisions	0	−247	0.6	−11,880
Estate and gift tax provisions	0	−204	0.5	−9,784
Miscellaneous[a]	37	469	1.2	518
Total effect	−1,565	−37,656	100.0	−481,118

Source: Joint Committee on Taxation, General Explanation of the Economic Recovery Tax Act of 1981, Washington, December 1981, table V-1, p. 380.

a. "Miscellaneous" includes tax-exempt financing for mass transit vehicles, tax-exempt treatment of obligations of fire departments, prepaid legal services exclusion, tax straddle, energy, and administrative and other provisions.

TABLE 1.16
Individual Income Tax Cuts as a Percentage of Income,
by Income Category, Calendar Years 1982–85

Calendar year	All households	Household income (in 1982 dollars)				
		Less than $10,000	$10,000– 20,000	$20,000– 40,000	$40,000– 80,000	$80,000 and up
1982	1.9	0.8	1.0	1.7	2.5	4.6
1983	3.5	1.3	1.9	3.2	4.6	6.7
1984	4.3	1.7	2.4	4.0	5.7	7.9
1985	5.2	2.3	3.0	4.9	6.7	8.4

Source: Congressional Budget Office.

Note: Individual income tax cuts from the Economic Recovery Tax Act of 1981 included in this table are the rate cuts, the deduction for two-earner married couples, and indexing.

(that is, income adjusted for inflation) into higher nominal tax brackets.[3] The reduction in federal tax revenue relative to what would have been received if the act had not been passed starts at $1.6 billion in fiscal year 1981 and rises to $199.2 billion in 1985.[4] Like the projected deficit figures, the largest reductions occur in 1984 and 1985. The effect of these changes is to produce a substantial reduction in income taxes on individuals.

EFFECTS ON STATE AND LOCAL REVENUES

The changes outlined above in the personal and corporate income and estate tax law may, without any action by state legislatures or city or county councils, affect the amount of state and local tax revenues. The largest effects are likely to be on state corporate income taxes as a result of the accelerated depreciation provisions, but state and local personal income and inheritance taxes may also be affected in several ways. This section describes those ways.

Piggybacking

In some states, a taxpayer's state personal income tax is calculated as a percentage of the income tax paid to the federal government; that is, the state tax is "piggybacked" on the federal tax structure. If the federal government lowers tax rates or otherwise reduces federal income taxes (as it has done), the personal income tax revenues of the state will automatically be lowered. The state must then raise nominal tax rates to generate the same revenue from the same income base. This forces state governments to take politically unpopular action to simply maintain tax revenues.

Automatic Acceptance of Federal Tax Regulations

Eighteen states and many localities adopt the federal individual income tax rules to simplify tax preparation by taxpayers. The tax laws in these states specify that, with certain exceptions, the state adopts the federal tax structure. Typical exceptions include the exclusion of dividends of corporations chartered in the state, the exclusion of the federal gasoline tax as a deduction, or the taxation of interest on municipal bonds. Similarly, many state corporate income tax laws copy federal law on rules for depreciation and the like. In these cases, changes in the federal tax code, such as the revision of the

---

3. Congressional Budget Office, *Baseline Budget Projections for Fiscal Years 1983-1987,* part 2 (Washington, D.C.: Government Printing Office, February 1982), p. 32.

4. These reductions amount to 1.2 percent of gross national product in 1982 and rise to 4.7 percent of GNP in 1985. This corresponds to a 2 percent reduction relative to GNP for the 1964 tax reduction after seven years of cumulation; *ibid.,* p. 25.

rules regarding depreciation and tax credits (more than the changes in the federal corporate tax rates) will result in a direct reduction of state or local revenues. To a lesser extent, the same is true for gift and estate taxes.

In these jurisdictions the state legislature or city council will have to "uncouple" the state tax law from the federal tax law to prevent an automatic drop in the state or local tax revenues.

Adoption of the Federal Tax Structure

Six states and some localities specifically adopt individual income and corporate tax provisions modeled after federal tax law, rather than defining the entire state or local tax structure in terms of the federal code. In these cases, the federal changes do not have any automatic impact on state or local revenues unless the state legislatures or city councils specifically adopt the new federal code. However, in many of these jurisdictions there may be pressure to make the local tax code conform to the new federal tax code.

Deductions

Three states allow deduction of federal taxes from state income tax, on the theory that double taxation of income is inappropriate. In such states the state income tax revenues will increase because of the federal tax rate cuts and the increases in deductions. Since these were previously deductible, the state revenues will increase by an amount equal to the state tax rate times the reduction in federal taxes. Even in these states, however, the rise in the personal income tax revenues may be offset by the changes in the corporate tax structure, particularly the depreciation provisions.

STATE LINKAGES

Unless a state changes the relation of its tax structure to the federal tax structure, the revenue losses during the 1981−82 biennium would be substantial. The Council of State Governments surveyed the states for estimates of the revenue effects. The results of the survey (see table 1.17) suggest that the states' revenue losses from ERTA's individual and corporate income tax provisions would amount to slightly more than $700 million over the biennium.[5] The change in the corporate tax structure, primarily the accelerated cost recovery system changes in the depreciation rules, accounts for almost $600 million of this amount.

---

5. The Council of State Governments, *Economic Recovery Act: Implications for State Finances in 1982* (Washington, D.C.: Council of State Governments, 1982), table 1.

TABLE 1.17

Anticipated Impact of ERTA on State Revenue
(millions of dollars)

	Fiscal 1981			Fiscal 1982			Biennium totals		
	Individual	Corporate	Total	Individual	Corporate	Total	Individual	Corporate	Total
Alabama (a)	+M	−M	0	+10.5	−4.0	+6.5	+10.5	−4.0	+6.5
Alaska	NT	−1.4	−1.4	NT	−3.2	−3.2	NT	−4.6	−4.6
Arizona	NP	NP	NP	−3.4	−0.7	−4.1	−3.4	−0.7	−4.1
Arkansas	0	0	0	0	0	0	0	0	0
California	0	0	0	0	0	0	0	0	0
Colorado	+0.9	−3.3	−2.4	+16.9	−10.8	+6.1	+17.8	−14.1	+3.7
Connecticut	−0.1	−6.4	−6.5	−0.3	−22.5	−22.8	−0.4	−28.9	−29.3
Delaware	NP	NP	NP	−0.5	−4.0	−4.5	−0.5	−4.0	−4.5
Florida	NT	0	0	NT	0	0	NT	0	0
Georgia	0	0	0	−44.0	−35.0	−79.0	−44.0	−35.0	−79.0
Hawaii (b)	+M	−1.9	−1.9	−M	−2.9	−2.9	−M	−4.8	−4.8
Idaho	0	0	0	−0.5	−2.5	−3.0	−0.5	−2.5	−3.0
Illinois	0	−11.8	−11.8	0	−75.1	−75.1	0	−86.9	−86.9
Indiana	NP	NP	NP	0	−5.0	−5.0	−M	−5.0	−5.0
Iowa	+3.0	−2.0	−5.0	−8.0	−7.0	−15.0	−11.0	−9.0	−20.0
Kansas	NP	NP	NP	+2.1	−7.0	−4.9	+2.1	−7.0	−4.9
Kentucky	NP	NP	NP	+4.2	−16.8	−12.6	+4.2	−16.8	−12.6
Louisiana	+1.3	−5.3	−4.0	+11.1	−10.6	+0.5	+12.4	−15.9	−3.5
Maine	NP	NP	NP	−0.5	−21.1	−2.6	−0.5	−2.1	−2.6
Maryland	0	0	0	+3.0	−8.1	−5.1	+3.0	−8.1	−5.1

Table 1.17, continued

	Fiscal 1981			Fiscal 1982			Biennium totals		
	Individual	Corporate	Total	Individual	Corporate	Total	Individual	Corporate	Total
Massachusetts	0	-5.0	-5.0	0	-15.0	-15.0	0	-20.0	-20.0
Michigan	-M	0	-M	-M	0	-M	-M	0	-M
Minnesota	NP	NP	NP	NP	NP	NP	NP	NP	NP
Mississippi	-M	-2.0	-2.0	-M	-7.0	-7.0	-M	-9.0	-9.0
Missouri (a)	-2.3	-3.5	-5.8	+6.0	-23.6	-17.6	+3.7	-27.1	-23.4
Montana	NP	NP	NP	+0.7	-1.8	-1.1	+0.7	-1.8	-1.1
Nebraska (a)	-M	-M	-M	-25.4	-8.7	-34.1	-25.4	-8.7	-34.1
Nevada	NT	NT	NT	NT	NT	NT	NT	NT	NT
New Hampshire	NT	-2.5	-2.5	NT	-4.5	-4.5	NT	-7.0	-7.0
New Jersey (a)	-M	-13.0	-13.0	-M	-39.0	-39.0	-M	-52.0	-52.0
New Mexico	0	0	0	-M	-1.5	-1.5	-M	-1.5	-1.5
New York	-2.0	-35.0	-37.0	-40.0	-75.0	-115.0	-42.0	-110.0	-152.0
North Carolina	0	0	0	0	0	0	0	0	0
North Dakota	NP	NP	NP	-0.5	-0.5	-0.5	-0.5	0	-0.5
Ohio	0	0	0	-12.8	-3.2	-16.0	-12.8	-3.2	-16.0
Oklahoma	NP	NP	NP	+7.7	-11.9	-4.2	+7.7	-11.9	-4.2
Oregon	0	0	0	0	0	0	0	0	0
Pennsylvania (b)	NP	NP	NP	-0.5	0	-0.5	-0.5	0	-0.5
Rhode Island	0	-5.0	-5.0	0	-5.0	-5.0	0	-10.0	-10.0
South Carolina	0	0	0	0	0	0	0	0	0
South Dakota	NT	NT	NT	NT	NT	NT	NT	NT	NT
Tennessee	NP	NP	NP	NT	-20.0	-20.0	NT	-20.0	-20.0
Texas	NT	NT	NT	NT	NT	NT	NT	NT	NT
Utah	-M	-M	-M	+4.7	-3.9	+0.8	+4.7	-3.9	+0.8
Vermont	-4.0	-2.5	-6.5	-8.0	-4.0	-12.0	-12.0	-6.5	-18.5
Virginia	NP	NP	NP	-3.8	-16.5	-20.3	-3.8	-16.5	-20.3

Table 1.17, continued

	Fiscal 1981			Fiscal 1982			Biennium totals		
	Individual	Corporate	Total	Individual	Corporate	Total	Individual	Corporate	Total
Washington	NT	NT	NT	NT	NT	NT	NT	NT	NT
West Virginia (a)	−M	−M	−M	−M	−M	−M	−M	−M	−M
Wisconsin (a)	−2.7	−8.7	−11.4	−15.2	−27.2	−42.4	−17.9	−35.9	−53.8
Wyoming	NT	NT	NT	NT	NT	NT	NT	NT	NT
Total	−11.9	−109.3	−121.2	−100.0	−490.1	−590.1	−111.9	−599.4	−711.3

Source: The Council of State Governments.

a. Information based on federal tax year rather than state fiscal year.

b. Not verified in follow-up survey.

+M	Minimal Gain
−M	Minimal Loss
NP	Not Provided
NT	No Tax

For states that piggyback their personal income taxes on the federal income tax, an increase in the state tax rate is required. States could also raise the corporate tax rate on the now lower base in order to maintain revenue. To overcome the effects of the depreciation changes, a state could allow corporations to deduct only a percentage of the depreciation allowed for federal tax purposes.

Tables 1.18 and 1.19 list the states whose tax structures were automatically linked to the federal structure in one way or another as of late 1981. Table 1.19 identifies states where there is currently a move to alter the linkage between the state and the federal tax code for the individual income tax and the corporate income tax.

The tables indicate that states are rather quickly attempting to change their laws in order to reduce their revenue losses. Of the eighteen states that automatically conformed to some or all of the federal personal income tax provisions at the time of the survey in late 1981, seven indicated that they may disconnect the state from the federal tax structure. Of the twenty-three states that do not automatically conform to the federal structure, twelve indicated that they may conform. The remaining nine states have no individual income tax. On the other hand, Georgia, Illinois, New Jersey, New York, and Wisconsin account for more than half the revenue loss.

Twenty-three states automatically conformed to some or all of the federal corporate tax provisions. At the time of the survey, three states had already acted to disconnect the state corporate tax from the federal structure and another five indicated that they might disconnect. Twelve of the twenty-two states that do not automatically conform to the federal corporate tax law indicated they may conform.   Five states have no corporate income tax.

The information contained in these tables was valid as of January 1982. The amount of activity on the part of state legislatures to change the relation of the state tax codes to the federal tax structure is noteworthy. A number of states are moving to change the relationship of state taxes to federal taxes to avoid the automatic revenue effects of the new federal tax system.

TABLE 1.18

Relationship of State Laws to ERTA: Individual Income Tax

State	Automatically conform to some or all	Do not automatically conform	Conform some ways by choice	May conform	May disconnect	No state individual income tax
Alabama		•				
Alaska						•
Arizona		•		•		
Arkansas		•				
California		•				
Colorado	•					
Connecticut	•				•	
Delaware	•					
Florida						•
Georgia		•		•		
Hawaii		•	•	•		
Idaho		•		•		
Illinois	•			•		
Indiana		•		•		
Iowa		•		•		
Kansas	•			•		
Kentucky		•	•			
Louisiana		•				
Maine		•			•	
Maryland	•					

Table 1.18, continued

State	Automatically conform to some or all	Do not automatically conform	May conform	May disconnect	Some action taken to disconnect	No state corporate tax
Massachusetts		•				
Michigan	•				•	
Minnesota		•				
Mississippi		•	•	•		
Missouri	•				•	
Montana	•				•	
Nebraska	•				•	
Nevada						•
New Hampshire						•
New Jersey		•				
New Mexico	•					
New York	•					
North Carolina	•					
North Dakota		•	•			
Ohio	•			•		
Oklahoma	•					
Oregon		•				
Pennsylvania		•				
Rhode Island	•					
South Carolina		•				
South Dakota						•
Tennessee						
Texas						•
Utah		•	•	•		
Vermont	•					•

Table 1.18, continued

State	Automatically conform to some or all	Do not automatically conform	May conform	May disconnect	Some action taken to disconnect	No state corporate tax
Virginia	●					
Washington					●	●
West Virginia		●				
Wisconsin		●	●	●		
Wyoming						●

Source: Council of State Governments.

TABLE 1.19

Relationship of State Laws to ERTA: Corporate Tax

State	Automatically conform to some or all	Do not automatically conform	May conform	May disconnect	Some action taken to disconnect	No state corporate tax
Alabama	●	●	●			
Alaska						●
Arizona		●		●		
Arkansas		●				
California	●	●				
Colorado	●					
Connecticut	●				●	
Delaware		●				
Florida		●		●		
Georgia		●		●		
Hawaii		●		●		
Idaho	●		●	●		
Illinois		●				
Indiana		●		●		
Iowa	●			●		
Kansas		●				
Kentucky		●	●	●		
Louisiana		●	●			
Maine		●				
Maryland	●					

Table 1.19, continued

State	Automatically conform to some or all	Do not automatically conform	May conform	May disconnect	Some action taken to disconnect	No state corporate tax
Massachusetts	•				•	
Michigan		•		•		
Minnesota		•		•		
Mississippi		•	•			
Missouri	•				•	
Montana	•	•			•	
Nebraska	•					
Nevada						•
New Hampshire	•					
New Jersey	•					
New Mexico	•					
New York	•					
North Carolina		•				
North Dakota	•					
Ohio	•					•
Oklahoma		•				
Oregon	•					•
Pennsylvania	•					
Rhode Island	•					
South Carolina		•				
South Dakota						•
Tennessee	•	•			•	
Texas		•	•	•		•
Utah						
Vermont	•					

Table 1.19, continued

State	Automatically conform to some or all	Do not automatically conform	May conform	May disconnect	Some action taken to disconnect	No state corporate tax
Virginia	•					
Washington						•
West Virginia		•		•		
Wisconsin	•					
Wyoming						•

Source: The Council of State Governments.

Appendix to Chapter 5
Economic Recovery Tax Act Changes

This appendix provides details on the provisions of the Economic Recovery Tax Act of 1981. It covers changes in personal income taxes, individual savings incentives, corporate income taxes, estate taxes, miscellaneous provisions, and tax straddles.

PERSONAL INCOME TAXES

The most notable changes in the personal income tax are the changes in the marginal rates and the indexing of the tax brackets beginning in tax year 1985. Individual rates were reduced by 5 percent as of October 1, 1981, and were to be reduced by 10 percent on July 1, 1982, and again in fiscal year 1983. The actual reductions from the 1981 base will be slightly over 1 percent for tax year 1981, 10 percent in 1982, 19 percent in 1983, and 23 percent in 1984. Starting in tax year 1985, the zero tax bracket (the level of income below which no taxes are paid), the tax brackets, and the personal exemptions will be indexed according to the annual increase in the consumer price index (CPI), so that federal tax rates on real income (adjusted for increases in the CPI) will remain constant.[1]

The act also makes the following changes:

---

1. The estimated revenue effects of the specific provisions discussed here are presented in tables 1.20–24.

Joint Return Deductions

A two-earner married couple filing a joint return may use a new deduction in computing adjusted gross income. This deduction allows the spouse earning the lower income to deduct 5 percent of income up to $1,500 of the first $30,000 of earnings. For tax year 1983 and beyond, the deduction rises to 10 percent with a maximum of $3,000.

Child Care Expenses

The maximum tax credit for child care is increased from $2,000 to $2,400 for taxpayers with one dependent and double those amounts for taxpayers with two or more dependents. The percentage of income that may be excluded for child care costs is raised from 20 percent to 30 percent for taxpayers with incomes of $10,000 or less. The rate then declines by one percentage point for each $2,000 of income until it reaches the minimum rate of 20 percent for taxpayers with incomes of $28,000 or more, or until the exclusion reaches the maximum noted above. The act also excludes from an employee's income amounts paid by an employer for child care assistance to a qualified program.

Unearned Income

The maximum rate on unearned income (income from sources other than wages and salaries) drops from 70 percent to 50 percent, and the maximum rate on capital gains declines from 28 percent to 20 percent.

Charitable Contributions

Taxpayers who do not itemize their tax returns may deduct 25 percent of the first $100 of charitable contributions. In tax year 1984 the contributions amount will be raised to $300. In 1985 the deduction will be 50 percent of all contributions and in 1986 the deduction will be 100 percent. The provision will expire after tax year 1986.

Other Provisions

The act provided income exclusions for individuals working overseas and extended the period during which a taxpayer who had sold a house could purchase another without paying capital gains from eighteen months to two years. It raised the lifetime capital gains exclusion from $100,000 to $125,000 for persons over fifty-five, provided that the house is a principal residence.

TABLE 1.20
Estimated Revenue Effects of Individual Income Tax Provisions
(millions of dollars)

Provision	1981	1982	1983	1984	1985
Rate cuts and rate reduction credit	—	−25,793	−65,703	−104,512	−122,652
Indexing	—	—	—	—	−12,941
Deduction for two-earner married couples	—	−419	−4,418	−9,090	−10,973
Child-care exclusion	—	−19	−191	−237	−296
20 percent capital gain maximum rate for 1981	−39	−355	—	—	—
Charitable contributions deductions for persons who do not itemize	—	−26	−189	−219	−681
Partial income exclusion from sources outside the U.S.	—	−299	−544	−563	−618
18-month period for rollover of principal residence increased to 2 years	a	b	b	b	b
One-time exclusion of gain increased to $125,000	a	−18	−53	−63	−76
Other	a	−18	−14	−16	−17
Total	−39	−26,947	−71,112	−114,700	−148,254

Source: Joint Committee on Taxation, *General Explanation of the Economic Recovery Tax Act of 1981 (P.L. 97-34)* (Washington, D.C.: Government Printing Office, December 1981), table V−3.

a. Negligible.
b. Less than $10 million.

INDIVIDUAL SAVINGS INCENTIVES

Individual Retirement Accounts (IRAs)

The law increased the amount that could be deducted for contributions to individual retirement accounts from $1,500 or 15 percent of the taxpayer's annual compensation (whichever is lower) to $2,000 or 100 percent of compensation. Persons who are covered by an employer retirement program can now set up IRAs. The law increased from $1,750 to $2,250 the deduction for spousal IRAs—that is, accounts set up by a worker with a nonworking spouse. This has the effect of raising to $4,000 the amount that a two-earner household may voluntarily contribute to a retirement account that is deductible from federal income taxation.

Keogh Plans

The amount deductible for a self-employed retirement (Keogh) plan rose from $7,500 to $15,000 (provided it is less than 15 percent of income). This has the effect of raising the allowable contribution at higher income levels but leaves the same the maximum proportion of income that may be sheltered.

Interest and Dividend Income

In the past, taxpayers could exclude from income the first $200 in interest and dividend income. Of dividend income, a single taxpayer can now exclude the first $100 and a couple can exclude $200. Of interest income, taxpayers can now exclude 15 percent, or up to $3,000 ($6,000 for a couple). As a result of these changes, a couple could exclude as much as $1,300, compared with a previous possible maximum of $400.

All-Savers Certificates

Banks and savings and loan institutions can issue savings certificates (all-savers) that earn 70 percent of the interest rate on one-year treasury certificates. Individuals can exclude from their taxable income up to $1,000 of the interest on these certificates ($2,000 for couples). These certificates are issuable only from October 1, 1981 through December 31, 1982.

TABLE 1.21
Estimated Revenue Effects of Individual Savings Provisions
(millions of dollars)

Provision	1981	1982	1983	1984	1985
Retirement savings	—	−229	−1,339	−1,849	−2,325
Increase in self-employment retirement plan deduction	—	−56	−157	−173	−183
Repeal of $200 exclusion of interest, 15% net interest exclusion	—	566	1,916	—	−1,124
Exclusion of interest on certain savings certificates	—	−398	−1,791	−1,142	—
Reinvestment of dividends in stock of public utilities	—	−130	−365	−416	−449
Employee stock ownership plans and other provisions	—	a	−61	−627	−1,548
Other	a	a	a	a	a
Total	—	−247	−1,797	−4,207	−5,629

Source: See table 1.20.

a. Negligible.

Other Investment Incentives

Public utilities can pay stockholders newly issued stock rather than dividends. Holders of this new stock can exclude from tax up to $750 per year ($1,500 for couples). This provision expires at the end of calendar year 1985. The law also changed the rules regarding tax credits for employer contributions to employee stock ownership plans and extended the exclusion of employee contributions to employer-provided prepaid legal service plans.

CORPORATE INCOME TAXES

Corporate tax rates were lowered, and numerous changes were made in the way that corporate income is calculated. The changes will reduce taxable corporate income and taxes and are intended to serve as an incentive to investment. This will reduce federal corporate income tax revenues and,

TABLE 1.22
Estimated Revenue Effects of Corporate Income Tax Provisions
(millions of dollars)

Provision	1981	1982	1983	1984	1985
Reduction in corporate tax rates	—	−116	−365	−521	−565
Accelerated cost recovery system and related provisions	−1,503	−9,569	−16,796	−26,250	−37,285
Tax credit for qualified building rehabilitation expenditures	−9	−129	−208	−240	−304
Investment credit for used property	−24	−61	−74	−85	−137
New jobs tax credit	—	−63	−13	57	117
Credit for increasing research activities	—	−448	−708	−858	−847
Charitable contributions of scientific property used for research	a	a	a	a	a
Suspension of regulations governing research expenditures	—	−57	−120	−62	a
Subchapter S shareholders changes and related provisions	a	a	a	a	a
Simplification of LIFO inventories and small business accounting	—	−68	−184	−192	−145
Other	−27	−216	−278	−285	−282
Total	−1,563	−10,727	−18,746	−28,436	−39,448

Source: See table 1.20.

a. Less than $5 million.

depending upon the linkage of federal and state corporate tax structures, state revenues. The major changes are as follows:

Corporate Tax Rates

The lowest corporate income tax rate, which applies to the first $25,000 of income, was reduced from 17 percent to 16 percent in the tax year beginning in 1982 and 15 percent in 1983 and beyond. The rate on the second $25,000 of corporate income was reduced from 20 percent to 19 percent in the tax year beginning in 1982 and 18 percent in 1983 and beyond. For fiscal tax year corporations, the changes are prorated.

Depreciation of Assets

Thirty categories of corporate assets, all with different allowable depreciation schedules, were combined into the following four categories for investments put in place after December 31, 1980.

1. Automobiles, light trucks, machinery, research and experimentation and pollution control equipment, and racehorses. The depreciable life of this class of assets is now three years; it was previously as long as four. In addition, a one-time tax credit of 6 percent is now allowed.

2. All other machinery and equipment that previously had a depreciable life of up to eighteen years and single-use farm structures such as henhouses will now be depreciated over five years. These assets will now be eligible for a 10 percent tax credit.

3. Public utility property with a previously depreciable life of eighteen and a half to twenty-five years, railroad tank cars, some mobile homes, and certain other structures such as theme amusement parks will now be eligible for depreciation over ten years and are eligible for a 10 percent investment tax credit.

4. Classes of public utility property with a previous depreciable life of over twenty-five years as well as all other buildings will now be depreciated over fifteen years. Public utility property is eligible for a 10 percent investment tax credit.

The law also allows for accelerated depreciation in the early years of the life of the asset and further allows for this accelerated rate to increase for assets put in place in calendar 1985 and beyond.

Tax Credits

Several changes were made to liberalize the use of tax credits. The most important and controversial of these is the provision liberalizing leasing laws and making it easier for firms with relatively small taxable profits (or none at all) to "sell" an asset—along with the investment tax credits and accelerated depreciation benefits that go with it—to another firm that does have taxable profits. The new owner leases the asset back to the original owner, but continues to reap the benefits of the tax credit and depreciation allowance. Further, the period during which tax credits can be carried forward was extended from seven to ten years so that new (and presumably unprofitable) firms could carry investment tax credits forward to later (and presumably more profitable) years.

The legislation also increased the investment tax credit for the rehabilitation of old buildings, which was previously 10 percent for nonresidential buildings thirty or more years old. The credit is now 15 percent for nonresidential buildings thirty to thirty-nine years old, 20 percent for nonresidential buildings forty or more years old, and 25 percent for residential or nonresidential buildings that have been certified as historic. (Buildings constructed on the site of a demolished historic structure are eligible for another form of accelerated depreciation.) The act also increased the maximum amount of used property purchases that is eligible for an investment tax credit. The new maximum was $100,000; it now is $125,000 through tax year 1984 and will be $150,000 in 1985.

The targeted jobs tax credit was extended for one year to cover jobs given to an expanded eligible population. AFDC recipients, registrants in the work incentive (WIN) program, economically disadvantaged Vietnam-era veterans over the age of thirty-five, and people who had completed public service employment (PSE) programs were added to the eligible population. At the same time, eligibility of cooperative education students was limited to those who were economically disadvantaged and, probably most importantly, retroactive certification of existing employees was eliminated. This represents an expansion of the eligible population and reflects the congressional intention of expanding job demand for disadvantaged workers in the private sector. Employers can take as a tax credit 50 percent of wages up to $3,000 for a new eligible employee in the first year of employment and up to $1,500 in the second year of employment. The maximum tax credit for the firm in any year is 90 percent of the firm's tax liability.

Research and Development

The law has several provisions that are designed to stimulate corporate spending in this country. Between July 1981 and 1985, 25 percent of any expenditure by corporations in excess of the average annual amount spent in the previous three years for research and development may be taken as a tax credit. Corporations that contribute new research equipment to colleges or universities can now take larger deductions against corporate income taxes. To encourage research and development in this country, the law allows firms to offset all their U.S. research and development costs against U.S. income only rather than against U.S. and foreign income.

Small Business Benefits

A small business with as many as twenty-five shareholders can be taxed as a partnership, so that corporate rates are applied to its net income and personal income rates are not applied to any net income paid out to shareholders. The previous limit was fifteen shareholders. Small businesses can deduct the cost of purchasing new or used machinery and equipment as a business expense, rather than depreciating the cost over several years. The limit on such deductions is $5,000 in tax years 1982 and 1983, $7,500 in 1984 and 1985, and $10,000 after 1985.

The law made it simpler for small businesses to use last-in-first-out (LIFO) accounting methods. In periods of inflation the use of LIFO accounting increases the cost of goods sold and, therefore, reduces taxable profits.

ESTATE TAXES

The tax act made changes in the provisions for gift and estate taxation that significantly reduce the taxation of these asset transfers. In fact, it is estimated that when the provisions are fully operative in calendar year 1987, only 1 percent of estates will be taxed.

The major changes are as follows:

1. The total of gifts and estates that is exempt from taxation will increase substantially, from the previous $175,625 to $225,000 from deaths occurring in calendar year 1982, $275,000 in 1983, $325,000 in 1984, $400,000 in 1985, $500,000 in 1986, and $600,000 in 1987 and beyond.

2. The existing limits on the amounts of gifts and estate transfers between spouses, and the sometimes arbitrary assignment of assets to one spouse or the other that resulted from them, were repealed.

3. The maximum tax rate on estates will be reduced from the previous 70 percent to 65 percent in 1982, 60 percent in 1983, and 55 percent in 1984. When the exemption and the lower maximum rate are fully implemented, the maximum rate will only apply to gifts and estates of $2.5 million or more.

4. The annual gift tax exclusion is raised from $3,000 to $10,000 per recipient. There is an unlimited exclusion for tuition and medical expenses.

5. The law also extended until January 1983 transitional exemptions on generation-skipping transfers.

TABLE 1.23
Estimated Revenue Effects of Estate and Gift Tax Provisions
(millions of dollars)

Provision	1981	1982	1983	1984	1985
Exemptions from taxation	—	a	−1,077	−1,981	−2,811
Unlimited marital deduction	—	a	−303	−304	−311
Reduction in maximum rates of tax	—	a	−172	−371	−556
Increase in annual gift tax exclusion; unlimited exclusion for certain transfers	—	−123	−204	−201	−187
Postponement of generation skipping tax effective date	b	b	b	b	b
Other	—	−81	−358	−361	−383
Total	—	−204	−2,114	−3,218	−4,248

Source: See table 1.20.

a. Less than $5 million.

b. Negligible.

MISCELLANEOUS PROVISIONS

Tax-Exempt Bonds for Local Government Transit Vehicles

Prior law allowed issuance of federal income tax-exempt bonds for the construction of mass transit facilities (terminals, stations) that were owned by a private firm or individual and leased to local governments. This has the effect of reducing the leasing cost to the local government. Under the new tax act, this privilege is extended to bonds for the purchase of transit vehicles. This means that a firm buying subway cars or buses for lease to a local government can use tax-exempt bond financing.

TABLE 1.24
Effects of Miscellaneous Provisions
(millions of dollars)

Provision	1981	1982	1983	1984	1985
Tax-exempt financing for vehicles used for mass commuting	—	a	−7	−29	−54
Tax-exempt treatment of obligations of certain volunteer fire depts.	a	a	a	a	a
Prepaid legal services exclusion	—	−16	−24	−26	−8
Tax straddles	37	623	327	273	249
Energy provisions	—	−1,320	−1,742	−2,242	−2,837
Administrative	—	1,182	2,048	1,856	718
Other	—	—	435	766	309
Total	37	469	1,037	598	−1,623

Source: See 1.20.

a. Less than $1 million.

Volunteer Fire Departments

Previous law allowed the use of tax-exempt bond financing for local governmental units that had the powers of taxation, eminent domain, or police power. The new law extends this use of tax-exempt bonds to volunteer fire departments that sell the bonds for the primary purpose of buying firehouse facilities or fire trucks, provided that they provide firefighting or emergency medical services in areas not covered by local government services but provided under contract to the appropriate local governmental unit; that is, areas in a local governmental jurisdiction in which volunteer units provide these services. This exemption applies to bonds issued after December 31, 1980.

Exclusion of Employer Prepaid Legal Service Costs

Previous law allowed employees to exclude from taxable income the amount their employer paid for prepaid legal services. This provision would have expired in 1981, but the act extends it to 1984. This means that employer contributions to prepaid legal service plans have the same status as employer contributions to pension plans through calendar year 1983.

TAX STRADDLES

A "tax straddle" is the purchase or sale of substantially equivalent securities, particularly commodities contracts, in both the long term and the short term. Until the passage of the 1981 tax act, the tax status of straddles had been unclear. The commodities provisions were originally put in the tax code to allow farmers to protect themselves from variations in the prices of commodities between planting and harvesting. However, they also had the effect of allowing investors to convert regular income to capital gains and to defer the taxation of income on capital gains. This phenomenon had been increasingly used and advertised by firms offering tax shelters and were thought to be disrupting commodities markets. Generally, the provisions of the 1981 act limit the deduction of short-term losses to that net of realized long-term capital gains and set limits on the loss (gain) carry forward or backward. That is, it limits the ability of the taxpayer to convert short-term to long-term capital gains and avoid taxation of income received from straddles.

6

Federal Deregulation and State and Local Governments

By Catherine Lovell

Congress enacts laws and the president signs them, but the job of interpreting what they mean and issuing regulations that put the intent of the laws into practice is up to federal agencies.

Because many federal laws affect state and local governments in one way or another, federal agencies have issued a large number of regulations with which state and local governments must comply. The number of regulations affecting local governments in particular grew rapidly during the 1970s, as many programs of direct grants to local governments were enacted. Regulations have both increased in number and widened in scope. They now touch on most aspects of state and local governments' operations. Many state and local officials feel that federal regulations have added to the costs of operating their governments and have unnecessarily limited their effectiveness in delivering programs and responding to the needs of their residents.

The result has been that these officials have joined representatives of business in complaining about federal regulation, and these complaints have had an impact in Washington. This chapter describes how that impact has been translated into several approaches to deregulation.

The chapter first outlines what federal regulations are intended to do, and how we can look at them from several perspectives. It then describes the proliferation of regulations affecting state and local governments, identifying the types of regulations that have been imposed. Finally, it describes the process by which regulations are issued and outlines five approaches that have been taken by recent administrations to try to ease the regulatory burden. The focus of this chapter is on regulations that apply to state and local governments, but because many efforts to reduce regulation of businesses also affect state and local governments, it occasionally discusses business deregulation.

THE REGULATORY PROCESS

The federal regulatory process begins with the enactment of a law. Often Congress writes its laws in broad terms; before agency administrators can put a law into operation, they must eliminate ambiguities, clarify standards, and develop procedures for implementation. They do these things in the process of making rules, which are called regulations. Throughout the life of the statute the administering agency continues to issue regulations that elaborate on the law and, sometimes, even change its meaning. The process of rule making involves preparing proposed rules, obtaining public comments on them, and issuing final rules that take the comments into account. The detailed steps in rule making are explained later in this chapter.

Dimensions of the Regulatory Process

The complete regulatory process may be thought of as having three dimensions: *statutory, administrative,* and *behavioral.* Regulations contain restatements of the provisions of a law; this is the statutory dimension. They also contain the agency's interpretations of legislative intent, and the agency's plans for implementing the law; this is the administrative dimension. After regulations have been issued, federal agencies must enforce them, which the agencies do for different regulations with varying degrees of vigor; this is the behavioral dimension.

The three dimensions are illustrated by experience over the past several years with the administration of the community development block grant (CDBG) program as it affects local governments. Section 104(b)(2) of the Housing and Community Development Act of 1974, which set up the program, required that participating jurisdictions give "maximum feasible priority to activities which will benefit low- and moderate-income families or aid in the prevention of slums and blight." Section 101(c) mandated that projects benefit "principally persons of low and moderate income." These terms were further defined in the law.

The administering agency—the Department of Housing and Urban Development (HUD)—had to establish operational meanings and develop enforcement mechanisms. In writing its regulations, HUD repeated the intent of the act—to aid persons of low and moderate income (the *statutory* dimension). For implementation purposes the regulations went further to define "low income" to mean less than 50 percent of the metropolitan median income, and "moderate income" to be between 51 percent and 80 percent of the median (the *administrative* dimension).

Neither the law nor HUD defined in quantitative terms the meaning of the terms "maximum feasible priority" or "principally benefits." As a result, there was neither a floor nor a ceiling to guide officials of a local government about how much of their grant they should direct to projects benefiting low-income residents, nor was there an objective measure against which HUD could evaluate a community's success in targeting benefits on low-income areas. Thus the amount of low-income targeting that HUD desired became a matter of the policy preferences of HUD officials administering the programs (the *behavioral* dimension). In fact, for the first two years of the CDBG program, under the Nixon administration, HUD required only that local officials certify that their CDBG program had given maximum feasible priority to activities that benefited low- or moderate-income families or helped eliminate slums or blight. Some HUD regional offices looked behind the certification to see where benefits actually accrued, but other offices did not—a further illustration of the behavioral dimension.

HUD enforcement practices changed when the Carter administration took over. New rules on low-income targeting were issued. The new HUD administrators no longer merely reviewed the procedures that local governments followed. Instead, HUD officials reviewed the substance of local programs, seeking more detailed verification that projects were actually designed to reach low- and moderate-income residents. The vigor with which the regulations were enforced as well as some of the administrative rules—both the administrative and behavioral dimensions—had changed greatly between the two administrations.

Examination of changes in regulatory processes and discussions of deregulation must consider all three dimensions—statutory, administrative, and behavioral. Regulations in large part are statutorily based, written to explain what laws mean and what affected parties must do to carry them out. Attempts at deregulation must, therefore, be directed partly at Congress and the number and character of laws its members write. Deregulation in its administrative dimension must focus on rule making that goes beyond the intent of laws or changes their meanings and is procedurally unsound, or produces rules that are unclear, duplicative, or foolish. For the behavioral dimension of deregulation, we must examine the size and intentions of agency staffs charged with enforcement of regulations.

GROWTH AND TYPES OF REGULATIONS

The number of federal regulations affecting state and local governments has grown significantly over the last fifteen years. Much of the growth has come about as a result of the increase in numbers of federal grants since 1960 and the growth in the 1970s of direct grants to local governments. As table 1.25 shows, more than 1,200 regulations affecting local governments were added between 1961 and 1978, of which more than half (663) were imposed between 1971 and 1975.

TABLE 1.25

Number of Federal Regulations Directly Affecting Local Governments, Selected Years, by Types

Type	Year of imposition or substantial amendment			
	1961−65	1966−70	1971−75	1976−78
Programmatic	8	42	92	66
Procedural	23	94	571	324
Total	31	136	663	390
Vertical	22	114	476	309
Crosscutting	9	22	187	81
Total	31	136	663	390

Source: Catherine Lovell, Max Neiman, Robert Kneisel, Adam Rose, and Charles Tobin, *Federal and State Mandating on Local Governments: Report to the National Science Foundation* (Riverside, Calif.: University of California, June 1979). Regulations were obtained from the *Code of Federal Regulations.*

Note: The figures represent a best estimate of the numbers of federal regulations that directly affected local governments in 1978.

As numbers of grants have grown and as Congress and the agencies have tried to correct problems in regulatory arrangements, regulations have grown not only more numerous but also more complex. As table 1.26 shows, the number of pages in the *Code of Federal Regulations* devoted to the general revenue sharing program tripled over six years, and for each of two block grant programs—CETA and CDBG—the number of pages quadrupled over a few years. As Congress gained experience with grant programs over the last decade, it has tightened program guidelines. When questions of statutory interpretations, problems in management, and allegations of abuse arose, the federal agencies administering the programs have added new regulations or expanded the old ones.

Total numbers of regulations, however, do not tell the full story; regulations differ in several ways. In thinking about federal regulations that affect state and local governments, we can classify regulations in three ways: (1) by enforcement basis, (2) by scope of application, and (3) by the kind of governmental process affected. The first two classifications help us understand the source and legal basis for imposing regulations and how the regulations are applied. The third classification is particularly useful in understanding the complaints of state and local governments about the scope and detailed nature of regulations, and is essential in determining what kinds of regulations may be needed and what kinds serve no purpose.

TABLE 1.26
Program Rules in the Code of Federal Regulations
(number of pages)

Year	GRS	CETA	CDBG
1973	21	—	—
1974	22	97	—
1975	22	154	56
1976	26	331	63
1977	43	291	79
1978	46	353	195
1979	66	487	202

Source: Donald F. Kettl, "Regulating the Cities," Publius, vol. 2, no. 2 (spring 1981). Data are from the U.S. Office of the Federal Register, Code of Federal Regulations, various years. For GRS, 31 CFR 51; for CETA, 20 CFR 675−689 and 29 CFR 93−99; and for CDBG, 24 CFR 58, 570−571.

Basis of Enforcement

Four out of five regulations that affect local governments (1,037, or 82 percent of the 1,260 that existed as of 1978) are imposed as *conditions of aid*. They can be imposed on a jurisdiction only so long as it accepts federal aid. Some condition-of-aid regulations require a recipient government to undertake certain kinds of activities; for example, to receive community development funds a jurisdiction must develop a housing assistance plan. Other condition-of-aid regulations detail specific procedures for carrying them out; for example, a jurisdiction must use certain data sources in preparing its housing assistance plan.

The other 20 percent of regulations affecting local governments are *direct order* regulations, which flow from the authority of the federal government to impose requirements on other governments. For example, the federal government, using its constitutional authority to "protect the public health," can impose clean air or clean water standards.

Scope of Application

A second useful distinction among types of regulations is the scope of their application. *Vertical regulations* apply specifically to one functional area, and *horizontal or cross-cutting regulations* are applied across functional areas.

An example of a vertical regulation is the requirement that a health program include a home visit component. An example of a horizontal regulation is the requirement that all government offices in the jurisdiction be made accessible to the handicapped.

Three-quarters (76 percent) of the regulations that affect local governments are vertical regulations, each applying to one function or program. Although cross-cutting regulations make up only about one-quarter of the regulations on the books, they have been particularly controversial.

The number of cross-cutting regulations has grown rapidly over the last fifteen years. This kind of regulation is not directly related to the program for which a grant is given but is attached to the grant as a condition of the aid.[1] These regulations grow out of some forty federal laws and are attached as conditions to grant programs which are used as the vehicles for broadening the applicability of the laws to states and local governments.

Among the cross-cutting regulations are the following:

- *Nondiscrimination* requirements growing out of the Civil Rights Act and, later, laws providing certain rights to the handicapped, to women, and to older people.

- *Environmental protection* laws and executive orders on such subjects as air and water protection, archeological and historic preservation, and protection for endangered species, wetlands, and wild and scenic rivers.

- *Labor standards,* including rules based on the Davis-Bacon Act to assure payment of prevailing wages, and procurement standards based on the Federal Procurement Policy Act.

- *Health, welfare, and safety protection* rules, in such areas as protection for human subjects in research, worker safety standards, and animal welfare.

- Rules arising from the Freedom of Information Act.

Many of the cross-cutting requirements have been considered particularly onerous by some state and local government officials who feel that it is inappropriate or inefficient to use specific service programs like highway building or water purification to meet social goals that they consider to be unrelated. Some state and local officials also disagree with the substance of some of the laws, or are experts in sewers or roads and know little about the intricacies of new social legislation. When the cross-cutting regulations accompany a sewer treatment plant grant, for example, the public works

---

1. For a study of cross-cutting regulations, see U.S. Office of Management and Budget, *Managing Federal Assistance in the 1980's* (Washington D.C.: Government Printing Office, 1980). For further discussion see Claude E. Barfield, Jr., "Unsnarling the Federal Grant System," *Regulation,* September/October 1981, pp. 37−46.

department must make sure that minority contractors have an opportunity to bid, that the plans meet handicapped access requirements, that the people displaced by the land acquisition process are moved and treated in accordance with regulations on relocation, that environmental impact assessments are completed, that the department hires and trains minority people, that its inspectors monitor all OSHA requirements on the job, that citizens are consulted on the project, and so forth. Clearly the costs for departmental activities are greater when they have to include the costs of meeting a broad spectrum of nationally defined social goals. Clearly, also, public works departments are not necessarily equipped to carry out the activities required to meet the broader goals. Understanding the incidence of cross-cutting regulations helps particularly in analyzing some of the concern about the quantity and scope of regulatory activity.

OMB Circulars as Cross-Cutting Regulations

The rapid growth in the size and diversity of federal aid programs and the increase in accompanying regulations has brought demands for simplification and standardization of financial and other procedural regulations. The Office of Management and Budget (OMB) has been working with grant-making agencies, the General Accounting Office (GAO), and representatives of state and local governments to develop a series of financial circulars that establish uniform policies and rules to be observed by all executive branch agencies, and to develop circulars that attempt to coordinate grant programs. The circulars are administered by OMB but are implemented through the regulations of the federal grant making agencies.

These regulations have become a type of cross-cutting requirement attached to all grants. Although they were designed to aid recipient governments, many state and local governments see them as regulations. The most important of these are the following:

- *OMB Circular A–102* establishes uniform financial and other administrative requirements for grants to state and local governments. It provides guidance about banking procedures; bonding and insurance; records retention; waiver of single state agency requirements; handling of interest earned on grant funds pending disbursement and other program income; how to calculate matching contributions, particularly in-kind contributions; standards for grantees' financial management systems; financial reporting requirements; monitoring and reporting program performance; budget revision procedures; grant closeout procedures; forms for applying for grants; property management systems; procurement standards; and audit standards.

- *OMB Circular A−87* provides uniform rules for determining costs applicable to grants and contracts with state and local governments. It defines allowable costs and sets forth the procedures by which costs are recovered. It also provides that one federal agency will negotiate grantees' indirect costs on behalf of all other federal agencies.
- *OMB Circular A−73* sets forth policies to be followed in the audit of federal operations and the audit of federal grants to state and local governments. Its objective is to encourage comprehensive audit planning and better coordination among federal, state, and local government auditors.
- *OMB Circular A−111* establishes policies and procedures to be followed in jointly funded assistance to state and local governments and nonprofit organizations.
- *OMB Circular A−95* attempts to coordinate grant proposals and provide governors and federal agencies with information about grants in any state by setting up machinery and procedures for state review and evaluation of grant proposals. It requires state or areawide clearinghouses for grant applications.

Governmental Process Affected

Another way of classifying regulations is by the process affected. There are two major types: programmatic and procedural. Each has several subtypes. *Programmatic* regulations are almost always based on a law and specify what must come out of a program operated by a jurisdiction. *Procedural* regulations are almost always based on administrative actions; they prescribe particular procedures that a jurisdiction must follow in the day-to-day operation of programs. In a sense, they specify what must go into a program's operations.

Table 1.27 shows various subtypes of programmatic and procedural regulations and their numbers in 1978. By far the largest number of regulations (83 percent) are procedural. Both programmatic and procedural regulations may be applied vertically or horizontally and may be either direct orders or conditions of aid.

Programmatic Regulations

Following are the subtypes of programmatic regulations:

Program regulations impose an action, responsibility, goal, service, or function but do not specify the quality or quantity. An example is a rule requiring all general-purpose local governments to adopt a general plan. This is a direct order that applies vertically. An example of a program regulation imposed as a condition of aid and applied horizontally would be the following:

TABLE 1.27
Programmatic and Procedural Regulations in 1978, by Type

Type	Percent	Number
Programmatic		
Program	9.9	125
Program quality	5.6	71
Program quantity	2.4	24
Procedural		
Reporting	12.5	158
Performance	36.7	463
Fiscal	12.5	165
Personnel	9.6	120
Planning and evaluation	6.1	77
Record keeping	4.5	57
Total	100.0	1,260

Source: Catherine Lovell, Max Neiman, Robert Kneisel, Adam Rose, and Charles Tobin, *Federal and State Mandating on Local Governments: Report to the National Science Foundation* (Riverside, Calif.: University of California, June 1979). Regulations were obtained from the *Code of Federal Regulations*.

Note: The figures represent a best estimate of the numbers of federal regulations that directly affected local governments in 1978.

> All general-purpose governments receiving revenue sharing funds must establish a program of affirmative action in the hiring of local personnel.

Program quality regulations specify either (1) the conditions and characteristics of each unit of goods or services delivered by a program, or (2) the kinds of groups or people eligible to receive the goods and services. Examples of quality regulations are the following:

> Each school lunch provided must contain food elements from each of the basic food sources.

> All hospitals participating in a program to increase the supply of hospital care must ensure that adequate laboratory and X-ray facilities are available.

Program quantity regulations specify the number of times a given unit of a good or service must be produced. An example of a program quantity regulation might be that there must be a certain number of toilets per square block of park area.

Procedural Regulations

Procedural regulations focus on how things must be done. There are six main subtypes of procedural regulations:

Reporting regulations require a jurisdiction to send data or information to some specified place or agency, or to publish information for the public. Examples might include rules requiring reporting of results of evaluation studies, documentation of eligibility for programs, and publishing public notices of governmental proceedings.

Performance regulations provide detailed instruction on how a program must be carried out. For example, a performance regulation might require that schools participating in a school lunch program provide some instruction in nutrition for the children, or that drug-treatment centers provide assistance in career planning to their clients.

Fiscal regulations specify how the fiscal resources attached to a particular program or grant must be organized, accounted for, or monitored. Examples are requirements to conduct audits, to adopt federal accounting procedures, to restrict equipment purchases, or to limit the amount of funds that can be spent on administrative overhead.

Personnel regulations specify how individuals employed in programs must be recruited, what their qualifications should be, and the like. Examples are rules that a program providing career planning and advice for drug addicts must retain a professional career planner, that employees in a program must be enrolled in social security, and that hiring practices must emphasize public notification of job opportunities.

Planning and evaluation regulations require that activities be coordinated with an overall program plan, that the plan be reviewed by some outside agency, or that the agency administering the program must review or assess the degree to which it is accomplishing what it is supposed to do.

Examples of *planning* regulations are a requirement that applications for health care assistance be submitted to a regional health systems agency for review, and a requirement that a jurisdiction show that proposed low-cost housing is consistent with local zoning rules before the project can be funded. Examples of *evaluation* regulations are a requirement that a drug use abatement program must follow up on its former patients to see how well the program reached its goals, and a requirement that a nutrition program use specified methods for assessing improvements in child health.

Record-keeping regulations are any requirements that oblige a government to retain information or data. Examples include requirements for keeping records of the numbers and names of participants in a program or the retention of patient treatment histories.

Procedural regulations tell state and local governments *how* to do things and are least palatable to them. Procedures are the most likely to be location and organization-related and the least amenable to generalization. A large part of the discontent about federal regulations is the mismatch between general procedural regulations and local situations.

REASONS FOR THE MOVEMENT TOWARD REFORM

States and local governments have always resisted or disliked federal regulations, for two main reasons. First, they object to the loss of autonomy made explicit by the regulatory relationship. The pervasiveness of regulatory activity has substituted prescription and compulsion for the autonomous negotiating relationship among the various governmental spheres which the traditional federalist defenders would insist is the touchstone of a democratic system.

Second, states and local governments object to the costs of the requirements placed upon them by the federal government. Although empirical research on fiscal impacts is not extensive, several studies have shown that costs are often substantial.[2] The work of the Federal Paperwork Commission was especially valuable in documenting the several-million-dollar cost of information-gathering regulations. The studies suggest that regulations force local governments to reorder their budget priorities, and that regulations play an increasingly important role in determining what local governments do and how they spend their money. State and local governments must often bend general rules to fit particular situations, and that is often costly. A key question raised by state and local governments is who should pay the costs when regulations require them to do things they would not do otherwise, or to do things in a different way than they think is most efficient.

The demand for regulatory reform by state and local governments has grown stronger over the last decade as the number of federal regulations has increased and as the range and scope of regulations have expanded.

---

2. For three studies of cost impacts, see Catherine Lovell and Charles Tobin, "The Mandate Issue," *Public Administration Review,* May/June 1981, pp. 318–330; Thomas Muller and Michael Fix, "The Impact of Selected Federal Actions on Municipal Outlays," Joint Economic Committee of Congress, October 1980; and The Academy for Contemporary Problems, *Impact of Federal Paperwork on State and Local Governments: A Report to the Commission on Federal Paperwork* (Columbus, Ohio: The Academy for Contemporary Problems, 1977).

The regulation issue for local governments has also been exacerbated by a configuration of forces that is pressing on them. They are caught between (1) demands from constituents who expect government to increase the quality and range of public service, while at the same time expecting local governments to protect diversity of interests and rights to community; (2) increased pressures from federal agencies to enlarge the scope and alter the processes of local government services; and (3) growing difficulties in extracting the necessary local revenues, partly as a result of restrictions on revenue bases and rates, partly as a result of economic downturns. This configuration of forces leads to more dependence on grants-in-aid and to greater vulnerability to external demands. It also leads to more desire for autonomy and to a search for the most economical way to provide services.

Excessive regulation seems to constrain state and local government options. State and local governments have also often felt closed out of the regulatory process and have complained about lack of consultation by federal agencies with them as regulations are developed. It is within this context that demands for regulatory reform come from state and local governments.

APPROACHES TO REFORM

Since the days of the Nixon administration, regulatory reformers have advocated or implemented various activities that fall within each of five general approaches. The particular approaches emphasized by an administration depend, of course, on the purposes of the reformers and the values that underlie those purposes. Reformers run the gamut from those who accept extensive federal regulation and merely want to make it as effective and flexible as possible to those who believe that federal regulation should be kept at an absolute minimum.

Following are the five approaches:

1. *Generating and sharing information during the rule-making process.* Advocates of this reform approach assume that regulatory actions will be more thoughtful and effective if there is more analysis and openness in the process and greater participation by those affected by the rules being made. They hold that possession of fuller information will ensure that all interested actors know what is likely to happen to them and that decision makers can then better foresee the results of their actions.

2. *Enlarging congressional control over rule-making processes.* Those who support this approach assume that federal agencies have a built-in dynamic that leads them to write new regulations, but that these regulations do not need to be as detailed and complex as they are in order to implement laws. They believe that agencies have been insufficiently sensitive to congressional intentions in their development of regulations.

3. *Strengthening executive oversight of agency rule making*. Proponents of this approach to reform also assume that federal agencies have a proclivity to write new rules, and that they show a control and professional bias, erring in the direction of overregulation. These proponents contend that the agencies develop strong biases from their functional perspectives and are insensitive to cost impacts and to the other general consequences of their regulatory actions, because they know little about the activities of other agencies and have no grasp of the overall regulatory burdens.

4. *Removing the federal government's need to be involved in regulatory activity*. Some reformers move from the assumption that much federal regulatory activity is harmful and intrusive economically or socially but that, so long as the federal government manages or funds programs, regulatory activity is inevitable. Therefore, they argue, in order to reduce federal regulatory activity, the government must reduce federal programs.

5. *Reducing enforcement intensity of existing regulations*. This reform stance is also based on the assumption that regulatory actions are intrusive and inflexible and, further, that regulatory relief can be obtained primarily by relaxing enforcement or introducing more flexibility into enforcement practices, because the body of regulations is now too large to amend or suspend quickly enough.

The following discussion outlines the major initiatives affecting state and local governments that have been undertaken during the Reagan and Carter administrations under each of these approaches.

Generating and Sharing Information During Rule Making

Reforms to enlarge information during the rule-making process have concentrated on increasing opportunities for public and interest-group participation, on making regulatory activities more visible, and on requiring analysis of economic and other impacts of regulations before they are promulgated.

At present, rule making encompasses five basic steps.

1. After a law is enacted, the responsible agency develops proposed regulations and publishes them in the *Federal Register*. In developing the regulations, the agency relies in part on legislative history, including committee hearings and floor debate, for its interpretations.

2. Interested parties comment in writing to a designated agency representative. Sometimes agencies hold hearings to obtain comments. (On some legislation, a congressional oversight committee must agree to the regulations before they can become final.)

3. The agency amends the proposed regulation in light of the comments and reissues it for comment, or issues it in final form in the *Federal Register*.

4. The regulation, when final, is published in the *Federal Register* and in the *Code of Federal Regulations*.

5. Administrators implement programs and, from time to time, amend the regulations or issue new ones.

In preparing and issuing regulations the agencies are governed by the Administrative Procedures Act, initially passed in 1946, which contains certain requirements for administrative agencies in their rule-making procedures. Congress designed these requirements to ensure that the fundamental rights of citizens are not violated by administrative actions. The act directs agencies to announce in the *Federal Register* any proposed new rules or any proposed changes in existing rules. Agencies are required to give interested parties the right to submit testimony or even to appear at agency hearings when a new rule or rule change is being considered. The act also establishes judicial review processes for those appealing rules.

The *Federal Register* is published every weekday of the year except federal holidays. The period during which affected parties can comment varies, but is usually thirty, sixty, or ninety days. In each instance, the *Register* gives detailed instructions on how and when a viewpoint can be expressed—for example, through written submissions or orally at a public hearing. Rule making is sometimes rapid but is more often an extended process. Each agency may set its own time limits for promulgating regulations and can take months reviewing comments or completing other steps, sometimes stretching the process out for years. Court challenges of a regulation can also prolong the process.

Public Participation

A first method of enlarging information during the rule-making process has been the attempt to facilitate public participation. President Carter's 1978 executive order on improving government regulation required agencies to write all regulations in plain English, to designate an agency contact person for each rule so that the public knows who to contact with questions; and to take explicit steps to encourage public comment and allow sufficient time for it.[3] An accompanying memorandum set up special procedures by which the national organizations of state and local governments were to be consulted on regulations.[4]   President Reagan, in his February 1981 executive order on federal regulation, continued instructions to the agencies about clarity but revoked requirements regarding special agency outreach techniques and made no mention of special procedures for consulting with state and local governments.[5]

Making Regulatory Activities More Visible

Presidents Carter and Reagan and Congress have taken steps to make regulatory activities generally more visible. President Carter in 1978 required agencies to publish at least twice a year in the *Federal Register* an agenda of significant regulations under development or review, so that the public could know what matters agencies have under consideration. He also established a Regulatory Council composed of representatives of all executive departments and agencies; one of its charges was to publish, at least every six months, a unified calendar of major regulations under consideration.[6]   In 1980 Congress, following President Carter's lead, passed the Regulatory Flexibility Act requiring agencies to publish a regulatory agenda every six months (April and October) in the *Federal Register* announcing which regulations they were considering and which they were reviewing for possible phaseout.[7]   The act also required that all notices of proposed rule making in the *Federal Register* must describe those groups to be affected by the rule; identify rules that the proposed rule might duplicate or affect; assure that the agency would consider alternatives to the proposed rule that would substantially reduce the economic and other impacts on individuals and small businesses, organizations, and governmental jurisdictions; and state the purposes, difficulties, and costs of complying with the regulation.

In his 1981 executive order, President Reagan reiterated the requirement that all agencies publish twice yearly an agenda of proposed regulations or regulatory changes.[8]   He created a Regulatory Information Service Center

---

3. Jimmy Carter, Executive Order 12044, *Federal Register*, March 24, 1978, pp. 12661–12665.

4. For a full discussion of these procedures and the history of problems with formalizing federal agency consultation with state and local government national organizations, see Margaret Wrightson, ''Regulatory Reform, Recent Federal Initiatives,'' in *Federal Regulation of States and Local Governments*, draft report, U.S. Advisory Commission on Intergovernmental Relations, Summer 1982.

5. Ronald Reagan, Executive Order 12291, *Federal Register*, February 19, 1981, pp. 13193–13198.

6. ''Memorandum for Heads of Executive Departments and Agencies, October 31, 1978, *Administration of Jimmy Carter*, pp. 1905–1906.

7. P. L. 96–354, September 19, 1980.

8. Executive Order 12291, *Federal Register*, February 19, 1981.

to standardize these agendas so that they contain the same types of data and can be computerized. The calendars of agendas organize the data by agency and by segment of the public (such as small businesses or state and local governments) that are to be affected.

The rule-making process is without doubt now more visible. It is easier to trace regulatory activity; the proposed rules and the calendars of regulatory considerations delineate those that may affect state and local governments and make it easier to find and understand regulations.

Analysis of Regulation Impact

Many proponents of regulatory reform have put greatest emphasis on regulatory impact analyses of various sorts. Such analyses were begun when President Ford introduced the "inflation impact statement" (later renamed "economic impact statement"), under which agencies were required to perform economic analyses of their major regulatory proposals.[9] President Ford designated the Office of Management and Budget (OMB) to oversee the process; OMB in turn delegated responsibility to the Council on Wage and Price Stability (CWPS). Neither OMB nor the CWPS had the authority to delay implementation of a rule or change it, so agency cooperation with the impact analysis program was partial at best.[10]

President Carter expanded the review and oversight process.[11] He replaced the concept of a "major" rule with the concept of a "significant" rule, presumably to allow agency heads to consider noneconomic but still significant impacts. A rule was to be classified as "significant" if it would cause (1) an annual effect on the economy of $100 million or more; (2) a major increase in costs or prices for individual industries, levels of government, or geographic regions; or (3) other significant impacts. President Carter's order created the Regulatory Analysis Review Group to help agencies analyze economic and other consequences of proposed "significant" rules and explore alternatives. Rather than doing strict cost-benefit analyses, agencies were to describe for the public the major alternative ways of dealing with the regulatory problem that had generated the proposed rule, and to provide an analysis of the consequences of each of the alternatives and a detailed

---

9. Gerald R. Ford, Executive Order 11821, *Federal Register* November 29, 1974, pp. 41501–41502.

10. Thomas D. Hopkins, acting assistant director for government operations and research, Council on Wage and Price Stability, interview with Katherine Burnick, March 31, 1977, cited in Katherine Burnick, "The Inflation Impact Statement Program and Executive Branch Coordination," draft for the American Bar Association Commission on Law and Economy Study of Federal Regulation, May 18, 1977.

11. Jimmy Carter, Executive Order 12044, *Federal Register,* March 24, 1978, pp. 12661–12665.

explanation of the reasons for choosing one alternative over the others. The analysis and the Regulatory Analysis Review Group's comments were to be made public before a proposal could be published in the *Federal Register*. In 1980, Congress passed the Regulatory Flexibility Act, incorporating the "significant rule" concept and the impact assessment requirement. The act directs agencies to ignore strict cost-benefit criteria and to do a broad analysis of alternatives.

Evaluations of the Carter administration's regulatory review program seem to agree that the program had more impact on regulatory decision making than the Ford administration's approach, both because the Carter program was more active and because the agencies, the Regulatory Analysis Review Group, and the Council on Wage and Price Stability were gaining a better sense of what was desired.[12]   In the final analysis, however, the Carter program's effects on regulatory growth were not great.[13]   While some agency decisions may have been improved by the introduction of new information, agencies did not have sufficient staff or staff capabilities to undertake adequate analyses, standards were inadequate or lines of oversight responsibility were blurred, and agency compliance was often less than adequate.[14]

President Reagan in his 1981 executive order continued the emphasis on regulatory impact analysis. His order set forth clear and largely economic standards for regulatory analysis and gave unambiguous power to OMB to guide and enforce the analysis process. The order returned to the Ford administration's concept of "major" rule, describing as "major" any regulation that would result in an annual effect on the economy of $100 million or more or a major increase in costs of prices for consumers, individuals, or local governments. Regulations were divided into "major" and "all other." Agencies are required to submit their regulatory impact analyses to OMB, which has the power to reject them. Analyses must meet the following detailed standards established by OMB:

---

12. For a discussion of various evaluations of the program see Margaret Wrightson, *op. cit.*

13. *Ibid.*

14. For a discussion of the shortcomings of the program see Christopher DeMuth, "Constraining Regulatory Costs: The White House Programs," *Regulation,* January/February 1980, p. 22; and George Eads, "Harassing Regulation: The Evolving Role of White House Oversight," *Regulation,* May/June 1981, p. 24.

1. There must be adequate information concerning the need for and consequences of the proposed action.

2. The potential benefits to society must outweigh the potential costs.

3. Of all the alternative approaches to the given regulatory objective, the proposed action must maximize the net benefits to society.

4. The chosen alternative must have the least costs.

5. The analysis must identify sources of regulatory authority.

6. There must be a detailed analysis of costs and benefits including costs estimates, benefit estimates, and net benefit estimates (in dollars where possible).

Agencies are required to make their preliminary and final regulatory impact analyses available to the public. Those effects that cannot be quantified must be explained, and those groups most likely to bear the costs must be identified.

Although it is too soon to evaluate the effects of the regulatory impact analysis efforts under the Reagan administration, it is clear that the review process has been strengthened and that commitment to the process is strong. President Reagan's order placed unprecedented implementation authority in the OMB and its Office of Information and Regulatory Analysis. OMB has estimated that for 1981 the office reviewed fifty major regulations out of a total of approximately three thousand new or amended regulations proposed. Full regulatory impact analyses were undertaken on only nineteen of these; reviews of the other thirty-one were waived for emergency or other conditions.[15] No record has been compiled of potential regulations that were not proposed due to the findings of the impact analyses.

Debate over the cost-benefit analysis requirement is growing.[16] Agencies have run up against the problems that have always plagued cost-benefit analysis when attempts are made to apply it to social programs, where numbers cannot really substitute for value judgments. Although analysts have made progress in recent years in cost-benefit methodology, dollar figures are still difficult to attach to the benefits of health, environmental, civil rights, and other social activities. A recent ruling by the Supreme Court may also slow down the use of cost-benefit analysis.[17] The Court ruled in June 1981

---

15. Office of the Vice President, *Year-End Summary of Actions Taken by the Presidential Task Force on Regulatory Relief,* December 3, 1981.

16. For one summary of the issues in this debate, see Steven Kelman, "Cost-Benefit Analysis, An Ethical Critique," *Regulation,* January/February 1981, and James V. DeLong, Robert M. Solow, Gerald Butters, John E. Calfee, Pauline Ippolito, and Robert Nisbet, "Defending Cost-Benefit Analysis: Replies to Steven Kelman," *Regulation,* March/April 1981.

17. "Washington Update—Policy and Politics in Brief," *National Journal,* June

that the Occupational Safety and Health Administration (OSHA) does not have to prove that the benefits of its regulations outweigh their costs. The Court noted that there was an "absence of any indication that Congress intended OSHA to conduct its own cost-benefit analysis before promulgating a toxic material or harmful physical agent standard." Instead, the Court held, Congress was "fully aware that the act would impose real and substantial costs on industry and believed that such costs were part of the cost of doing business."

In the intergovernmental context, in particular, skeptics have complained that regulatory impact analysis does not seem suited to most of the rules issued by the Department of Health and Human Services (HHS), the Department of Education, and other agencies to control the use of federal grants.[18] Agencies have also expressed concern about the increasing amounts of paperwork they must generate with each new regulation to satisfy OMB's requirements.[19] The General Accounting Office (GAO) has estimated that the required analyses and reviews of rules will cost the agencies between $10 million and $20 million per year.[20]

Enlarging Congressional Control Over Rule Making

A second approach to regulatory reform is augmenting congressional control over rule-making processes. Understandably, the major impetus for this approach comes from Congress. The Senate in March 1981 passed a bill (S. 1080) that would provide the first major overhaul of the Administrative Procedures Act since it was enacted in 1946. The bill's most important and controversial feature calls for a two-house legislative veto of proposed regulations. Under the bill, the implementation of most rules would be delayed forty-five days while congressional committees reviewed them. If a committee recommended disapproval of a regulation, each chamber would have an additional thirty days to act. A majority of both houses would have to reject a rule for it to be "vetoed." The president would not be able to counteract the congressional veto. The measure would apply the veto across the board to all agencies except the Department of Defense and the Internal Revenue Service, and to all rules except those dealing with rates, wages, prices, or mergers. Opponents of the veto provision argue that the timing is wrong for such a proposal, since a decision is pending before the U.S. Supreme Court on the constitutionality of the legislative veto.[21] As a safeguard, the Senate

---

20, 1981, p. 1130.

18. *Ibid.*

19. *National Journal,* May 2, 1981.

20. "At a Glance: A Weekly Checklist of Major Issues," *National Journal,* June 27, 1981, p. 1179.

21. For a discussion of that case, see Laura B. Weiss and Elder Witt, "Battle

adopted an amendment to sever the veto provision if the Supreme Court finds the legislative veto unconstitutional.

The bill also would require agencies to perform cost-benefit analyses of major new regulations and would authorize OMB to establish guidelines for the cost-benefit tests. The bill would place some limits on OMB powers. OMB would be able to review the procedures followed by the agency but would not be able to comment on the substance of a rule.

The measure would strengthen the role of the courts by instructing judges not to presume that an agency's interpretation of a law is necessarily correct. This provision would place a greater burden on the agency to support its position in any appeal about a regulation. Under the current Administrative Procedures Act and legal precedents, judicial deference is given to agency expertise. S. 1080, like the Regulatory Flexibility Act, includes provisions designed to increase public participation and requires a review of major rules every ten years.

There is some doubt that the measure will pass in the House, although a companion bill (H.R. 746) cleared the House Judiciary Committee February 25, 1982 and was on the calendar for floor consideration as of this writing. The measure is generally supported by the business community and opposed by consumer groups.[22] Backers of the proposals argue that the veto power would act as a check on overregulation; that it would trim the broad, vague grants of power given many agencies in their enabling legislation; and that it would transfer power from insulated bureaucracies back to elected representatives where it belongs.[23] Opponents say that Congress would have problems giving regulations adequate review. Best estimates are that 7,500 to 9,000 new regulations are issued each year; dealing just with the major ones would overload Congress. Opponents also raise the constitutional issue of separation of powers.[24]

Strengthening Executive Oversight of Rule Making

A third approach to reform is strengthening executive oversight of agency rule making. This approach has included steps to increase the power of OMB to oversee the agencies in regulatory matters, the introduction of a "paperwork budget," and the regulatory review activities under President Reagan of the Task Force on Regulatory Relief (the Bush Commission).

Over Legislative Veto Coming to a Head February 22 Before Supreme Court," *Congressional Quarterly,* February 6, 1982, pp. 200–202.

22. Diana Granat, "Senate Unanimously Passes Broad Regulatory Reform," *Congressional Quarterly,* March 27, 1982, p. 701.

23. Michael Wines, "A Heavy Load," *National Journal,* January 2, 1982, p. 34.

24. *Ibid.*

Increasing OMB's Oversight Powers

The powers of OMB to oversee the agencies in regulatory matters have grown with each administration. President Carter gave OMB the responsibility for implementing his regulatory executive order, but OMB did not develop strong procedures for controlling agency rule making. President Reagan's executive order placed unprecedented coordination and implementation authority in the OMB, which now works in tandem with the Bush Commission (discussed below).[25] Agencies are required to submit all proposed rules, major and minor, to OMB for its approval before they are first published in the *Federal Register,* and all final major rules before their final publication in the *Register.* Proposed major rules must be submitted sixty days before their first publication, along with their full regulatory impact analysis. Proposed minor rules must be submitted ten days prior to publication. OMB has the power to designate any rule as major. OMB also has the power to suggest to the agencies that existing rules be terminated.

The OMB approval process, under the Reagan administration, operates as follows. Agency regulatory officers (designated for this purpose) send proposed and final rules to OMB once they have been completely reviewed and approved in the agency.[26] OMB keeps track of each submission by computer; each is subjected to a triple review process by an OMB desk officer, by a budget examiner, and by staff from the Regulatory Analysis Branch. The reviewer's job is to determine that the need for the regulation has been established, that sufficient alternatives have been considered, and that benefits and costs have been compared. When an OMB reviewer raises an issue, attempts are made to work out the differences informally. So far, in the 20 percent of the cases where problems have arisen, they have been solved informally.[27] Once regulations are approved by reviewers, OMB informs the agencies that they may proceed with publication in the *Register.*

Agency heads may disregard OMB suggestions, but they cannot publish a rule until the agency has responded to the OMB director's views and has incorporated those views and the agency's response in the rule making file.[28] In cases where the congressional committee has included an oversight role for itself in the legislation authorizing the program, proposed rules must also be sent to the committee for their approval.

---

25. *Washington Post,* "OMB Now a Regulator in Historic Power Shift," May 5, 1981, p. A1.

26. For the details of this process I am indebted to Margaret Wrightson, *op. cit.*

27. *Ibid.*

28. *Regulatory Eye,* vol. 3, no. 9, p. 5, and interview by Margaret Wrightson of ACIR with Thomas Hopkins, deputy director of the Regulatory Analysis Division, Office of Management and Budget, December 7, 1981, as cited in Wrightson, *op. cit.*

Rule making for the new community development block grant program, in which the congressional oversight committee does play this role, illustrates the process. In 1981, Congress gave states the option of administering the nonentitlement, small-city portion of the program. HUD then wrote rather detailed proposed regulations governing the states' administration of the program. OMB reviewers altered the HUD proposed rules significantly by shortening them, making them more general, and leaving much more flexibility to the states in the management of the program than HUD had proposed.[29]   After negotiation between HUD and OMB, HUD on November 20, 1981, published the amended regulations as the proposed regulations for the program.

Because the community development legislation requires congressional oversight of HUD regulations pertaining to that program, HUD then sent the proposed new rules to the House Banking and Urban Affairs Committee, which had the option of passing a resolution of disapproval by March 6, 1982. In this case, the committee did not like OMB's alterations; many of its members felt that the alterations made the program "more like a general revenue sharing program than the program they had intended."[30]   Two days before the deadline, the committee and HUD agreed that HUD would issue as final rules the OMB-amended rules as published, but would propose amendments, within two weeks, to meet the major objections of the committee. Final rules more acceptable to Congress were published on April 8, 1982.

It is early and difficult to evaluate the extent to which the expanded powers of the OMB have affected the content and quantity of regulations. Most observers agree that there has been some reduction in numbers, length, specificity and complexity of regulations issued, although these estimates are, for the most part, based on a reduction in the number of pages in the *Federal Register* in 1981 compared with 1980. By the last months of 1981, however, production of new rules was running about 90 percent of 1980 by one estimate.[31]   During the first 100 days of the OMB's rule review efforts, only about 8 percent of the rules reviewed by OMB were found to be inconsistent with the president's regulatory principles.[32]   Certainly the OMB process is tougher and more thorough than it has been in the past. It has received, so

---

29. See discussion of the community development block grant program in part 2 of this volume.

30. Interview by author with committee staff member, February 24, 1982.

31. David Walker, Albert Richter, and Cynthia Cates Colella, "The First Ten Months: Grant-in-Aid, Regulatory and Other Changes" in *Intergovernmental Perspective,* published by U.S. Advisory Commission on Intergovernmental Relations, vol. 8, no. 1 (winter 1982).

32. Staff Report to the Presidential Task Force, June 6, 1981.

far, extraordinary cooperation from the agencies. Review of new rules and strengthening the oversight powers of OMB, no matter how effective, can only slow the process of growth in numbers of regulations and perhaps improve their quality. Other methods are needed to reduce the absolute numbers.

Paperwork Reduction

Attention to excessive paperwork requirements began with President Nixon's appointment of a Commission on Federal Paperwork, which was charged with developing ways to reduce the paperwork load. In 1977, the commission issued a number of volumes of analyses of paperwork burdens and recommended ways to reduce duplicative, unnecessary, and unreasonably burdensome information collection. The commission reported that the federal government had about 5,000 reporting requirements on which recipients of federal aid, businesses, and individuals must spend 768 million person-hours a year.[33] They estimated that paperwork requirements on grant programs amounted to between 1 percent and 10 percent of total program outlays; for most programs, paperwork costs ranged between 5 and 7 percent.

President Carter implemented some of the recommendations of the commission with a memorandum to all agency heads that strengthened the powers of OMB in oversight of all executive agency forms.[34] OMB was authorized to clear all forms, and to veto a form or order the form changed. The executive order also established the information collection budget (ICB) process, which requires each agency to submit to OMB all the forms expected to be used in the upcoming fiscal year, with an estimate of the number of hours that would be spent filling them out. The final paperwork budget allocated to each agency prescribes ceilings for each agency and specifies which forms must be eliminated or reduced.

Richard Neustadt has estimated that the Carter administration was able to use this method to cut paperwork in the government by 15 percent in the two years between 1977 and 1979, but then ran out of easy targets.[35] In 1980, Congress passed the Paperwork Reduction Act, which set up the OMB Office of Information and Regulatory Affairs, formalized the ICB process, and further augmented OMB's power by requiring that agency to determine,

---

33. For a discussion of the commission's work as it affected state and local governments, see Academy of Contemporary Problems, *op. cit.*

34. Jimmy Carter, Memorandum for Heads of Executive Departments and Agencies, *Administration of Jimmy Carter in 1977*, February 16, 1977, pp. 177–178.

35. Richard Neustadt, "Taming the Paperwork Tiger," *Regulation*, January/February 1981.

before approving any form, whether an agency has to collect the information to properly perform its function.

The OMB paperwork reduction process and the use of the ICB are still in their infancy, so little evaluation of their effectiveness has been made. OMB has reported that for the agencies under OMB control, paperwork burdens were decreased by 9 percent during 1981, whereas burdens imposed by agencies not under OMB control rose by 2 percent.[36] The Reagan administration is continuing the antipaperwork activities.

Review of Existing Regulations—the Activities of the Bush Commission

As one of his first acts after his inauguration in January 1981, President Reagan established a task force on regulatory relief with Vice President George Bush as chairman. In addition to its general oversight of new regulations, which it exercises through the OMB, the commission's main purpose has been intensive review of existing regulations. Members of the commission are the secretaries of the treasury, labor, and commerce; the attorney general; the OMB director; the Council of Economic Advisor's chairman, and an assistant to the president for policy development. Each agency was asked to appoint one of its top administrators to keep in touch with the task force. The commission is staffed by the OMB.

The commission began its review efforts by inviting businesses, labor organizations, state and local government officials, and others to help identify "burdensome, unnecessary, and counterproductive federal regulations." The commission received 2,500 individual suggestions and comments from about 300 individuals and groups, among them the National League of Cities, the National Association of Counties, the U.S. Conference of Mayors, the National Conference of State Legislatures, the National Conference of Governors, and various state and local governments. Each of these groups submitted lists of what they considered to be the most objectionable regulations.

During 1981 the Bush Commission designated 100 existing regulations for review.[37] As a result of commission activities, by the close of 1981 agencies had issued proposed or final regulatory changes on 38 of the 100 existing regulations. Table 1.28 classifies the 100 regulations by economic sector. Twenty-five of the regulations have a primary impact on state and local governments, of which six have been reviewed and acted upon. They

---

36. Margaret Wrightson, "Regulatory Reform: Recent Federal Initiatives," in *Federal Regulation of States and Local Governments,* draft report, U.S. Advisory Commission on Intergovernmental Relations, summer 1982.

37. Office of the Vice President, *Year-End Summary of Actions Taken by the Presidential Task Force on Regulatory Relief,* December 30, 1981.

TABLE 1.28

Regulations Designated for Review by the Bush Commission, 1981, by Impact and Type

Groups feeling primary impact	Type of regulation						
	Economic	Environmental	Health and safety	Equal opportunity	Energy	Other (a)	Paperwork requirements	Total
State and local governments	3	5	2	5	1	5	4	25
Small businesses	5	1	3	2	0	1	0	12
Auto industry	0	17	11	0	2	4	0	34
Other businesses and nonprofit organizations	5	7	8	1	2	1	5	29
Total	13	30	24	8	5	11	9	100

Source: Office of the Vice President, *Year-End Summary of Actions Taken by the Presidential Task Force on Regulatory Relief,* December 30, 1981.

a. Urban and community policies and assistance, work programs, voluntary standards, and coordination of federal programs.

are the following:

Protections for the Handicapped. Section 504 of the Rehabilitation Act of 1973 required that the handicapped be assured access to mass transit, airports, roads, and railroads. In implementing the law the Department of Transportation (DOT) issued a regulation requiring that all new buses purchased with federal funds be equipped with wheelchair lifts and that new and existing rapid rail transit systems be made accessible to wheelchair users and other handicapped persons, often through the installation of elevators.[38] At the request of transportation agencies and state and local governments, the Bush Commission reviewed the regulation. As a result, DOT in July 1981 issued an interim rule substituting a "local option" provision for the controversial requirements. Local areas had to certify to the department that they were making "special efforts" consistent with DOT guidelines to provide transportation service for handicapped persons. The U.S. Court of Appeals for the District of Columbia opened the door for this revision by ruling that section 504 itself did not require extensive physical improvements.[39]

Davis-Bacon Amendments. The Davis-Bacon Act and related acts require that workers employed by contractors and subcontractors engaged in federally funded or assisted construction projects be paid the wages prevailing in the geographical area. In determining the prevailing wage, the Department of Labor has almost always used union scales, which are higher than actual average wages if both union and nonunion workers are taken into account. State and local governments have insisted for some time that the regulations require them to pay higher wages than needed, thus adding to their construction costs. These regulations have been slated for major review by the commission.

In the meantime, the Labor Department has revised several of the regulations interpreting Davis-Bacon, reducing reporting requirements, and allowing increased use of semiskilled "helpers" who can be paid at lower wage scales. The department also made some changes in the way it determines prevailing wage rates. These changes will save money for both contractors and governments.

Standards for a Merit System of Personnel Administration. Nineteen federal grant programs require state and local governments to maintain merit systems for the workers who administer the program. The Office of Personnel Management (OPM) prescribes standards for these systems, which are supposed to avoid political favoritism in hiring and promotions.

---

38. *Federal Register,* July 20, 1981, pp. 37488–37494.

39. *American Public Transportation Association* vs. *Lewis,* U.S. Court of Appeals for the District of Columbia, case 80–1497, May 26, 1981.

Under Bush Commission prodding, OPM has been reviewing the regulations with a view to eliminating unnecessary provisions and revising unduly burdensome ones. In the meantime, the administration has submitted a bill (S. 1042) that would eliminate all statutory merit personnel requirements established as a condition for the receipt of federal grants by states and local governments.

OMB Circular A—95. The commission and OMB have conducted a review of A—95, which, as noted earlier, required metropolitan and regional bodies to review and comment on areawide implications of federal aid programs. OMB was expected to issue a drastically revised circular in summer 1982 repealing most of the requirements. A—95 requirements have been deleted from the block grants enacted as part of the 1981 reconciliation act.

Civil Rights. Many of the civil rights regulations affecting discrimination against minorities and on the basis of sex have been under major review. The Office of Federal Contract Compliance Programs has published a proposed rule that would substantially change affirmative action regulations for government contractors and federally assisted local government contractors. These revisions would exempt smaller entities from the rules, reduce compliance requirements, and change definitions of "underutilization," which is a concept used to determine whether a group has suffered from employment discrimination. Under Bush Commission direction, the Justice Department is leading a major review of the affirmative action policies of many departments and agencies.

Urban and Community Impact Analyses. The urban and community impact analyses executive order, issued in 1978 by President Carter, required impact statements from federal agencies designing programs and regulations for urban areas. President Reagan canceled it after review by the Bush Commission. The commission and studies by OMB and GAO found the impact reports burdensome, redundant, and minimally effective. The National League of Cities called the urban impact statements a "potentially useful process" and expressed concern at the order's cancellation.[40]

The Bush Commission's early achievements make clear the difficulties of bringing about major regulatory reform through reviews of individual regulations. In its first nine months of work, the commission achieved major changes in only nineteen regulations, many of which aroused opposition. Few of the changes directly affected state or local governments. More thorough evaluation of the commission's effect will have to wait until it has had more time to work, however. One possible effect of the commission's review activity will be its influence on future regulatory actions.

---

40. Judy Anders-Michalski, "Reagan Rescinds Order for Impact Statements," *Public Administration Times,* April 1, 1982.

The above discussion of reform approaches, which have focused on strengthening executive oversight of agency rule-making processes, shows that there has been increasing attention to rule-making processes over the last four administrations. Strong attempts have been made by the executive branch to reduce paperwork imposed by agencies and to make agencies more "self-conscious." The executive branch has attempted to control its own rule makers through the delegation of extraordinary oversight powers to OMB. However, careful evaluation of the effectiveness of the efforts remains to be undertaken. Both the Carter administration and the Reagan administration have used the kinds of management reforms discussed in this section. The Reagan administration is using two other approaches as well, which require some discussion.

Reducing Federal Government Programs

A fourth approach to federal regulatory reform—one which in the long run may be most important for state and local governments—is reducing or abolishing federal programs, or devolving functions or grant programs to the states. Some OMB officials say openly that they are not concentrating on fundamental reforms of the regulatory processes as they affect grant programs because they do not expect many direct federal grant programs to be around in a few years. Some observers believe that the major deregulatory effort of the Reagan administration as it affects state and local governments will be an amalgam of budget cuts and block grants to states. The new block grant regulations, for example, are only ten pages in length; they replace hundreds of pages of complex regulations for the old categorical programs. Attempts have been made to remove as many regulations as possible from block grants, as states begin to administer the programs. OMB has even waived its normal requirements so that states, in administering block grants, need not follow OMB circulars A−87 (cost principles for state and local governments), A−102 (uniform administrative requirements), and A−95 (evaluation, review, and coordination of grant programs). The block grants do still carry some statute-based regulations as well as the major cross-cutting requirements discussed earlier, but the regulations do not prescribe how states are to implement these requirements.

Local governments realize that, under this strategy, deregulation at the federal level lays the groundwork for new regulation by the states. Block grants, for example, require states to make contractual assurances that they will meet the various statutory conditions that govern the expenditure of block grant funds. In the absence of federal regulations, the states will need to develop regulations to clarify and interpret what laws mean. Without the A−87 and A−102 circulars, states will have to develop their own rules for administrative and financial control procedures and rules for enforcing the major cross-cutting laws.

Clearly, doing away with a program is the most effective way of eliminating regulation. It is not so clear whether reducing the amount of money allocated to a program will contribute to reducing regulation. There is little reason to think so. Having states administer a block grant program can certainly reduce federal regulation, but must increase rule making by the states. Some observers also expect that the courts will become more active in interpreting federal statutes.[41] According to these observers, the numerous federal laws that establish cross-cutting requirements as well as the statutory demands of the grant programs themselves will encourage close scrutiny of both federal and state spending decisions by affected clients and interest groups.

Reducing Enforcement Intensity of Existing Regulations

The final approach to deregulation—reducing enforcement intensity—is the most difficult to use, to identify when it is done, and to assess. The *Washington Post* in 1981 reported: "The Reagan administration is systematically cutting back its enforcement of hundreds of federal regulations."[42] According to the *Post*'s survey, many key federal agencies are relaxing their once-vigorous oversight of business and local governments. The *Post* cites reductions in enforcement personnel and instructions to act more leniently in the National Highway Traffic Safety Administration, OSHA, the Department of the Interior, the Department of Labor, the Department of Agriculture, and the Environmental Protection Agency. In the EPA, for example, the Office of Enforcement has been abolished and its functions split up among several other offices. The number of enforcement attorneys is to be reduced by three-quarters, from two hundred to forty. EPA has substantially reduced the number of cases referred to the Justice Department for prosecution.

The *Post* also reported that the administration was considering reorganizations that would centralize all civil rights enforcement programs in the Justice Department, abolishing the Department of Labor's Office of Federal Contract Compliance and considerably diminishing the activities of the Equal Employment Opportunity Commission.

---

41. See, for example, Thomas J. Madden and Patrick R. Harkins, "The Federal Courts and the New Block Grants," in *Assistance Management* (published by the National Assistance Management Association), vol. 1, no. 1 (February 1982).

42. Caroline E. Mayer, "U.S. Relaxing Enforcement of Regulations," *Washington Post,* November 15, 1981, p. F-1.

According to the administration, the proposed changes are being considered for budgetary reasons. Labor representatives, consumer groups, environmentalists, and other public interest groups argue that reductions in enforcement are part of the overall campaign by the administration to reduce overregulation.[43]

As a deregulation strategy, relaxation of enforcement can be only partly effective. Obviously, there is room for more flexibility and common sense in rule enforcement, and perhaps no harm would be done if many ill-advised procedural regulations could be ignored with impunity. On the other hand, if agencies avoid even-handed enforcement of important regulations, entities that have been treated differently may appeal to the courts to enforce equal treatment. And certainly, if agencies fail to enforce regulations that implement laws, interest groups representing those protected by the regulatory interpretations of laws—such as the handicapped, the aged, minorities, and women—or groups with a public mission, like environmental coalitions, will file lawsuits in attempts to force compliance. Furthermore, Congress may move in to fill enforcement voids if it finds agencies too lax in those areas it considers important.

CONCLUSIONS

As the Reagan administration ended its first year, the record showed less substantial reform in regulatory relations between the federal government and states and local governments than many state and local governments wanted or expected. During the first year, several major regulations that had been most objectionable to state and local governments had been revised or rescinded, and the general climate in which agencies consider new regulations was more sensitive to the impacts of regulations. Several major block grants had been enacted, consolidating a number of categorical grants and reducing drastically the number of regulations. In spite of these changes, very real tensions still exist between the pursuit of equity and national purposes, on the one hand, and the need for autonomy and diversity in local governments. To the extent that regulations are interpretations of statutes, they cannot be altered. It would be difficult—and wrong—for regulatory reform to attempt to subvert congressional purposes although, of course, political dialogue will always continue over how broadly inclusive national purposes should be.

Whether state and local governments could ever be completely satisfied with regulatory arrangements between them and the federal government is questionable, because of the ambiguous relationships that exist among the levels of government and the distinctive perspectives of each. Yet, because

---

43. *Ibid.*

the Reagan administration has expanded the regulatory reform agenda, the time may be ripe for serious reexamination of major aspects of regulatory relationships among federal, state, and local governments. Reform can at least be focused on reducing the number and scope of regulations and increasing the sensitivity of procedural regulations by substituting incentive systems and bargaining models for command and control blueprints. The Reagan administration, like the three administrations before it, has done little fundamental thinking—at least as publicly reported—about how such incentive systems or bargaining models might be designed.

In the meantime, if federal regulations are simplified and more discretion left to the states, there is a strong indication that attempts will be made to use the courts to force both the federal agencies and the states to be more specific in their rule making. In the case of social legislation, those interests that are not protected by implementing regulations have promised that they will bring suits to attempt to force agencies to implement the statutes more directly. Already, these interest groups feel that there has been too much deregulation in social areas and that deregulation is merely a code word for selective elimination of whatever regulations do not suit the values of the administration—particularly those that advance social equity. They point to the number of such regulations on the Bush Commission's review lists.

It is too early to judge the Reagan administration's regulatory reform activities thoroughly. The study of the Reagan domestic program described in this volume provides an opportunity for continuing observation of changes in regulatory activities and resulting changes in the form and content of regulations. The three dimensions of regulatory activity—statutory, administrative, and behavioral—will continue to be analyzed to see whether they remain as reduced and simplified as intended by the administration. Also, the major state regulations that replace federal regulations, as programs devolve to the states through the block grants, will be compared to the federal regulations they replace. Finally, interest group responses to deregulatory efforts will be observed and analyzed.

The administration has, during its first year, intensified discussions about the need for regulatory reform and given legitimacy to calls for reform. It has begun some reforms and has promised more. What the reforms will be and what groups will benefit from the changes remains to be observed.

PART 2

Descriptions of Forty Major Budget Reductions Affecting State and Local Governments

By Rita Seymour, Catherine Eschbach,
John Gunther-Mohr, Charles Cameron,
Dwight Dively, and John W. Ellwood

Introduction to
Budget Reduction Descriptions

The Omnibus Reconciliation Act of 1981 affected spending levels in 232 of the budget's 1,314 accounts. The following pages describe the changes that were made in forty of these accounts.

HOW THE ACCOUNTS WERE CHOSEN

The forty accounts that are described in the following pages made up 64.7 percent of the budget authority savings achieved by the Reconciliation Act of 1981 and 67.9 percent of all nondefense budget authority reductions achieved during the first session of the 97th Congress. They contain the largest dollar reductions in programs directly or indirectly affecting state and local governments.

In choosing these accounts for further study the authors sought to identify three classes of changes that could affect the finances, politics, and services of state and local governments. The first class includes budgetary changes in those accounts which provide federal grants to state and local governments. Twenty-seven out of the forty accounts fall into this category. They include twenty-two accounts that provide direct grants to states and localities—such as highway grants, employment and training grants under CETA, and the nine block grants—and five federal income support programs—medicaid, the housing subsidy programs, and aid to families with dependent children—that, because they are administered by state and local governments, are classified as federal grants by the Office of Management and Budget (OMB). Each of these accounts either had its budget authority or outlays reduced by $100 million with the passage of the reconciliation act or, as with the nine new block grants, incorporated significant programmatic changes that could affect American federalism.

The second class of activity affected accounts that provided aid to institutions in both the public and private sector. Reductions in these accounts would affect the finances, politics, and services of states and localities because they operate such institutions. Although federal support for higher education is not classified as a grant to states and localities, reductions in such support would affect public universities, which receive state and local funding. Should the student loan program be reduced, for example, states and localities would either have to increase their appropriations for the colleges attended by these students, raise tuition and fees, or decrease the services offered by these institutions.

The final class of effect is the most ambiguous. Eleven of the accounts described in this section fund programs that are totally funded and administered by the federal government—medicare, unemployment compensation, trade assistance benefits, food stamps, the special milk program, child nutrition programs, the supplementary security program, the rehabilitation loan fund, the disaster loan fund, the subsidy to Conrail, and the Northeast Corridor track improvement program. These accounts were included because reductions in their funding levels would place great political pressure on at least some state and local governments to support these services.

Of the budget accounts that had either their budget authority or outlay funding levels reduced by at least $100 million by the Reconciliation Act of 1981, three categories are not included in the following descriptions: most of the major social insurance entitlements such as social security, disability insurance, and the various federal workforce retirement programs; certain fixed-cost programs such as farm price supports, the payment to the postal service, and the U.S. contribution to international organizations; and most programs directly run by the federal government such as the various energy supply and construction accounts, the strategic petroleum reserve, and the pay comparability increase for the federal civilian and military workforce.

It should also be noted that changes in off-budget expenditures, off-budget direct loans and loan guarantees, tax expenditures, and expenditures by government sponsored enterprises are not analyzed. In addition, only those regulatory changes affecting the implementation of the changes in the forty budget accounts are described.

HOW TO USE THESE DESCRIPTIONS

The forty descriptions follow a common framework. They are listed by federal budget function. Since the Legislative Reorganization Act of 1946, the accounts of the federal budget have been grouped by types of activity. Currently there are nineteen budget functions ranging from the national defense function to the health function to interest on the public debt. The accounts described in this section fall into seven of these nineteen functions—energy; natural resources and environment; transportation; community and regional development; education, employment, training, and social services; health; and income security.

The descriptions are listed in the order in which the accounts would appear in the federal budget. To find a given description the reader may go to the table of contents of this book or examine the last three digits in the budget account number at the top of the summary table that accompanies each description. These three digits are the subfunction number for that account.

Each section begins with a description of the nature of the programs and their funding levels prior to the passage of the Omnibus Reconciliation Act of 1981. This is followed by a section setting out the programmatic and funding level changes that were brought about with the passage of the reconciliation act. Since many of these accounts had to receive an appropriation in order to be funded for fiscal year 1982 and since others had to be reauthorized after the passage of the reconciliation act, the next section sets out the programmatic and funding changes that were made in 1981 after the passage of the reconciliation act. The next section sets out those administrative regulations which were issued in 1981 to implement the reconciliation act changes. The final section presents the authors' assessments of the effects of these changes. It also includes a brief analysis of further changes (if any) sought by the Reagan administration in its fiscal year 1983 budget.

Each section contains a summary table that sets out the budgetary modifications made in 1981 that will affect the account in fiscal years 1982, 1983, and 1984. All modifications are measured from the Congressional Budget Office current policy baseline, which was produced in December 1980. The first two rows of each summary table set out that baseline for budget authority and outlays for the three year period.

The next two rows of the table set out the CBO cost estimates of the changes in budget authority and outlays brought about by the passage of the reconciliation act. These estimates, which were produced during July and August of 1981, are presented in terms of dollar levels after reconciliation and in terms of percentage reduction in dollars from the CBO baseline. The cost estimates are presented for fiscal years 1982, 1983, and 1984. In some cases the reconciliation act incorporated multiyear changes. In others the Congressional Budget Office cost estimators projected out the fiscal year 1982 changes through 1984. These differences are noted in the various descriptions.

The two rows of the table set out the CBO estimate of the fiscal year 1982 levels of budget authority and outlays after all congressional action during 1981 (during the first session of the 97th Congress). Because the continuing resolutions that were passed during the first session of the 97th Congress have been extended through fiscal year 1982, these estimates should be accurate through fiscal year 1982, with the exception of funding level changes brought about by changing economic conditions, the passage of supplemental appropriations, or the enactment of rescissions. No figures appear for fiscal years 1983 and 1984 in these two rows since Congress has yet to enact appropriations for these periods.

AUTHORSHIP OF DESCRIPTIONS

Rita Seymour wrote the sections on guaranteed student loans, student financial assistance, medicare, trade adjustment ssistance, unemployment compensation, special milk, food stamps, supplemental security income, and aid to families with dependent children.

Catherine Eschbach prepared the sections on energy conservation grants, the youth conservation corps, wastewater treatment grants, federal highway programs, the northeast rail corridor improvement program, the Conrail subsidy, the mass transportation programs, the air transportation programs, and medicaid.

John Gunther-Mohr wrote the sections on the nine block grants: community development; elementary and secondary education; social services; community services; primary care; maternal and child health services; preventive health and health services; alcohol, drug abuse, and mental health; and low-income energy assistance. He also provided the introduction to the health block grants.

Charles Cameron was responsible for the sections on impact aid, compensatory education assistance, assisted housing, and public housing subsidies.

Dwight Dively was responsible for the rehabilitation loan fund, the programs of the Economic Development Administration, and the child nutrition programs. He also assisted the other authors as a general editor of their work.

John W. Ellwood wrote the sections on the urban development action grant program, the disaster loan fund, the two accounts which funded the CETA programs, and the refugee assistance program.

The material in this section was prepared under the supervision of Rita Seymour and John W. Ellwood, with Ms. Seymour handling most of the work during the latter stages of its preparation. Finally, Carol Camp and Claire Laporte prepared early drafts of several sections.

ENERGY CONSERVATION

Program Description

The Department of Energy conducts energy conservation programs in three areas. The first is the only one that directly affects state and local governments. The department channels funds through the states to provide grants for low-income housing weatherization, energy conservation for schools and hospitals, general conservation measures, and state energy conservation and emergency planning and management. Second, it provides grants for technology development, both to develop specific products and to perform basic research. Third, the department provides grants to establish standards and to provide technological assistance and information. Typical projects in this area include setting building standards, providing residential and commercial conservation services through utility firms, and establishing the federal government's own management efforts. Budget authority for 1981 totaled $709 million dollars, of which $430 million was attributable to state and local grants. The accompanying table contains CBO estimates for all programs in the account. Of these estimates, approximately 89 percent of the funding went for grants to state and local governments.

Reconciliation Act Changes

Reconciliation did not alter the scope of conservation activities funded through this account; it only reduced their levels for fiscal years 1982, 1983, and 1984. Total conservation program authorization for fiscal year 1982 was $376 million, of which $336 million was designated for state and local programs. State and local grants were limited to $387 million in 1983 and $399 million in 1984.

Appropriations and Other Changes

The funding for 1982 state and local conservation grants was substantially reduced in the appropriation process. The total amount available was that appropriated for 1982 plus 1981 deferrals and transfers. Altogether, approximately $240 million was available for fiscal year 1982 ($55 million through appropriations and $185 million through 1981 deferrals).

The appropriation process cut some conservation programs more than others. Conservation programs for schools and hospitals and appropriate technologies had their funds reduced more than 75 percent of an estimated current policy level. All other conservation programs except the energy

CBO Baseline and Effect
of Congressional Action During Calendar 1981
(in millions of dollars and percentages)
Account No. 89-0215-272

Category	FY1982 Dollar Level	FY1982 Percent Change	FY1983 Dollar Level	FY1983 Percent Change	FY1984 Dollar Level	FY1984 Percent Change
CBO Baseline						
Budget						
authority	850	—	904	—	959	—
Outlays	874	—	926	—	973	—
Reconciliation Act						
Budget						
authority	545	−36	575	−36	593	−38
Outlays	837	−4	671	−28	616	−37
Final FY 1982 Expenditures After All Changes						
Budget						
authority	145	−83	—	—	—	—
Outlays	741	−15	—	—	—	—

invention and weatherization programs were reduced more than 50 percent of estimated current policy.

Administrative Regulations

No regulations have been forthcoming relevant to the reconciliation act changes.

Assessment

The energy conservation program has been growing steadily at about 20 percent per year for the past five years. However, as a result of action taken in 1982, this trend has been abruptly reversed. The entire conservation program was reduced to less than half of its 1981 actual level. In 1982, $234 million was appropriated for energy conservation. The 1983 budget request clearly demonstrates that the program is targeted for severe reductions again in 1983. The 1983 budget requested only $27 million for the entire conservation program. The request specified that 1983 would be the last year for funding for the low-income weatherization and for the energy savings investments in schools and hospital programs. The reduction in funding is consistent with the administration's view that conservation has been and will continue to be achieved through the marketplace. The increased price of energy is viewed as the best mechanism for energy conservation.

The cuts in grants to state and local governments will directly reduce their ability to operate existing conservation programs. Many states operate programs that have established states as the primary mechanism for providing end-users with information and technical assistance on conservation techniques. The 1982 reductions and the proposed 1983 near-elimination of the grants to states will either halt these programs or will force states to finance them.

YOUTH CONSERVATION CORPS

Program Description

The Youth Conservation Corps (YCC) provides summer jobs on federal and state lands for youths aged fifteen to eighteen. Funds go to the Interior Department, the Department of Agriculture, and the states which provide these summer jobs. The jobs are typically minor construction, maintenance, and visitor services at parks and recreational areas. Though the program has never been large (outlays have never exceeded $65 million), it grew rapidly at the outset and has stabilized in recent years. In 1981, outlays totaled $19 million.

Reconciliation Act Changes

The reconciliation act specified that no funds could be appropriated to carry out the Youth Conservation Corps Act of 1970 for fiscal years 1982, 1983, or 1984, which effectively eliminated the program. Approximately $1 million will be spent for this program in fiscal year 1982 from prior-year appropriations.

Appropriations and Other Changes

In fiscal year 1981, the Supplemental and Rescission Appropriations Act reduced funds available to the YCC by $34 million. This rescission reduced the outlay estimate for fiscal year 1981 from $60 million to $26 million and in fiscal year 1982 from $8.4 to $1.4 million.

Administrative Regulations

No regulatory changes occurred, as the program was completely eliminated.

Assessment

During the debate on the reconciliation act, it was assumed that the program would be reauthorized at a later date. Though this program is a politically popular one, the chances for reauthorization are slim. No funds were requested in the 1983 budget.

CBO Baseline and Effect
of Congressional Action During Calendar 1981
(in millions of dollars and percentages)
Account No. 14-0109-302

Category	FY1982 Dollar Level	FY1982 Percent Change	FY1983 Dollar Level	FY1983 Percent Change	FY1984 Dollar Level	FY1984 Percent Change
CBO Baseline						
Budget authority	60	—	60	—	60	—
Outlays	60	—	60	—	60	—
Reconciliation Act						
Budget authority	0	−100	0	−100	0	−100
Outlays	12	−80	0	−100	0	−100
Final FY 1982 Expenditures After All Changes						
Budget authority	0	−100	—	—	—	—
Outlays	1	−98	—	—	—	—

WASTEWATER TREATMENT GRANTS

Program Description

This program provides grants-in-aid to municipalities for building publicly owned wastewater treatment works as authorized by the Clean Water Act. It is the largest program administered by the Environmental Protection Agency (EPA).

This program is essentially a construction program. Funding restrictions are imposed by budget authority limitations, but actual expenditures in a given year are better viewed through the outlay estimates, which reflect the slower spend-out rates associated with construction projects. Hence, the cuts in budget authority made this year will not affect the outlay estimates until 1983, 1984, and 1985. In 1981, the actual program level was set at $3.3 billion, but $1.7 billion was rescinded, so the final level was only $1.6 billion and the outlays were $3.9 billion. The 1980 actual funding level was $3.4 billion in budget authority and $4.3 billion in outlays.

Reconciliation Act Changes

The reconciliation act limited the authorization of appropriation to $40 million for fiscal year 1982. The $40 million covers only the program's administrative expenses. The administration's request for grant funding was contingent upon congressional reform of the allotment formula and other aspects of the municipal wastewater treatment grant program. Once the reforms were enacted, the administration would request $2.4 billion for fiscal year 1982. The reconciliation act did not specify projected funding levels for 1983 or 1984.

Appropriations and Subsequent Changes

In December 1981, Congress passed an authorization bill that included many of the changes the administration had requested and authorized $2.4 billion for each of the fiscal years 1982, 1983, 1984, and 1985. As of April 1982, no appropriation had passed. Though $2.4 billion was authorized, states cannot spend any of that money until an appropriation is passed.

The law made a number of programmatic changes that will significantly affect the operation of the construction grant program. The categories of projects available for funding were limited to the construction stages of secondary and more advanced treatment, interceptors, and correction of infiltration and inflow problems. Costs incurred in the planning and design phases of

CBO Baseline and Effect
of Congressional Action During Calendar 1981
(in millions of dollars and percentages)
Account No. 68-0103-304

Category	FY1982 Dollar Level	FY1982 Percent Change	FY1983 Dollar Level	FY1983 Percent Change	FY1984 Dollar Level	FY1984 Percent Change
CBO Baseline						
Budget						
authority	3,600	—	3,920	—	4,200	—
Outlays	4,320	—	4,215	—	4,105	—
Reconciliation Act						
Budget						
authority	40	−99	2,420	−38	2,420	−43
Outlays	4,245	−2	3,685	−13	2,925	+29
Final FY 1982 Expenditures After All Changes						
Budget						
authority	0[a]	−99	—	—	—	—
Outlays	4,089	−5	—	—	—	—

a. Due to late authorization, program has yet to receive an appropriation for fiscal year 1982.

these projects will be reimbursed from the construction grant. Grants approved before October 1, 1984 will continue to receive 75 percent federal share for construction and will be eligible for any necessary subsequent grants at 75 percent federal share. Grants approved after October 1, 1984 will receive only 55 percent federal share of the cost of construction.

A provision was made for governors to use up to 20 percent of a state's annual allotment to fund projects that would otherwise be ineligible under the new restrictions. Funding for innovative and alternative processes and techniques was made part of the permanent authority of the EPA and the federal share of these grants was specified to be 20 percentage points higher than the prevailing federal share. Significantly, the law specified that states set aside between 4 percent and 7.5 percent of their allotment to fund this increased federal share for innovative grants.

The law also amended the Federal Water Pollution Control Act to allow for an extension of the deadline for achievement of secondary treatment by municipalities from 1983 to 1988. The amendment eliminated the requirement that all municipalities achieve the best practicable waste treatment technology by 1983.

There were several other changes made, but it is doubtful that they will have a significant cost-saving effect for the states.

Assessment

The program has been subject to criticism for a number of years. The number of active projects had remained around 11,000 over the last five years, but is expected to drop to 10,000 in 1982 and to 6,500 in 1983. Though budget authority rose sharply in 1978, it has been falling rapidly since then. Actual outlays over that same period rose, but began to fall in 1981.

As reflected in the outlay figures, actual construction funds to the states grew until very recently. In 1981, the grant program was reduced. The EPA estimated that as a result seventeen states would run out of construction grant money in fiscal year 1981 and approximately nine other states would use more than 80 percent of their allotment. The $2.4 billion limit for 1982 suggests that in some states some high-priority projects   will not be funded.

In general, wastewater grants will continue to be funded at greatly reduced levels. This will cause increasing problems for states and municipalities as they try to comply with legal requirements for clean water. The most likely solution to this problem will be legislation relaxing environmental standards and their compliance dates. Some relaxations were made in the authorization bill, but more are likely to be considered.

The 1983 budget proposed funding this program at the same dollar level, $2.4 billion, at which the program was funded in 1982. The wastewater program may be included as part of the federalism initiative proposed for 1983. The future funding levels for wastewater construction will depend on the states' response to the federalism initiative.

FEDERAL AID TO HIGHWAYS

Program Description

The highway aid program provides financial assistance to states for building and maintaining highway systems and for urban and rural transportation programs. Programs funded include the construction and maintenance of the interstate system, construction and reconstruction of a state's primary highway system, aid for planning and construction of local roads, replacement and rehabilitation of bridges, safety programs, and provisions for emergency relief. The largest single program in this account is interstate highway construction, which accounted for 39 percent of the $7.98 billion authorization level in fiscal year 1981.

The highway aid program is financed through the highway trust fund with revenues from the federal gasoline tax and other transportation-related excise taxes. The funding mechanism is important because it allows the authorizing committees greater autonomy in setting the level of program activity. The authorizing legislation for this program, the Surface Transportation Act of 1978 and the Federal Aid Highway Act of 1981, contains contract authority that allows states to enter into obligations in advance of an appropriation. The contract authority contains the federal promise to pay. An appropriation is required before funds can be spent, however, so an appropriation serves to liquidate existing federal obligations.

A unique provision of the highway trust fund allows the appropriations committees some control over the timing of obligations. Each year the appropriations committees determine the amount of contract authority that can be obligated in that year. Generally, the obligational authority falls short of the total amount of contract authority available for obligation. Because all contract authority will eventually be obligated, however, this mechanism controls the timing but not the level of total program activity.

Reconciliation Act Changes

To exert control over expenditures from the highway trust fund, the reconciliation act reduced the obligational authority from the $9.6 billion contained in the CBO baseline to $8.2 billion. It further limited obligations in fiscal year 1983 to $8.8 billion. This limitation excluded obligations for emergency relief in both years. (The reconciliation act had no effect on budget authority, which is simply an estimate of new contract authority for this account.) The reductions in obligational authority were estimated to reduce outlays by 6 percent in fiscal year 1982, 9 percent in fiscal year 1983, and 13

147

**CBO Baseline and Effect
of Congressional Action During Calendar 1981
(in millions of dollars and percentages)
Account No. 20-8102-401**

| | FY1982 | | FY1983 | | FY1984 | |
| | Dollar | Percent | Dollar | Percent | Dollar | Percent |
Category	Level	Change	Level	Change	Level	Change
CBO Baseline						
Budget						
authority	7,854	—	8,600	—	9,320	—
Outlays	8,285	—	9,000	—	9,700	—
Reconciliation Act						
Budget						
authority	0	0	0	0	0	0
Outlays	7,785	−6	8,160	−9	8,455	−13
Final FY 1982 Expenditures						
After All Changes						
Budget						
authority	8,279	+5[a]	—	—	—	—
Outlays	8,065	−3	—	—	—	—

a. Budget authority increased as a result of the Federal Aid Highway Act of 1981.

percent in fiscal year 1984. Because obligation ceilings are set annually in the appropriations process, the limits contained in the reconciliation act can be further reduced by the appropriations committees.

The reconciliation act took additional steps to control the timing of expenditures from the trust fund. The act specified that no more than one-fourth of the obligation ceiling can be obligated during the first quarter of the year. Within this overall limitation, states are also prohibited from obligating more than 35 percent of their allocation during the first quarter of the fiscal year. The secretary of transportation was directed to provide funds to a state if necessary to prevent lapses of funding previously appropriated and to redistribute unobligated funds to other states that are able to obligate the funds.

Appropriations Changes

The Department of Transportation and Related Agencies Appropriations Act restricted fiscal year 1982 obligational authority for the highway aid program to $8.0 billion. This is $200 million less than the amount contained in the reconciliation act. (The appropriations act also provided $8.0 billion to liquidate existing obligations.)

Assessment

Actions taken during the 97th Congress will slow down but not reduce total federal funding for this program. For fiscal year 1983, however, the administration proposes a significant overhaul of the program by restricting highway aid to the interstate system. The financial solvency of the trust fund has recently been called into question because expenditures have exceeded revenues in each of the past three fiscal years. The budget, therefore, has proposed that the financial responsibility for urban and rural highway systems be returned to state and local governments. The administration has also proposed that some trust fund revenues be turned over to the states but this might threaten trust fund solvency further.

TRUST FUND SHARE OF HIGHWAY SAFETY PROGRAMS

Program Description

This account provides the funding mechanism for two Department of Transportation programs. First, it funds highway safety research and development conducted by the department. Second, it funds the state and community highway safety program, which will be discussed in this section. The highway safety program provides a series of matching grants to assist states in establishing and improving highway safety programs and in enforcing the national speed limit. These grants are focused on programs that control the drinking driver, improve the quality and availability of emergency medical service, and help reduce accidents. In fiscal year 1981, $197 million was provided in grants to state and local governments.

Reconciliation Act Changes

The reconciliation act dramatically reduced the amount of funding available for highway safety programs. The act authorized the appropriation of $100 million for each of the fiscal years 1982, 1983, and 1984. This represented budget authority reductions of $100 million, $114 million, and $127 million respectively from the CBO baseline. In addition, the reconciliation act rescinded $173 million of contract authority in fiscal year 1982. Therefore, the total program reduction in fiscal year 1982 was $273 million. Because outlays take place through another account, the outlay savings from these reductions are not demonstrated in the accompanying table. Over time, the total outlay savings will equal total budget authority savings, $514 million.

The reconciliation act also imposed some program requirements on the safety program. Out of the $100 million annual authorization, $20 million is earmarked for enforcement of the 55-mph speed limit. If surveys show that more than 50 percent of a state's motorists violate the 55-mph speed limit, the state's apportionment of federal highway funds will be reduced by up to 5 percent in fiscal years 1982 and 1983 and up to 10 percent in later years. The reconciliation act continued the requirement that a state spend 2 percent of its funds to encourage the use of safety belts.

**CBO Baseline and Effect
of Congressional Action During Calendar 1981
(in millions of dollars and percentages)
Account No. 69-8016-401**

Category	FY1982		FY1983		FY1984	
	Dollar Level	Percent Change	Dollar Level	Percent Change	Dollar Level	Percent Change
CBO Baseline						
Budget authority	200	—	214	—	227	—
Outlays	0	—	0	—	0	—
Reconciliation Act						
Budget authority	−73[a]	−137	100	−53	100	−56
Outlays	0	0	0	0	0	0
Final FY 1982 Expenditures After All Changes						
Budget authority	−73	−137	—	—	—	—
Outlays	0	0	—	—	—	—

Note: Outlays are made through another account.

a. The reconciliation act reduced current year authority by $100 million and also rescinded $173 million in prior year contract authority.

Appropriations Act Changes

Because this is a trust fund, the appropriations act simply ratified the steps taken during the reconciliation process.

Assessment

The reconciliation act significantly reduced grants to states for highway safety. The final fiscal effect of this reduction will depend on whether states attempt to reinstitute these programs with state funds. The new Reagan budget proposed no significant reductions in the program in fiscal year 1983.

NORTHEAST CORRIDOR IMPROVEMENT PROGRAM

Program Description

The Northeast Corridor improvement program was created to improve passenger and freight rail service in the corridor between Washington, D.C. and Boston. Its goal is to facilitate safe, dependable high-speed service. The program provides funds for track improvement, bridge repairs, elimination of grade crossings, station improvements, electrification, installation of signaling and communication systems, and construction of railway maintenance facilities. In fiscal year 1981, the actual program level was $350 million.

Reconciliation Changes

The reconciliation act directed the secretary of transportation to complete planned construction of the corridor. The act also authorized funds for fiscal years 1982 and 1983. The authorization level reflected a 48 percent savings in budget authority in fiscal year 1982 and a 40 percnt savings in fiscal year 1983 from the CBO baseline. However, since this is a construction program, outlay savings resulting from the reconciliation act will not become evident for several years.

Appropriations Changes

The Department of Transportation and Related Agencies Appropriations Act reduced the amount of funding available for the Northeast Corridor program in fiscal year 1982 by $30 million from the amount allowed in the reconciliation act.

Assessment

Reconciliation and appropriation actions changed the focus of this program from creating a faster train system to completing a reliable and serviceable rail system. The authorization reduction will be achieved mainly by repairing rather than replacing the signaling system and by canceling the project to electrify lines north of New Haven. As a result of these changes, travel times in the corridor will be slower than they would have been had all the originally planned improvements been made; the difference is expected to be ten minutes from Washington to New York and thirty minutes from New York to Boston.

The 1983 major construction programs that are scheduled include electrification repair in the vicinity of New York City, improvements to Providence

CBO Baseline and Effect
of Congressional Action During Calendar 1981
(in millions of dollars and percentages)
Account No. 69-0123-401

Category	FY1982 Dollar Level	FY1982 Percent Change	FY1983 Dollar Level	FY1983 Percent Change	FY1984 Dollar Level	FY1984 Percent Change
CBO Baseline						
Budget authority	386	—	309	—	0	—
Outlays	315	—	315	—	315	—
Reconciliation Act						
Budget authority	200	−48	185	−40	200	NA
Outlays	307	−3	272	−14	233	−26
Final FY 1982 Expenditures After All Changes						
Budget authority	170	−56	—	—	—	—
Outlays	306	−3	—	—	—	—

station, and rehabilitation of the Portal Bridge in New Jersey and the Sus-quehanna River Bridge in Maryland. It is unlikely that the $115 million pro-posed in the 1983 budget will be sufficient to complete the plannned pro-jects. Amtrak has assumed and will probably continue to assume responsibility for the management and the construction of the Northeast Cor-ridor improvements, as the federal share of the construction program declines.

CONRAIL

Program Description

Conrail is a private corporation that was created out of the Penn Central and six other bankrupt railroads in an attempt to preserve freight and commuter passenger service in the Northeast and Midwest. Although the corporation was supposed to be self-sustaining, Conrail has required subsidies every year since its creation on April 1, 1976. The federal subsidies are used for two purposes. First, the subsidies are used to make major improvements in plant and equipment and to cover losses incurred in the initial phases of the operation. Second, the subsidies are used to provide labor protection benefits to Conrail employees. To finance program operations, Conrail uses internally generated funds, money from private sources, and federal subsidies. In 1981, actual budget authority totaled $569 million.

Reconciliation Act Changes

Since 1976, the federal government has been supporting Conrail's freight and commuter services and currently owns an estimated $2.3 billion in Conrail stock. The reconciliation act not only restricted the value of Conrail securities that could be bought in fiscal year 1982 to $263 million but, more importantly, set out a plan for selling existing securities. Thi action was taken in the expectation that Conrail would be able to make a profit in 1982 without federal support.

The reconciliation act specified a number of provisions for the sale. First, the board of directors of the U.S. Railway Association must determine whether Conrail is profitable. If the board finds that it is, the secretary of transportation must try to sell the U.S. government's share of common stock in Conrail. Second, if after June 1, 1984, the secretary is unable to sell the shares as a single block, one of two alternatives may occur. The employees of Conrail may submit a plan for the purchase of Conrail or, more likely, Conrail may be sold in parts to existing railroads.

The reconciliation act specified a number of changes that were aimed at improving Conrail's profitability and hence its salability as an entity by the 1984 deadline. As a result of action taken in both the 1980 Staggers Act and the reconciliation act, Conrail is now able to sell or abandon unprofitable lines. This ability enables Conrail to improve its own financial condition and hence its chances of being sold as an entity. The reconciliation act also allowed Conrail to spin off its commuter services either to local transit authorities or to the newly created Amtrak Commuter Services Corporation. Amtrak Commuter was established to operate the commuter services that

CBO Baseline and Effect
of Congressional Action During Calendar 1981
(in millions of dollars and percentages)
Account No. 98-0111-401

	FY1982		FY1983		FY1984	
Category	Dollar Level	Percent Change	Dollar Level	Percent Change	Dollar Level	Percent Change
CBO Baseline						
Budget						
authority	560	—	500	—	300	—
Outlays	460	—	500	—	300	—
Reconciliation Act						
Budget						
authority	455	−19	262	−48	0	−100
Outlays	125	−73	439	−12	153	−49
Final FY 1982 Expenditures						
After All Changes						
Budget						
authority	0	−100	—	—	—	—
Outlays	250	−46	—	—	—	—

Conrail had been obligated to provide. However, local transit authorities were provided the opportunity to establish their own commuter service if they notified Amtrak of their intentions by April 1, 1982.

The reconciliation act also made significant changes in Conrail's labor protection plan in order to increase Conrail's profitability. Conrail's labor protection plan had provided furloughed employees with large income allowances and all employees with generous health and welfare benefits and compensation for moving and retraining costs. The act limited benefit payments established by previous legislation to $20,000 per individual. Reconciliation also enabled Conrail to terminate certain excess employees, but required Conrail to pay them $350 for each month of active service up to a total of $25,000. Among other changes to Conrail's labor benefit plan, the act barred state laws or regulations that mandated the number of Conrail employees. Finally, the reconciliation act authorized a total of $400 million for labor benefits until expended.

Appropriations and Other Changes

Appropriations actions lowered the amount available to Conrail in fiscal year 1982 from the reconciliation authorization limit. Of this total, $25 million was appropriated for rail rehabilitation, $110 million was appropriated for new labor provisions, and $85 million was appropriated for Conrail operations. Transfer of commuter services from Conrail was financed by a one-time appropriation in 1982 of $45 million.

As a result of appropriations action, Conrail's labor benefit programs were accounted for in a new income security budget account.

Assessment

Conrail made a profit in 1981. All expectations are that it will not request funding for its operations for fiscal year 1983 or 1984. Funding for the labor provisions is expected to continue, but will diminish to zero after Conrail is sold in 1984. Upon Conrail's sale, the federal government will no longer subsidize the service. Hence, additional operating subsidies have not been requested by Conrail or proposed by the administration for 1983. The proposed 1983 labor protection level was $20 million.

PUBLIC MASS TRANSPORTATION

Program Description

The Urban Mass Transportation Administration (UMTA) operates under the authority of the Urban Mass Transportation Act of 1964. Its overall objectives are to assist in the development of improved mass transportation facilities, equipment, techniques, and methods; to encourage the planning and establishment of areawide urban mass transportation systems; and to help state and local governments in financing such systems.

The major emphasis of UMTA funding is to provide grants or loans to help communities acquire, improve, and maintain capital equipment and facilities and to provide operating subsidies.

UMTA is involved in several other program areas. One such program involves research, development, and demonstration of all phases of urban mass transportation. Major projects in this area are advanced-technology rapid rail cars, an operational "people mover," and new techniques of traffic management, among others. Most of these projects are conducted under contracts with private organizations; public bodies, including state and local governments; and expert individuals. Another program area is university research and training in urban transportation analysis, planning, engineering, and operations. UMTA also provides grants to governmental bodies to provide fellowship training for persons employed in public transportation positions.

Allocations for UMTA's programs are based on formulas. Funds are apportioned to urban areas by a formula based half on population and half on population density. The federal matching share for funds used for capital purposes is up to 80 percent; for operating purposes it is up to 50 percent.

The actual level of program funding in fiscal year 1981 was $4.6 billion.

Reconciliation Act Changes

The reconciliation act did not specify program changes; it merely achieved its reductions by cutting programs across the board. In fiscal year 1982, capital subsidies were lowered to $1.5 billion from $1.6 billion; formula grants were reduced to $1.48 billion from $1.76 billion; and rural transit grants were reduced to $.75 billion from $1.2 billion. This was a 26 percent reduction in budget authority from the CBO baseline in fiscal year 1982. In fiscal years 1983 and 1984 reductions are a projection of the 1982 reduction because reconciliation limited funding in fiscal year 1982 only.

CBO Baseline and Effect
of Congressional Action During Calendar 1981
(in millions of dollars and percentages)
Account No. 69-1119-401

	FY1982		FY1983		FY1984	
Category	Dollar Level	Percent Change	Dollar Level	Percent Change	Dollar Level	Percent Change
CBO Baseline						
Budget authority	5,090	—	5,507	—	5,914	—
Outlays	4,090	—	4,340	—	4,450	—
Reconciliation Act						
Budget authority	3,792	−26	3,661	−34	3,443	−42
Outlays	3,892	−5	3,630	−16	3,095	−30
Final FY 1982 Expenditures After All Changes						
Budget authority	3,495	−31	—	—	—	—
Outlays	3,792	−7	—	—	—	—

Because UMTA grants primarily support capital projects, outlay savings will occur slowly over time. The estimated outlay reduction resulting from reconciliation was only 5 percent in fiscal year 1982, growing to 30 percent by fiscal year 1984.

Appropriations Process Changes

The appropriations process cut more from UMTA's budget. In the two largest UMTA programs—discretionary capital and operating grants—the appropriation act reduced the budget authority for new and obligated but unexpended funds from $1.71 billion to $1.68 billion and from $1.43 billion to $1.37 billion respectively. The bill also reduced the authorization for appropriation whereby states could withdraw previously approved interstate highway segments and apply the authorized funds to transit projects. The program was reduced from $560 million to $538 million.

Altogether, the 1982 budget authority was reduced 31 percent and the outlay estimate was reduced 7 percent. Significantly, the bulk of the reduction in budget authority will not be noticed for several years since the spend-out rate is slower for construction projects.

Administrative Regulations

No new regulations have been generated as a result of the recent action in this area; however, on December 17, 1981, UMTA issued a notice proposing a comprehensive review of urban transportation planning in light of the administration's efforts to eliminate federal government intrusion into state and local affairs. Related to this action, the Department of Transportation's semiannual regulatory agenda indicated that UMTA might review its regulations concerning equipment maintenance.

Assessment

Over the last few years, UMTA's budget authority and outlays have been growing. From 1979 to 1980, actual budget authority and outlays grew 36 and 50 percent respectively. The rate of growth from 1980 to 1981 for budget authority was 45 percent and 20 percent for outlays. Estimates for the 1982 and 1983 levels of funding demonstrate a reversal of this growth trend.

As a result of action taken in fiscal year 1982, funding for both capital assistance and operating assistance was deeply cut (32 percent from the CBO baseline). The 1983 budget proposal for UMTA funding was $3.1 billion. This reduced level and the other program changes proposed by the administration reflect the larger effort to return responsibility and decision making to the state and local governments, to retarget public funding to capital improvements of existing transit systems, and to eliminate subsidies that undermine local incentives for efficient program administration.

States and localities will undoubtedly be significantly affected. To compensate for the reductions, transit operators will have to choose between reducing services, raising fares, and seeking nonfederal sources of revenues. Localities that had planned to begin construction of new transit systems will probably have to abandon those plans or seek alternative financing. It appears likely that states will be called upon by their major city transit authorities and by their rural communities to provide financial assistance.

GRANTS-IN-AID TO AIRPORTS

Program Description

The grants-in-aid to airports program provides funds to air carriers and general-aviation airports. Funds are used for the construction and reconstruction of runways, taxiways, aircraft aprons, and public-use portions of terminals. Funds were also used for land acquisition for airport development and noise abatement. In fiscal year 1981, $469 million was expended for this program.

The grants are financed through the airport and airways trust fund, with approximately 90 percent of the program costs provided by taxes on passenger tickets and other minor excise taxes. This funding mechanism is important because it allows the authorizing committees greater autonomy in setting the level of program activity. Authorizing legislation for this program contains contract authority, which means that funds can be obligated in advance of an appropriation. The contract authority constitutes the federal promise to pay but an appropriation is required before payment can be made. For this program, therefore, the appropriation serves to liquidate an existing federal obligation.

A unique provision of the trust fund allows the appropriations committees some control over the timing of the obligations. The appropriations committees annually limit the amount of contract authority available for obligation in that year. This limit is generally much less than the total amount of contract authority available for obligation. Because all contract authority will eventually be obligated, however, this mechanism controls the timing, but not the level of total program activity.

Reconciliation Act Changes

The authorizing legislation for this program expired at the end of fiscal year 1980. The program was not reauthorized in the reconciliation act. The act did limit the total amount which could be obligated out of the trust fund to $450 million in fiscal year 1981 and to a total of $1,050 million for fiscal years 1981 and 1982. The reconciliation act made no programmatic changes in this account.

163

**CBO Baseline and Effect
of Congressional Action During Calendar 1981
(in millions of dollars and percentages)
Account No. 69-8106-402**

Category	FY1982		FY1983		FY1984	
	Dollar Level	Percent Change	Dollar Level	Percent Change	Dollar Level	Percent Change
CBO Baseline						
Budget authority	789	—	872	—	942	—
Outlays	674	—	770	—	842	—
Reconciliation Act						
Budget authority	600	−24	663	−24	716	−24
Outlays	522	−23	593	−23	640	−24
Final FY 1982 Expenditures After All Changes						
Budget authority	0	−100	—	—	—	—
Outlays	485	−28	—	—	—	—

Appropriations and Other Changes

Late in the summer of 1981, an authorization bill for fiscal year 1981 was enacted which provided $450 million of contract authority for fiscal year 1981. As of April 1982, no authorization for 1982 had been enacted. The House and Senate were debating two separate bills dealing with air transportation. The House bill maintains the traditional structure of distribution of funds between large and small airports. The Senate bill drops the largest airports from eligibility and allows them to negotiate with the airlines for development funds by charging them user fees. The differences between the two versions of the bill had yet to be resolved.

Although the authorization bill had not been enacted, the Department of Transportation and Related Agencies Appropriations Act set an obligation limit of $450 million for fiscal year 1982. The fiscal year 1982 limit represented a reduction of $150 million from the $1,050 million allowed in the reconciliation act. (The appropriations act also provided $471 million to liquidate existing obligations.)

Administrative Regulations

Since no law has been passed, no regulations have been issued.

Assessment

New program activity has been halted until some decision is reached on the attempts to "defederalize" the large airports by forcing them to raise funds from the commercial airlines using their facilities. In the interim, the program will have to draw down its balance, which is estimated to be $4.7 billion for fiscal year 1982. Though impacts on state and local governments in fiscal year 1982 are unclear, the longer the debate continues the more likely it is that there will be pressure on state and local governments to assist in funding airport development and planning.

The Reagan budget proposed an increase in general aviation excise taxes to be used to purchase new equipment for the air controllers and to increase the proportion of air controllers' salaries that are funded through the trust fund. Other programs are maintained at their current level.

COMMUNITY DEVELOPMENT BLOCK GRANT

Program Description

The community development block grant (CDBG) program provides grants to local governments for general community development. The funds are used primarily for development of residential neighborhoods (including provision of social services in those neighborhoods), rehabilitation of housing for low- and moderate-income families, physical improvements of neighborhood infrastructure, and economic development (including commercial rehabilitation). Cities have used funds to repair sewer and water systems, to provide street amenities and improvements, and to fund community organizations. Before the reconciliation act, funds were provided principally for the benefit of low-income persons.

Two forms of grants are supported by this program. *Entitlement grants* allocated by formula go to large cities and urban counties. *Discretionary grants,* which in fiscal year 1981 were administered by the Department of Housing and Urban Development (HUD), are allocated to small cities through statewide competitions. The HUD secretary's discretionary fund also provides grants to recipients and projects that might not receive assistance through the regular grant allocations. In fiscal year 1981, 2,850 localities received assistance at a cost of $3.675 billion.

Reconciliation Act Changes

Although CDBG has been a block grant since its inception, the reconciliation act further increased the states' authority over the program by giving them the option to administer the nonentitlement, small cities portion of the program. In addition, the act reduced the application requirements local governments must meet to receive funds and expanded the list of activities that may be undertaken with CDBG funds. By reducing HUD's level of involvement in local affairs, the reconciliation act was intended to reduce paperwork requirements and federal control, thereby improving program performance. The reconciliation act achieved savings by limiting the authorization of appropriations to $4,166 million for fiscal years 1982 and 1983, of which up to $500 million was set aside for the urban development action grant (UDAG) program, described in a separate section.

The reconciliation act lowered the CDBG budget authority by 7 percent in fiscal year 1982 and 15 percent in fiscal year 1983. (In 1984, CBO estimated a 21 percent budget authority reduction, although this is not specified in the act.) Because community development grants are used in construction,

167

**CBO Baseline and Effect
of Congressional Action During Calendar 1981
(in millions of dollars and percentages)
Account No. 86-0162-451**

	FY1982		FY1983		FY1984	
Category	Dollar Level	Percent Change	Dollar Level	Percent Change	Dollar Level	Percent Change
CBO Baseline						
Budget						
authority	3,960	—	4,329	—	4,644	—
Outlays	4,750	—	4,270	—	4,300	—
Reconciliation Act						
Budget						
authority	3,666	−7	3,666	−15	3,666[a]	−21
Outlays	4,720	−1	4,107	−4	3,894	−9
Final FY 1982 Expenditures						
After All Changes						
Budget						
authority	3,456	−13	—	—	—	—
Outlays	4,128	−13	—	—	—	—

a. The reconciliation act did not authorize spending in 1984; the figure is a CBO estimate.

outlay savings occur at a slower pace: 1 percent in fiscal year 1982, 4 percent in fiscal year 1983, and 9 percent in fiscal year 1984. Because the CDBG program requires an appropriation, further cuts can be achieved in the annual appropriations process.

Phasing

States were able to exercise their option to administer the small city portion of the program beginning on October 1, 1981. In fiscal year 1982, states received allotments once applications were received by the secretary of HUD. HUD will continue to administer the entitlement portion.

Distribution Formula

Nonentitlement cities—those under 50,000 in population or not included in standard metropolitan statistical areas—began to receive 30 percent of the funds appropriated for the CDBG program in fiscal year 1982. Previously, small cities received a share of approximately 25 percent. Funds allocated to small cities increased in fiscal year 1982 while funds allocated to entitlement cities and the secretary's discretionary fund declined.

The allocation formula itself is unchanged both for entitlement and non-entitlement portions of the program.

If an entitlement city or county fails to meet the requirements of the program, the funds will be reallocated to other cities and counties in the same metropolitan area in the next fiscal year. Previously, funds were immediately available for reallocation to entitlement and nonentitlement jurisdictions in the same metropolitan area.

Application Process

To receive funds under the small city portion of the program, states must (1) engage in planning for community development, (2) provide technical assistance to localities, and (3) consult local officials about the method of distributing the funds.

Both entitlement and nonentitlement jurisdictions are no longer required to file a housing assistance plan (HAP), which laid out a specific three-year program for which the community would be held accountable by HUD. Instead, a less specific statement of objectives is required that lays out proposed uses of funds. In addition, recipients of CDBG funds are required to (1) furnish information to citizens about uses and amounts of available funds, (2) publish their proposal, and (3) hold one or more public hearings.

Entitlement cities and counties fall under stricter requirements than non-entitlement jurisdictions. The statement of objectives for such cities must (1) assess the housing assistance needs of low-income persons, (2) specify a realistic annual goal for the number of dwelling units or low-income persons to be assisted, and (3) indicate the general locations of proposed housing for lower-income households.

Program Management

Each recipient of CDBG funds must file a performance report concerning the use of funds, and an assessment by the recipient of the relationship of such use to the objectives specified in the application. The secretary of HUD has the power to review the statements and adjust funds if violations occur. Withheld funds can be reallocated through the procedure set out in the distribution formula section (above).

Eligible Activities

Private, for-profit entities may now receive direct assistance to carry out economic development activities. This increase in flexibility allows cities to support economic development projects initiated by private real estate developers. Only 10 percent of CDBG funds may be used to provide public services within any jurisdiction. This new requirement may be waived by the secretary of HUD in fiscal years 1982 through 1984. Activities previously supported under Section 701 of the Housing Act of 1954 (planning grants) may be supported with CDBG funds.

Matching Requirements

States are required to provide funds for community development purposes equal to 10 percent of the amount made available by HUD for nonentitlement jurisdictions. States may deduct 50 percent of administrative costs in nonentitlement jurisdictions from their matching funds. This deduction can amount to no more than 2 percent of the total allocation, however.

Appropriations Process Changes

No programmatic changes were made in the appropriations process. The HUD Appropriations Act reduced budget authority from $3,666 million to $3,456 million, a cut of 6 percent below the reconciliation act level. The full reduction from the CBO baseline to the appropriations limit was $504 million or 13 percent.

Administrative Regulations

On April 8, 1982 HUD issued a rule establishing the policies and procedures for the state CDBG program. As described earlier, states may elect to administer the small city portion of the program. The rule allows states a great deal of flexibility in designing their own methods of distributing funds and in interpreting statutory requirements by establishing the policies and procedures for their programs.

The HUD regulations give no procedural guidance for fulfilling program requirements, but do require states to honor multiyear commitments to local governments for local development plans already made by HUD. The preamble to the rule makes clear that states must give "maximum feasible priority to activities which will benefit low- and moderate-income families or aid in the prevention or elimination of slums or blight," as specified in the reconciliation act.

HUD does not prescribe cost principles and other financial management procedures, as had been required under community development programs in the past. States are exempted from the procedural requirements of OMB circular A−87 ("Cost Principles for Grants to State and Local Governments") and A−102 ("Uniform Requirements for Grants to State and Local Governments," which prescribes assurances that recipient governments must make regarding the cross-cutting laws on civil rights, fair labor standards, historic preservation, environmental protections, etc.). States may apply equivalent procedures of their own for financial management and enforcement of the cross-cutting laws or they may elect to follow A-87 and A-102.

The regulations also enumerate the cross-cutting laws that the states must enforce as conditions of their grants to local governments, including applicable sections of the Civil Rights Act of 1964, the Davis-Bacon Act on wages and other labor standards, the National Environmental Policy Act of 1969, and the Lead-Based Paint Poisoning Prevention Act. Guidance on applicability of provisions of the Hatch Act and of Executive Order 11246, which imposes equal employment opportunity obligations, has been deferred for a later regulation.

States must set up methods for determining whether the local units have satisfied the performance requirements of the reconciliation act and whether funds have been used appropriately. HUD will, in turn, audit each state's performance on timely distribution of funds, compliance with certifications on requirements of the act and applicable cross-cutting laws, and reviews and audits by the states of their funded units.

Assessment

The most important effect of the reconciliation act is to change the program requirements of this existing block grant. While the final regulations have not yet been issued, the intent of the act and the administration's efforts to date has been to reduce HUD's control over the program. States will have to meet fewer requirements in spending block grant funds, but will have to establish their own guidelines and procedures.

Regulatory delays have discouraged most states from taking over the block grant. As of April 1982, thirty-six states had not yet decided to administer the small city part of the block grant—more states than have hesitated on any other block grant. States have complained that the delays have reduced planning time and time to consult local officials. Another factor behind states' reluctance to assume control of the block grant is the strong possibility that funds available for the program will decline in the next few years as pressure to reduce the budget deficit continues.

Local governments have been concerned that states will not sensitively administer the small cities program. Local governments have adjusted to HUD's administrative requirements and are unsure what different procedures the states will require, if any.

The fiscal year 1983 Reagan budget proposals call for funding of $3.456 billion, the same level approved in the 1982 appropriations act.

URBAN DEVELOPMENT ACTION GRANTS

Program Description

The urban development action grant (UDAG) program allocates grants to units of local government to promote private investment in distressed areas.

Grants are made only for particular projects in which some public improvement or financial concession is needed to secure participation of a private investor. The Department of Housing and Urban Development awards grants several times a year. In some rounds, proposals submitted by large cities compete with one another, while other rounds are restricted to proposals from smaller cities (those with populations of less than 50,000). In each round, HUD selects projects on the basis of (1) the merit of the proposal and (2) the degree of economic stress in the city or urban county applying for the grant. A jurisdiction may win several grants if it comes out ahead of other cities competing in a particular round. In fiscal year 1981, the program received $675 million in budget authority. Approximately 350 grants were awarded, averaging slightly less than $2 million each.

Reconciliation Act Changes

The reconciliation act reauthorized the UDAG program for fiscal years 1982 and 1983. It lowered the program's authorization of appropriations limit to $500 million for each of these two years. This represents a budget authority reduction of 26 and 31 percent below the current policy base in those years. Outlay reductions will occur at a slower pace, dropping by 2 percent in fiscal year 1982 and 12 percent in fiscal year 1983.

The reconciliation act authorized a separate UDAG account only through fiscal year 1983. If Congress does not reauthorize the program or provide budget authority for fiscal year 1984 and beyond, any unobligated UDAG budget authority will be added to the community development block grant (CDBG) budget account.

Previous law required the Department of Housing and Urban Development to maintain reasonable balance among the number of awards for commercial, industrial, and neighborhood projects. In 1978 and 1979, for example, 33.7 percent of the awards went for commercial projects, 35.5 percent went for industrial projects, and 30.7 percent went for neighborhood projects (most of which involved housing). The reconciliation act struck the requirement for this balance.

CBO Baseline and Effect
of Congressional Action During Calendar 1981
(in millions of dollars and percentages)
Account No. 86-0170-451

Category	FY1982 Dollar Level	FY1982 Percent Change	FY1983 Dollar Level	FY1983 Percent Change	FY1984 Dollar Level	FY1984 Percent Change
CBO Baseline						
Budget						
authority	675	—	729	—	779	—
Outlays	744	—	715	—	700	—
Reconciliation Act						
Budget						
authority	500	−26	500	−31	500	−36
Outlays	727	−2	627	−12	464	−34
Final FY 1982 Expenditures						
After All Changes						
Budget						
authority	440	−35	—	—	—	—
Outlays[a]	500	−33	—	—	—	—

a. Outlay number for FY 1982 incorporates an unofficial CBO reestimate. Earlier outlay estimates were too high; thus the 33 percent reduction figure is inflated. Actual final outlay reduction was in the 2−4 percent range.

Appropriations and Other Changes

The HUD appropriation for fiscal year 1982 granted $440 million in budget authority to the UDAG program. This represented a $60 million reduction from the authorization of appropriation limit contained in the reconciliation act. Thus, the total effect of congressional action during the first session of the 97th Congress was to reduce UDAG's budget authority by 35 percent below CBO's fiscal year 1982 current policy level.

The CBO outlay estimates for the effect of this additional reduction are overstated. When CBO produced its outlay estimates for current policy and the effect of the reconciliation act's changes, it overestimated the speed with which past UDAG budget authority would become outlays. Thus, the $744 million figure for current policy outlays and the $727 million figure for the outlay level after the passage of the reconciliation act are each approximately $220 million too high. A better estimate of the total effect of congressional action would be that the $235 million reduction in budget authority caused an outlay reduction of about $21 million. This represents a total outlay decline of 3 percent below CBO's fiscal year 1982 current policy level.

Administrative Regulations

Aside from the changes enacted in the reconciliation act, no significant administrative regulation changes have been made.

Assessment

The Reagan administration has recommended an additional 8 percent reduction in UDAG's fiscal year 1983 budget authority below CBO's current policy level. This apparent reduction is caused by the fact that CBO's current policy projections increase program funding to take account of assumed increases in the price level. In nominal dollar terms, therefore, the Reagan administration is calling for a continuation of the UDAG program at current funding levels.

Different people have different interpretations of the effect of eliminating the requirement for a reasonable balance among commercial, industrial, and neighborhood awards. Most observers see a shift from neighborhood projects to the other two categories. If past patterns hold, the shift will be to commercial projects in metropolitan cities and urban counties and to industrial projects in small cities. The difference of opinion comes over the judgment of whether the decline in the proportion of neighborhood projects implies a shift away from efforts to help the poor. Those who see this decline point out that neighborhood awards are the major category for directly helping low-income individuals. Others, however, point out that data for awards during 1978 and 1979 indicate that almost 60 percent of the housing units built or rehabilitated with UDAG awards are for middle- and upper-income residents.

REHABILITATION LOAN FUND

Program Description

The rehabilitation loan fund, sometimes referred to as the section 312 housing program, provides low-interest loans for the rehabilitation of single- and multifamily dwellings as well as a small number of commercial properties. The loan fund is specifically intended to promote the revitalization of distressed areas. President Carter's proposed budget estimated that 12,500 units would be rehabilitated using 1982 funding.

This program is a revolving fund, which means that both loan repayments and new budget authority provide funding for new loans. The rehabilitation loan fund goes through the normal appropriations process. Budget authority for fiscal year 1981 was $130 million, and outlays were estimated at $162 million.

Reconciliation Act Changes

The omnibus reconciliation act essentially abolished this program. The authorization of appropriation was removed for 1982 and subsequent years, so no new budget authority can be granted. The repayments to the loan fund can be reissued as new loans in fiscal year 1982, but not in future years. Thus, by fiscal year 1983, this program will be eliminated.

Appropriations Changes

Since the authorization of appropriation was removed, no funds were appropriated.

Assessment

The rehabilitation loan fund will have been eliminated by the end of fiscal year 1982. These funds will not be available to improve housing in distressed areas. Although the program was not large, there may be some increased pressure on public housing funds as a result of its elimination. The effects on states and localities will vary depending upon the extent of their housing programs.

CBO Baseline and Effect
of Congressional Action During Calendar 1981
(in millions of dollars and percentages)
Account No. 86-4036-451

Category	FY1982 Dollar Level	FY1982 Percent Change	FY1983 Dollar Level	FY1983 Percent Change	FY1984 Dollar Level	FY1984 Percent Change
CBO Baseline						
Budget						
authority	137	—	147	—	156	—
Outlays	147	—	140	—	142	—
Reconciliation Act						
Budget						
authority	0	−100	0	−100	0	−100
Outlays	−13	−109	0	−100	0	−100
Final FY 1982 Expenditures After All Changes						
Budget						
authority	0	−100	—	—	—	—
Outlays	−66	−145	—	—	—	—

ECONOMIC DEVELOPMENT ADMINISTRATION PROGRAMS

Program Description

The Economic Development Administration (EDA) is empowered to carry out the provisions of the Public Works and Economic Development Act of 1965. This act created a variety of grants, loans, and loan guarantees designed to stimulate business activity and thus reduce substantial and persistent unemployment in economically distressed areas.

There are seven major types of EDA programs. By far the most important are *development grants,* which provide funds for the construction of public works and community facilities. This program typically supports such projects as railroad sidings, access roads to industrial parks, tourist facilities, and water or sewer systems, and is designed to encourage commercial and industrial development. Federal funds generally cover 50 percent of the cost of any project; state or local governments provide the rest. About 64 percent of total EDA obligations in fiscal year 1981 were for development grants.

A second category is *planning grants,* which provide money to local development organizations in regions designated by the secretary of commerce as "redevelopment areas." These funds are to be used to obtain professional planning and support services. Third, *technical assistance grants* are given to local governments and nonprofit groups to support the collection and analysis of information needed by development projects. Each of these programs received about 6 percent of fiscal year 1981 obligations.

Economic adjustment grants are the fourth type of EDA program, and are designed to assist areas suffering severe and sudden economic disruptions. Funding levels have been quite low: less than $13 million in fiscal year 1981, or about 3 percent of total EDA obligations.

Direct loans are the fifth category, representing about 13 percent of fiscal year 1981 EDA obligations. This program provides low-interest loans to depressed areas for purposes similar to the development grants program. In addition, a loan guarantee program exists to help firms located in redevelopment areas gain access to credit markets. Payments for defaults on such guarantees commanded about 8 percent of total obligations.

The final program is a small *research and evaluation* effort designed to aid EDA administrators in analyzing and planning new programs. Its funding level is minimal.

The EDA programs have in general been targeted effectively toward economically depressed areas. Over 70 percent of EDA money has been spent in counties with high unemployment, low average incomes, or declining populations. However, the number of jobs created has not been significant by national standards.

Outlays for the program stood at $502 million in fiscal year 1981, while budget authority was $437 million after a rescission of $188 million had been made. Since much of the program involves construction grants, outlays tend to lag behind changes in budget authority. EDA programs go through the normal appropriations process.

Reconciliation Act Changes

President Reagan proposed eliminating all EDA programs in fiscal year 1982. Although it did not go that far, the reconciliation act set an authorization of appropriations limit for fiscal year 1982 of $290 million, a total that included both the EDA grants and program administration. CBO estimated that this would mean an authorization of $265 million for EDA programs, which is a reduction of 57 percent from the budget authority baseline. Outlays would be reduced by only 2 percent because of the delays involved in construction projects.

CBO Baseline and Effect
of Congressional Action During Calendar 1981
(in millions of dollars and percentages)
Account No. 13-2050-452

Category	FY1982 Dollar Level	FY1982 Percent Change	FY1983 Dollar Level	FY1983 Percent Change	FY1984 Dollar Level	FY1984 Percent Change
CBO Baseline						
Budget authority	623	—	670	—	712	—
Outlays	548	—	605	—	641	—
Reconciliation Act						
Budget authority	265	−57	283	−58	291	−59
Outlays	537	−2	422	−30	359	−44
Final FY 1982 Expenditures After All Changes						
Budget authority	199	−68	—	—	—	—
Outlays	515	−6	—	—	—	—

In addition, the reconciliation act mandated that no new projects be approved unless they can be completed with funds authorized in fiscal year 1982. Unless this provision is changed and more funds are granted next year, budget authority will be zero from fiscal year 1983 onward; outlays will continue for a time until projects are completed. The baseline shown in the table assumes that the program will continue to be authorized at its new, lower level. Within the group of projects which can be completed with 1982 funds, the secretary of commerce is to approve projects according to the following priorities:

1. Projects for which applications have been authorized to be filed as of the date of the reconciliation act get highest priority.
2. Projects for which preliminary application materials have been authorized to be filed get second priority.
3. All other projects get the lowest priority.

No guidelines on the allocation of funds among the various EDA programs were included in the act.

Appropriations Changes

The appropriations process resulted in further cuts in EDA funding. Fiscal year 1982 budget authority was limited to $199 million, which was 25 percent below the authorization limit. Outlays were estimated at $515 million, or 4 percent below the level of the reconciliation act. Thus, the total cuts from the CBO baseline amount to $424 million in budget authority (68 percent) and $33 million in outlays (6 percent).

Administrative Regulations

No significant changes have been made in the administration of the program, except for compliance with the mandates to fund only those projects that will not require money in future years and to set priorities for projects based on their status in the application process.

Assessment

The EDA grant programs have been sharply cut back for fiscal year 1982. The figures in the table for fiscal years 1983 and 1984 assume funding will continue at levels reflecting current policy as defined by the 1982 authorization. However, the administration is once again requesting the elimination of all EDA programs in fiscal year 1983, arguing that its general economic plan will be more effective in creating jobs than categorical grant programs.

Because the reconciliation act allows funding for those projects needing money only in fiscal year 1982, and gives highest priority to projects already planned, it is unlikely that any new development efforts will be supported.

Given these restrictions and the administration's stated policy, it is probable that the EDA programs will not be reauthorized for fiscal year 1983.

DISASTER LOAN FUND

Program Description

The disaster loan fund was originally established by the Small Business Act of 1958. Prior to the passage of the reconciliation act, the Small Business Administration (SBA) provided subsidized loans to individuals and businesses that were victims of either physical or nonphysical disasters.

Physical disaster loans were made to property owners to rehabilitate property damaged by natural disasters such as floods, hurricanes, tornadoes, and earthquakes. Nonphysical disaster loans were made to small businesses that needed assistance in complying with various federal or state statutes and regulations and to small businesses suffering economic loss because of displacement or economic injury. Loans to assist small business in complying with pollution control, meat and poultry inspection, and occupational safety requirements fall into the first type of nonphysical disaster loans, while loans to assist small business in overcoming economic loss caused by the closing of federal offices and military bases fall into the second category.[1]

The disaster loan fund is a revolving loan fund. Each year the SBA makes loans from the fund, which is replenished by the repayment of past loans. In recent years repayments of past loans (reflows) have averaged $800 to $900 million per year. New loan obligations were $1,237 million in fiscal year 1980, $1,522 million in fiscal year 1981, and $640 million in fiscal year 1982. Congress is required to enact new budget authority for the gap between reflows and new obligations. In fiscal year 1981, $315 million in new budget authority was granted.

Although the fund is not an entitlement, prior to the Reagan administration it was treated as such. No limit was placed on loans, and requests for new budget authority were sent to and enacted by the Congress without review. When the fund needed additional budget authority, OMB simply transmitted the SBA request to the appropriations committees, which routinely granted the requested authority.

---

1. Congressional Budget Office, *Federal Credit Activities: An Analysis of President Reagan's Credit Budget for 1982* (Washington: Congressional Budget Office, April 1981), pp. 78-79.

CBO Baseline and Effect
of Congressional Action During Calendar 1981
(in millions of dollars and percentages)
Account No. 73-4153-453

Category	FY1982		FY1983		FY1984	
	Dollar Level	Percent Change	Dollar Level	Percent Change	Dollar Level	Percent Change
CBO Baseline						
Budget authority	180	—	205	—	275	—
Outlays	767	—	92	—	218	—
Reconciliation Act						
Budget authority	0	−100	14	−93	33	−88
Outlays	160	−79	−135	−246	−33	−115
Final FY 1982 Expenditures After All Changes						
Budget authority	0	−100	—	—	—	—
Outlays	64	−92	—	—	—	—

Reconciliation Act Changes

The reconciliation act sought to achieve savings by eliminating the non-physical criteria for obtaining loans under the program and by raising the interest rate on loans to near or above the cost of money to the government (the interest rate the government must pay for debt of comparable maturity—usually long-term bonds and five- to seven-year notes).

The figures in the accompanying table overstate the outlay savings for this program. President Carter's fiscal year 1982 budget assumed that the disaster loan program would require a $780 million supplemental appropriation for fiscal year 1981. In its March 1981 reestimates, the Reagan administration withdrew the request for the supplemental appropriation. However, the Congress required that the CBO keep the $750 million in fiscal year 1981 budget authority and the resulting $500 million in fiscal year 1982 outlays in its fiscal year 1982 current policy baseline. When the supplemental appropriation was withdrawn, therefore, the Congress was able to take credit for a $500 million outlay savings.

Congress was able to reduce the fund's new budget authority for fiscal year 1982 to zero by agreeing to the Reagan administration's goal of limiting fiscal year 1982 new obligations to $440 million. Repayments of past loans were expected to be large enough to cover the fund's needs.

Narrowing the Definition of Acceptable Loans

The reconciliation act narrowed the definition of "disaster" to include only physical disasters and economic disasters resulting from physical catastrophes. The administration was empowered to (1) make loans to repair or replace damaged or destroyed property, if the losses were not covered by insurance; (2) refinance mortgages or liens against destroyed or damaged property; and (3) make loans to small businesses suffering economic loss as a result of physical catastrophe. Economic disaster loans are limited to those small businesses that cannot obtain credit elsewhere. Approximately a quarter of the savings are due to these changes.

Higher Interest Rates

Approximately three-quarters of the savings achieved by the reconciliation act are attributable to increasing the interest costs of disaster loans. Raising the interest cost not only decreases the amount of government subsidy per loan but also discourages many who would have applied for loans under the old rules. As a result of the higher rates and a year with a lower than normal rate of physical disasters, the number of new loans has declined sharply since the passage of the reconciliation act.

Maximum interest rates on every type of disaster loan were raised. Prior to the enactment of the reconciliation act, eligible homeowners paid interest rates of 3 percent regardless of whether they could obtain credit elsewhere. Businesses unable to obtain other credit paid 5 percent, while those businesses that could obtain other financing paid the government's cost of money plus up to one percentage point.

Under the new provisions, homeowners who cannot obtain credit elsewhere will have to pay interest rates of half of the government's cost of money, plus up to one percentage point. The total interest cost for such homeowners cannot exceed 8 percent, however. The interest ceiling for businesses, which are unable to obtain credit elsewhere, is also set at 8 percent.

Homeowners who are able to obtain credit elsewhere will have to pay interest rates equal to the cost of money to the government, plus up to one percentage point. Businesses, which are able to secure credit elsewhere, will have to pay interest rates no higher than private market rates and no higher than the guaranteed business loan rate.

The reconciliation act limited the amount of disaster loans for business applicants to 85 percent of the total loss from the disaster. A ceiling of $500,000 was placed on individual disaster loans.

Appropriations and Other Changes

No further reductions were made in the program by the appropriations committees. The $96 million outlay reduction in the accompanying table is a CBO reestimate to take into account declining loan activity.

Administrative Regulations

No regulatory changes have been made in the program.

Assessment

The administration has successfully sought to make the disaster loan program very unattractive for most prospective lenders. The true extent of the reductions cannot be estimated, however, until the program has to deal with a period of normal or greater than normal physical disasters.

In 1981 the administration sought to limit new obligations to $440 million. At present it appears that this goal will be exceeded by $220 million. In its fiscal year 1983 budget the administration is requesting a statutory limit on direct lending of $440 million.

IMPACT AID

Program Description

The impact aid program provides construction and operating grants to school systems in which there are large concentrations of children of federal employees. The rationale for the impact aid program, which dates back to 1950, is that large federal installations, such as military bases, may add to local demand for services without contributing to the local tax base. The program provides a type of payment in lieu of taxes. In fiscal year 1981, payments were made to more than 700 school districts.

The program makes payments directly to local school districts. The program distinquishes between type A children, whose parents both live on federal property and work there, and type B children, whose parents either work or live on federal property but not both. Of the 2.2 million students in districts receiving aid in 1981, 15 percent were type A. Most type A children are children of military personnel or are Indian children living on Indian lands. Most type B children either live in low-rent housing or in private homes.

Impact aid is an appropriated account. Unlike most education programs, it is not "forward-funded." The fiscal year 1982 budget, for example, affects schools during the 1981-82 school year rather than in the following one.

Reconciliation Act Changes

The reconciliation act phased out aid for type B children over a three-year period. Accordingly, the act achieved rather dramatic savings over the CBO baseline: a 45 percent reduction in budget authority in fiscal year 1982, rising to a 53 percent reduction in fiscal year 1984, with savings in outlays rising from 37 to 52 percent over the same period. In other words, budget authority was effectively cut in half and estimated outlay reductions totaled $1.3 billion over the three-year period. The reconciliation act made certain other small changes; for example, the operation of schools on military bases has been transferred to the Department of Defense.

CBO Baseline and Effect
of Congressional Action During Calendar 1981
(in millions of dollars and percentages)
Account No. 91-0102-501

Category	FY1982 Dollar Level	FY1982 Percent Change	FY1983 Dollar Level	FY1983 Percent Change	FY1984 Dollar Level	FY1984 Percent Change
CBO Baseline						
Budget authority	866	—	939	—	1,014	—
Outlays	837	—	923	—	998	—
Reconciliation Act						
Budget authority	475	−45	475	−49	475	−53
Outlays	524	−37	475	−49	475	−52
Final FY 1982 Expenditures After All Changes						
Budget authority	437	−50	—	—	—	—
Outlays	488	−42	—	—	—	—

Appropriations Changes

The appropriations process achieved some small additional savings in impact aid, raising total savings in budget authority and outlay in fiscal year 1982 to 50 and 58 percent, respectively.

Administration and Regulation

No regulations have yet appeared in this area.

Assessment

The impact aid program has been politically popular, particularly among districts near military bases. Furthermore, school districts like the program because there are virtually no strings attached to local use of the money. Nonetheless, every president since Eisenhower has sought to curtail the program, criticizing its massive distribution of funds without reference to need and its loose definition of federal impact. For example, many employees of federal installations already pay local property taxes. A recent study of federal impact aid equalization found that the construction program "has no fiscal equalizing tendencies'' while the maintenance program often ''serves as a large subsidy for the more wealthy.'' In essence, then, the Reagan administration has succeeded in imposing curbs long sought by prior administrations.

Only about 5 percent of the nation's school districts received impact aid last year, but clearly the amount received by these districts was substantial, on the order of $1 million per district. In those districts—generally near military bases or other concentrations of federal employees—the 50 percent reduction in impact aid will be felt. The demise of the program will not mean much for most districts, however.

Since impact aid was largely without ''strings,'' one might expect that impact aid money has been disproportionately used for administration. Whether cuts will now be taken in administration or in services is an open question. In its 1983 budget, the Reagan administration proposes to end all payments to type B children immediately, rather than phasing the payments out gradually. Additionally, payments for type A children would be approximately 80 percent of the 1982 level. Budget authority would be set at $288 million and outlays at $340 million.

ELEMENTARY AND SECONDARY EDUCATION BLOCK GRANT

Program Description

Before the reconciliation act, twenty-nine small programs, authorized by the Elementary and Secondary Education Act (ESEA), funded a wide variety of services and aid programs provided largely by state and local educational agencies (see table). The programs included special aid for school districts implementing desegregation plans (emergency school aid), project grants for gifted and talented children, and formula grants for strengthening management of state education agencies. Four of the twenty-nine programs were formula grants; the rest were project grants. In fiscal year 1981, the budget authority appropriated for all programs totaled $561 million.

Reconciliation Act Changes

The reconciliation act consolidated the twenty-nine programs in a single block grant, a larger number than any other block grant established by the reconciliation act. Through the consolidation of programs and simplification of administration, the reconciliation act gives states greater control over the kinds and quality of services provided.

The block grant will continue to support services and purposes provided by the twenty-nine earlier programs. The purposes specified in the act are (1) improvement of elementary and secondary schools in reading, mathematics, and writing; (2) improvement of education facilities and training for teachers and support staff, and (3) support of special projects, which range from education in the use of the metric system to health and environmental education.

The block grant is forward funded, which means budget authority is available from July 1 of one fiscal year through September 30 of the following fiscal year. For example, funds appropriated by Congress in fiscal year 1983 and included in the 1983 federal budget totals may be obligated from July 1, 1982 through September 30, 1983. Congress allows the budget authority to be obligated over a fifteen-month period so that school districts may receive their funding allocation before the start of the school year.

The reconciliation act limited the authorization of appropriations for fiscal years 1982, 1983, and 1984 to $589 million in each year. The CBO was unable to provide the exact effect of these changes. However, very roughly, budget authority was reduced by 30 percent from the CBO current policy baseline over the three-year period.

CBO Baseline and Effect
of Congressional Action During Calendar 1981
(in millions of dollars and percentages)
Account No. 91-0105-501

Category	FY1982 Dollar Level	FY1982 Percent Change	FY1983 Dollar Level	FY1983 Percent Change	FY1984 Dollar Level	FY1984 Percent Change
CBO Baseline						
Budget authority	764	—	833	—	910	—
Outlays	NA	—	NA	—	NA	—
Reconciliation Act						
Budget authority	589	−23	589	−29	589	−35
Outlays	NA	NA	NA	NA	NA	NA
Final FY 1982 Expenditures After All Changes						
Budget authority	470	−38	—	—	—	—
Outlays	NA	NA	—	—	—	—

Distribution Formula

Block grant funds will be distributed to state educational agencies according to each state's share of the national school-age population. Each state will receive a minimum of 0.5 percent of the total remaining after funds are set aside for the territorial United States and the secretary of education's discretionary fund is established. The states must pass through a minimum of 80 percent of their allocation to local educational agencies (LEAs) to be used at their complete discretion. The state allotments to the LEAs are to be made according to relative enrollments in public and private schools, adjusted to provide greater per-pupil allocations to LEAs that have the greatest numbers or percentages of children whose education imposes a higher than average cost per child. Adjustment factors could include (1) children from low-income families, (2) children living in economically depressed urban or rural areas, and (3) children living in sparsely populated areas. The secretary of education must approve adjustment factors.

Application Process

States are required to file applications with the secretary of education every three years. Applications must designate the state education agency as the agency responsible for program administration, provide for consultation with an advisory committee appointed by the governor (including representatives of the state legislature), set forth the planned allocation of funds reserved for state use among authorized activities, provide for public dissemination of information, and provide for annual evaluations beginning in fiscal year 1984.

LEAs are required to file applications with the state education agency every three years. Applications set forth planned allocation of funds among the activities authorized, provide for consultation with parents and teachers in the design and implementation of programs, and contain other assurances as specified in law.

Phasing

States had to take over administration of the block grant by October 1, 1982, or as soon as possible. (The act makes no other provisions for transition.)

Transferability

No provisions for transfer of funds are included in the act.

Audit Requirements

The provisions of title XVII will apply as follows: State education agencies are required to keep such records and provide such information to the secretary as required for fiscal audit and evaluation. LEAs are likewise required to make such information available to the state. Audit provisions currently required by the General Education Provisions Act apply to block grant funds.

Other Requirements and Provisions

Maintenance of effort provisions require that the expenditure for "the provision of free public education for the preceding fiscal year was not less than 90 percent . . . aggregate expenditures for the second preceding fiscal year." For example, expenditures in fiscal year 1983 may not be less than 90 percent of fiscal year 1982 expenditures. If that level is not reached, a prorated reduction will be made in payments to the state. The act requires that federal funds supplement, not supplant, state and local funds.

Provisions are included to ensure that private school children have the same access to programs and activities as public school children.

An amount not to exceed 6 percent of funds appropriated each year is allotted to the secretary for programs of national significance, including the national diffusion network program, which provides funds to encourage the rapid dissemination and adoption of improved educational practices, products, and programs. However, the secretary must first fund the inexpensive book distribution program (as carried out through "Reading is Fundamental"), the national program of arts in education, and the alcohol and drug abuse education program at a level not less than each program's fiscal year 1981 level.

The secretary can withhold block grant funds if it is found that the state has failed to comply substantially with the block grant requirements.

Appropriations Process Changes

Because the Labor, Health and Human Services, and Education Appropriations Act has not been passed, funding for the ESEA block grant is being provided under a continuing resolution. The continuing resolution reduced budget authority from $589 million to $470.4 million, a cut of 20 percent below the reconciliation act limit. The total cut from the CBO baseline to the appropriation limit was $394 million or 38 percent.

Several programs eligible to be funded under the block grant were granted separate budget authority in fiscal year 1982. These separately authorized programs are: follow-through ($19.4 million), biomedical sciences for disadvantaged students ($2.9 million), law-related education ($1 million), and career education ($9.6 million). The Department of Education can fund these programs separately from the block grant, although states can support the four programs with their block grant allocations.

Administrative Regulations

Proposed regulations for the block grant have been published, and now the Education Department is summarizing comments. The regulations, when published in final form, will be descriptive in nature and will not interpret or extend the language included in the reconciliation act. For example, the regulations will not describe the adjustment factors states should use to shift assistance to school districts with high educational costs per child. State adjustment factors probably will be reviewed on a case-by-case basis.

Assessment

The CBO baseline does not take into account rescissions made over the summer of 1981 and the trend toward lower funding levels for education programs that began before 1981. Therefore, the baseline is much greater than the funds actually distributed to school districts in 1981, and may over-estimate the funding levels for 1982, 1983, and 1984 that would have been available before the Reagan program.

The most important change caused by the block grant is the distribution formula. In fiscal year 1981, the distribution of aid under the twenty-nine project and formula grants was uneven. Some school districts received sub-stantial aid—especially those adept with grant applications—and most received little or no aid under any of the project grants. The block grant's population-based formula will smooth the previously uneven distribution of aid. A few school districts will lose large amounts of aid while many school districts will gain relatively smaller amounts.

Another important shift inherent in the change from project to block grant is the increased certainty of funding. With project grants, school districts and state educational agencies could not assume they would receive funding even for two or three years; future applications might be rejected. Under the block grant formula, state educational agencies can better estimate funding over a two- or three-year period, assuming Congress appropriates sums close to the authorized amounts.

Countering the increased certainty of funding under formula grants, future appropriations for the education block grant are likely to fall below the budget authority levels presented in the summary table.

The Reagan 1983 budget proposals call for budget authority of $433 million, a reduction of almost $40 million from the amount approved under the continuing resolution in 1982.

Programs Consolidated into Block Grant

Program	Fiscal 1981 budget authority (millions of dollars)	Type of grant	Type of recipient	Authorizing statute
Basic skills improvement	31	Project & formula	State and local educ. agencies, public and non-profit orgs.	ESEA, title II
Metric systems education	1	Project	State and local educ. agencies, public and non-profit orgs.	ESEA, title III
Law-related education	1	Project	State and local educ. agencies, public and non-profit orgs.	ESEA, title III
Arts education	3	Project	State and local educ. agencies, public and non-profit orgs.	ESEA, title III
Consumers education	1	Project	State and local educ. agencies, public and non-profit orgs.	ESEA, title III
School library resources	161	Formula	State educ. agencies	ESEA, title IV
Improvement in local educational practice	66	Formula	State educ. agencies	ESEA, title IV
International under-standing program	2	Project	State and local educ. agencies, public and non-profit orgs.	ESEA, title III

Programs Consolidated into Block Grant, continued

Program				
Magnet schools (Emergency School Aid Act)	30	Project	Local educ. agencies	ESEA, title VI
Pre-college teacher development in science programs	2	Project	Colleges & universities	P.L. 81-507, 94-378, 96-88
Biomedical sciences for disadvantaged students	3	Project	Colleges & universities	ESEA, title III
Cities in schools	3	Project	State & local public & non-profit orgs.	ESEA, title III
PUSH for excellence	1	Project	Urban local educ. agencies	ESEA, title III
Education for gifted and talented children	6	Project	State educ. agencies	ESEA, title IX
Community education (community schools)	3	Project	Local educ. agencies, non-profit & public entities	ESEA title VIII
Ethnic heritage studies	2	Project	Public & non-profit educ. agencies	ESEA, title IX
Alcohol and drug abuse education program	3	Project	Local school districts	Alcohol & Drug Abuse Education Act
Teacher centers	9	Project	Local educ. agencies, colleges	Higher Educ. Act, title V
Follow through	33	Project	State and local educ. agencies, colleges	Economic Opportunity Act
Strengthening state management	38	Formula	State educ. agencies	ESEA, title V

Programs Consolidated into Block Grant, continued

Program	Fiscal 1981 budget authority (millions of dollars)	Type of grant	Type of recipient	Authorizing statute
Educational television and radio programming	6	Project	State and local educ. agencies, public and nonprofit orgs.	ESEA, title III
National diffusion program	10	Project	State and local educ. agencies, public and nonprofit orgs.	ESEA, title III
Career education	10	Project	State and local educ. agencies, public and nonprofit orgs.	P.L. 95-207
Teacher corps	22	Project	State and local educ. agencies	Higher Education Act
Grants to school districts (Emergency School Aid Act)	33	Project	Local educ. agencies	ESEA, title VI
Grants to nonprofit organizations (Emergency School Aid Act)	5	Project	Nonprofit agencies	P.L. 95-561
Educational TV & radio (Emergency School Aid Act)	4	Project	Public & nonprofit agencies	ESEA, title VI
Special programs and projects (Emergency School Aid Act)	76	NA	Guidance and counseling	ESEA, title IV-D

COMPENSATORY EDUCATION ASSISTANCE

Program Description

Title I of the Elementary and Secondary Education Act (ESEA) of 1965 has become the cornerstone of federal aid to the nation's elementary and secondary schools, providing financial assistance for compensatory instruction to educationally disadvantaged children in low-income areas. In fiscal year 1981, title I received a $3.5 billion appropriation and provided assistance to over 90 percent of the nation's school districts.

Title I provides grants to state and local educational agencies through two programs—basic grants and concentration grants. *Basic grants* provide funds to local education agencies based on a legislated formula and provide funds to state educational agencies for migrant children and for handicapped, neglected, and delinquent children in state institutions. *Concentration grants* provide additional funds in counties with a high proportion of children from low-income families. Additionally, state education agencies receive some money for students in state institutions.

The method for distributing funds has reflected a compromise between an approach stressing poverty and an approach stressing educational disadvantage. More specifically, prior to the reconciliation act, title I funds were distributed as follows: First, money was allocated by the federal government to local school districts based on census enumerations of school children from low-income families, the number of recipients of free lunches, or the number of AFDC recipients. Further allocations then occurred within each school district. Such allocations had to meet the approval not of the federal government directly, but of the state educational agency operating within federal guidelines and regulations. These allocations within school districts involved a two-step process. First, school districts had to specify which schools were eligible to receive title I funds. Schools could be ranked both on the basis of poverty and on the basis of educational deprivation among students. Districts then had to distribute funds to schools on the basis of number and needs of students, as determined by educational criteria. Where there were high concentrations of poor students (75 percent or more), title I projects could be schoolwide.

Title I imposes three kinds of requirements on local school systems: first, the school district must not replace locally funded programs with title I programs; second, the district must use title I programs to supplement—that is, expand and improve—existing programs and to meet special needs that would not otherwise be met; and third, the amount of state and local funds used in a title I school must be comparable—that is, roughly equal—to the average amount of such funds used in the district's schools that do not receive title I funds.

Title I, like most education programs, is "forward funded" so that school districts can plan ahead financially. In other words, the budget allocations for fiscal year 1982 will not affect schools until school year 1982-83, and fiscal year 1982 outlays largely reflect budget action in the prior fiscal year.

Reconciliation Act Changes

In the reconciliation act, title I became part I of the new Education Consolidation and Improvement Act, which replaces ESEA. Funds are authorized to part I beginning in fiscal year 1983. Major structural changes in the program were avoided but states were granted more control.

With regard to funding, the reconciliation act authorized an appropriation of $3.5 billion in budget authority in each fiscal year 1982, 1983, and 1984 for this program. Of the $430 million savings over the CBO baseline in fiscal year 1982, approximately $420 million represents cuts in title I. Because title I is forward funded, fiscal year 1982 outlays were largely determined last year and, accordingly, outlay savings in fiscal year 1982 were quite modest.

In addition to these changes in funding, Congress made some structural changes. In general, changes replace specific provisions with broader, less specific ones and limit the authority of federal administrators to issue regulations. For example, the reconciliation act retains the focus on low-income areas but "permits" instead of "requires" that school districts focus on children in greatest need. The act repeals the authority to focus on areas having high concentrations of educationally deprived children; also, the new law does not contain specific authority for schoolwide projects. Previously, local educational agencies could skip the highest-ranked areas under certain circumstances; under the reconciliation act they must focus on the highest-ranked areas. Pages and pages of explanation of the comparability rule were reduced to a simple statement of the rule.

Appropriations Process Changes

Appropriations have traditionally been much lower than authorizations for title I, and this year was no exception. Budget authority was trimmed an additional 17 percent from the reconciliation level, lowering appropriated budget authority from $2,914 million, supplied though a continuing resolution. The level in the continuing resolution reflected the so-called Conte substitution, that is, a 4 percent reduction from the funding level in the appropriations bill passed by the House.

CBO Baseline and Effect
of Congressional Action During Calendar 1981
(in millions of dollars and percentages)
Account No. 91-0105-501[a]

	FY1982		FY1983		FY1984	
Category	Dollar Level	Percent Change	Dollar Level	Percent Change	Dollar Level	Percent Change
CBO Baseline						
Budget authority	3,961	—	4,376	—	4,851	—
Outlays	3,475	—	3,810	—	4,210	—
Reconciliation Act						
Budget authority	3,531	−11	3,513	−20	3,506	−28
Outlays	3,437	−1	3,434	−10	3,517	−16
Final FY 1982 Expenditures After All Changes						
Budget authority	2,914	−26	—	—	—	—
Outlays	3,358	−3	—	—	—	—

a. This budget account contains the title I program, the follow through program, aid programs for migrants and residents of the territories.

Administrative and Regulatory Changes

Because of forward funding, outlay savings will not occur until next year.

An important aspect of change in the ESEA program is regulatory activity. The administration intends to abolish the Department of Education, replacing it with an education foundation. Although the administration needs congressional approval to proceed with this plan, some employees have been released or transferred and others are leaving voluntarily. Therefore, some programs experts anticipate that federal oversight of title I funds may be cursory. No regulations for the new title I program have yet appeared; interested parties are referred to the statute for guidance.

Assessment

Title I grew extremely rapidly during the 1970s, but peaked several years ago and has been declining since. Although title I funds represent only a small portion of educational expenditures in any state, they are targeted toward low-income or educationally disadvantaged students. Reductions may therefore have a significant effect on schools containing large numbers of these students. Similarly, ending concentration grants will disproportionately affect schools that had been receiving them.

Education authorities have pointed to two other phenomena that may occur as school districts implement the cuts. First, earlier studies of schools raise the possibility that school districts may cut services more than administration, shielding administrators from reductions while generating local pressure to offset reductions. Second, some experts have suggested that the demise of the Department of Education as a regulatory presence may create the opportunity for some school districts to treat title I funds as general aid to education rather than money targeted on the poor and educationally disadvantaged. On the other hand, some knowledgeable observers believe that most districts will simply continue to follow existing patterns of distributing title I funds despite the inability of federal authorities to monitor local behavior.

In its fiscal year 1983 budget, the Reagan administration proposes further reductions in funding for chapter I (title I). Budget authority would be set at $1.9 billion while outlays would total $2.6 billion.

GUARANTEED STUDENT LOANS

Program Description

The guaranteed student loan (GSL) program provides students with the financial means to study at the postsecondary institution of their choice. The program provides federal subsidies to private and state lenders who make long-term, low-interest, noncollateral loans to students. Prior to reconciliation, eligibility was not based on financial need: any student who was enrolled at least half-time in an eligible institution could apply for a loan.

Although the loans are extended by private sources, the federal government subsidizes the program in three ways. First, the government insures or reinsures the loans against default. Second, it pays the lender the interest due while the student is in school, and for up to one year afterward. Third, the government pays the lender a special allowance on all loans outstanding. (In fiscal year 1981, the special allowance equaled the difference between the interest charged to the student and the average ninety-one-day treasury bill rate plus 3.5 percent.) In fiscal year 1981, budget authority for this account totaled $2.5 billion, 66 percent of which covered the special allowance.

The GSL program is an appropriated entitlement. All eligible persons are entitled to receive loans. Although an appropriation is required before federal funds can be spent, eligible students can sue if funds are not forthcoming. Therefore, GSL expenditures are not controlled in the appropriations process; rather, eligibility criteria, established in the authorizing legislation, and existing economic conditions determine the level of spending.

Reconciliation Act Changes

The reconciliation act sought to control federal spending by changing several provisions of the Higher Education Act. These amendments reduced budget authority by an estimated $479 million in fiscal year 1982, $855 million in fiscal year 1983, and $1,353 million in fiscal year 1984. The major program changes affected eligibility criteria, the parent loan program, administrative fees, the special allowance, and lending by the Student Loan Marketing Association.

Base Eligibility on Financial Needs

The reconciliation act required institutions to evaluate the financial need of applicants from families with incomes above $30,000. The secretary of education is responsible for creating the needs analysis system to be used by institutions.

**CBO Baseline and Effect
of Congressional Action During Calendar 1981
(in millions of dollars and percentages)
Account No. 91-0230-502**

Category	FY1982		FY1983		FY1984	
	Dollar Level	Percent Change	Dollar Level	Percent Change	Dollar Level	Percent Change
CBO Baseline						
Budget authority	3,082	—	3,664	—	4,103	—
Outlays	3,006	—	3,525	—	3,998	—
Reconciliation Act						
Budget authority	2,603	−16	2,809	−23	2,750	−33
Outlays	2,683	−11	2,759	−22	2,742	−31
Final FY 1982 Expenditures After All Changes						
Budget authority	1,774	−42	—	—	—	—
Outlays	2,451	−18	—	—	—	—

Amend Parent Loan Program

A parent loan program was established by the Education Amendments of 1980. The reconciliation act raised interest rates on loans to parents from 9 to 14 percent, effective October 1, 1981. If the twelve-month average interest rate on a ninety-one-day treasury bill drops below 14 percent, the parental rate will decline to 12 percent. If the interest rate increases above 14 percent, the parental rate will increase to 14 percent. In addition, the act made independent and graduate students eligible to borrow under the parent loan program. (Because of the broader focus, the name of the parent loan program was changed to the auxiliary loan program in the fiscal year 1983 budget.)

Restructure Administrative Fee

The reconciliation act eliminated the $10 institutional allowance, which had been paid to universities for administering each loan. At the same time, the act allowed institutions to charge a reasonable fee to offset administrative costs. The act established a loan origination fee of 5 percent, paid by the student.

Reduce Special Allowance

Prior to reconciliation, the special allowance payment to lenders was rounded up to the nearest one-eighth percent. This provision was eliminated for loans made on or after October 1, 1981.

Extend Lending Authority

The Education Amendments of 1980 authorized the Student Loan Marketing Association ("Sallie Mae") to make loans in areas where there is a severe shortage of student loan capital. Under this legislation, both the secretary of education and the affected state had to agree that there was a shortage of capital before Sallie Mae could extend a loan. The reconciliation act authorized Sallie Mae to extend loans in states where there is no state guarantee or nonprofit agency or where students are unable to obtain loans. Secretarial and state approval is no longer required. The act also extended other areas of Sallie Mae authority.

Appropriations and Other Changes

Because the Labor, Health and Human Services, and Education Appropriations Act has not yet been enacted, funding for this program is being provided by a continuing resolution. Under the resolution, the program is funded at $1.8 billion, which falls far short of program costs. A supplemental appropriations request of $1.3 billion is currently pending before Congress.

Administrative Regulations

Regulations implementing provisions of the reconciliation act were issued on September 18, 1981. These regulations contained tables for the needs analysis requirement.

Assessment

The Middle Income Assistance Act of 1978 eliminated financial need as a criterion for eligibility for the GSL program. As a result, federal expenditures grew from $879 million in fiscal year 1979 to $2.3 billion in fiscal year 1981. Reversing this growth trend became a goal of the Reagan administration. Savings proposals contained in the reconciliation act are estimated to reduce program spending by 11 percent in fiscal year 1982, 22 percent in fiscal year 1983, and 31 percent in fiscal year 1984.

Legislative changes made in the reconciliation act are not expected to significantly alter the program. The institution of a needs analysis for families with incomes over $30,000 is not expected to reduce student access to a college education but may limit the range of institutional choices available to students in some families. It is unlikely that increasing the parental interest rate will reduce borrowing because a 14 percent rate is still below the current market rate. Nor are graduate and independent students likely to borrow from the parent program, as the GSL program provides larger subsidies. Other provisions affecting borrowers or lenders are marginal and will not change behavior.

The fiscal year 1983 budget proposes more dramatic changes in the GSL program. The administration estimates fiscal year 1983 savings of approximately $900 million, or 37 percent of the budget authority required under current legislation. Proposals include: (1) increasing the loan origination fee from 5 percent to 10 percent; (2) restricting loan eligibility to financial need by instituting a needs analysis for all students; (3) increasing the insurance premium paid on guaranteed student loans to the federal government; (4) limiting the special allowance to two years after leaving the postsecondary institution; and (5) eliminating graduate and independent students from GSL eligibility. These students would continue to be eligible to borrow under the parent loan program, as authorized by the reconciliation act. However, the subsidies available through the parent program are much lower than subsidies available through the GSL program.

STUDENT FINANCIAL ASSISTANCE

Program Description

The original purpose of the student assistance program was to provide lower-income persons with access to a college education. Although this continues to be a program goal, assistance is now provided to middle-income individuals as well. Financial assistance is provided through grants-in-aid, part-time employment, and deferrable loans. At each participating university, a financial aid office determines the type and amount of assistance available to each student. In fiscal year 1981, $3.8 billion was appropriated for this program.

Financial assistance is provided through three grant programs and two self-help programs. The largest program, Pell grants, accounted for more than two-thirds of total program obligations in fiscal year 1981. To be eligible for a Pell grant, a student must be enrolled at least half-time in a college or postsecondary vocational institution. These grants vary in size depending upon the expected family contribution and student expenses. Students with exceptional financial need are eligible for additional assistance through the supplemental educational opportunity grant program. Grant assistance is also provided through the state student incentive grant program, in which the federal government encourages states to provide grants to needy students by matching state expenditures dollar for dollar.

The final two programs are self-help programs. The college work-study program provides part-time employment to eligible students. The federal government contributes 80 percent of the student wages; the rest is paid by the educational institution, the employer, or some other donor. The national direct student loan (NDSL) program extends long-term, low-interest loans to students with financial need. (Graduate students are also eligible for these loans.) The NDSL program is financed by an annual federal capital contribution, repayments on past loans, and the institutions' matching grants.

All student assistance programs are authorized by the Higher Education Act of 1965, as amended. The Education Amendments of 1980 contain specific authorization levels for each program for fiscal years 1981 through 1985. Before these funds can be spent, however, an appropriation is required. Funds are appropriated annually in the Labor, Health and Human Services, and Education Appropriations Act. Federal expenditures on student assistance are, therefore, controllable in the appropriations process.

CBO Baseline and Effect
of Congressional Action During Calendar 1981
(in millions of dollars and percentages)
Account No. 91-0200-502

Category	FY1982 Dollar Level	FY1982 Percent Change	FY1983 Dollar Level	FY1983 Percent Change	FY1984 Dollar Level	FY1984 Percent Change
CBO Baseline						
Budget authority	4,483	—	4,841	—	5,223	—
Outlays	4,600	—	4,553	—	4,779	—
Reconciliation Act						
Budget authority	3,933	−12	4,083	−16	4,283	−18
Outlays	4,546	−1	4,121	−9	4,056	−15
Final FY 1982 Expenditures After All Changes						
Budget authority	3,352	−25	—	—	—	—
Outlays	3,519	−24	—	—	—	—

Reconciliation Act Changes

The reconciliation act reduced federal expenditures on student assistance by limiting the annual appropriation for each of the five programs. Total appropriations were limited to $3.9 billion in fiscal year 1982, $4.1 billion in fiscal year 1983, and $4.3 billion in fiscal year 1984, which represent budget authority reductions of 12 percent, 16 percent, and 18 percent respectively.

The reconciliation act also made several minor program changes, including (1) reducing the administrative fee for Pell grants from $10 to $5 per student; (2) increasing the interest rate charged on the NDSL from 4 to 5 percent; (3) disallowing guaranteed student loans from the expected family contribution when determining eligibility for student assistance; and (4) mandating the secretary of education to set a series of assessment rates on the Pell family contribution schedule.

Appropriations and Other Changes

Because the Labor, Health and Human Services, and Education Appropriations Act has not yet been enacted, funding for this account is being provided by a continuing resolution. This resolution included $3.4 billion for this account, thereby reducing the student assistance program an additional 15 percent below the amount called for in the reconciliation act. The continuing resolution also contained a number of administrative details on Pell grants. For example, the resolution limited a student's financial award to a maximum of $1,800 per year.

Administrative Regulations

The regulations instituting the provisions of the reconciliation act were published in the federal register on January 6, 1982. These regulations covered the family contribution schedule, instituting a progressive percentage requirement on discretionary family income considered to be available for the student's education.

Assessment

The Middle-Income Student Assistance Act of 1978 expanded program eligibility to include students from middle-income families. Prior to this time, student assistance had been targeted toward lower-income individuals. Largely as a result of the expanded scope, federal expenditures for student assistance increased by nearly 60 percent from 1978 to 1981. Reversing this growth trend became a goal of the Reagan administration, resulting in reconciliation and appropriation actions that reduced the program by 25 percent in fiscal year 1982.

As financial resources become scarce, it will be increasingly difficult to assist both income groups. The reconciliation act did not deal with this issue; it simply reduced available funding without examining eligibility or other program criteria.

The fiscal year 1983 budget proposes a significant reduction in the student assistance program. Budget authority declines from $3.4 billion in fiscal year 1982 to $1.8 billion in fiscal year 1983. The budget proposes the complete elimination of the supplemental educational opportunity grant program and the state supplemental incentive grant program. In addition, no federal capital contribution is requested for the national direct student loan program. The requests for the Pell grants and the work-study program are 23 percent and 25 percent below the 1982 level.

TEMPORARY EMPLOYMENT ASSISTANCE

Program Description

Title VI of the Comprehensive Employment and Training Act (CETA) was meant to overcome countercyclical unemployment. Public service employment (PSE) jobs funded under title VI were open to the low-income unemployed and persons in families receiving public assistance when the national unemployment rate rose above 4 percent. To be eligible, a person had to be unemployed for at least ten out of the twelve weeks prior to the time of application and be a member of a family that had been receiving public assistance or whose family income was less than or equal to the Bureau of the Labor Statistics' lower living standard (LLS).

Reconciliation Act Changes

Title VI has been eliminated. In fiscal year 1981 it was originally funded at $729 million in budget authority, leading to $1,011 million in outlays. At the request of the Reagan administration, Congress rescinded $234 million of the fiscal year 1981 budget authority. This led to an outlay drop of $43 million in fiscal year 1981.

The reconciliation bill eliminated the rest of the program. Since some budget authority remains from prior years, outlays of $26 million will be generated in fiscal year 1982 as the program is shut down.

Appropriations Changes

Since the program was abolished by the reconciliation act, no funds could be appropriated.

Assessment

This program was winding down before the reconciliation act was passed, as evidenced by the rescission of fiscal year 1981 budget authority. Thus, some of the impacts of the program's elimination were felt before 1982.

**CBO Baseline and Effect
of Congressional Action During Calendar 1981
(in millions of dollars and percentages)
Account No. 16-0173-504**

Category	FY1982		FY1983		FY1984	
	Dollar Level	Percent Change	Dollar Level	Percent Change	Dollar Level	Percent Change
CBO Baseline						
Budget authority	1,129	—	1,218	—	1,317	—
Outlays	1,118	—	1,209	—	1,307	—
Reconciliation Act						
Budget authority	0	−100	0	−100	0	−100
Outlays	26	−98	0	−100	0	−100
Final FY 1982 Expenditures After All Changes						
Budget authority	0	−100	—	—	—	—
Outlays	10	−99	—	—	—	—

OTHER CETA PROGRAMS

Program Description

This budget account funds all of the programs authorized by the Comprehensive Employment and Training Act (CETA) with the exception of the cyclical public service employment program, which was authorized under title VI of the act. In fiscal year 1981, the programs funded under this account received an appropriation of $7.1 billion, resulting in outlays of $6.8 billion. The various parts of CETA funded through this account can be grouped into five categories.

Public Service Employment to Counter Structural Unemployment

Title II-D of CETA, like title VI, provided federal funds to state and local governments to administer public employment programs. CETA had two employment programs. Title II-D was intended to combat structural employment problems; title VI (see preceding section) dealt with cyclical employment problems. Actually, the two programs were quite similar, providing jobs to persons in families receiving public assistance and to low-income unemployed persons. In 1978, Congress amended the CETA authorization to increase its targeting toward the poor, eliminate fiscal substitution by recipient jurisdictions, increase the amount of transition to unsubsidized jobs, and reduce the levels of fraud and abuse. The 1978 changes were fairly effective in accomplishing these goals.[1]

General Training Programs

Titles II-A, II-B, and II-C currently authorize training programs for persons of all ages. Services include institutional and on-the-job training, work experience, vocational education and counseling, remedial education, and job placement services. As with the PSE programs, the training efforts are administered by state and local prime sponsors.

Special Programs for Youth

Titles IV and VIII authorize programs solely directed at the needs of young people. Title IV authorizes the youth community conservation and improvement projects (YCCIP) program, the youth employment and training programs (YETP), the summer youth employment program (SYEP), and the

---

1. Description quoted from Congressional Budget Office, *An Analysis of President Reagan's Budget Revisions for Fiscal Year 1982* (March 1981), pp. A-49.

job corps. Title VIII authorizes the young adult conservation corps (YACC).

National Programs

Title III of CETA authorizes additional employment and training assistance to special groups who face particular disadvantages in the labor market. They include Indians, other native Americans, veterans, older workers, displaced homemakers, migrant and seasonal farm workers, criminal offenders, persons of limited English-speaking ability, and workers dislocated due to increases in imported goods.

Private-Sector Programs

Title VII of CETA authorizes funds to establish private industry councils, whose function is to encourage local industry to become more involved in employing and training unemployed and underemployed low-income persons.

Reconciliation Act Changes

The reconciliation act eliminated the public service employment programs which had been authorized under CETA (titles II-D and VI), failed to reauthorize the young adult conservation corps (under title VIII), and lowered the authorization of appropriation limits for most of the remaining programs. From the Congressional Budget Office's current policy baseline, these changes caused a 53 percent reduction in this account's budget authority level in fiscal years 1982 and 1983, and a 58 percent drop in fiscal year 1984. The CBO estimated that the account's outlays would decline by 41 percent in fiscal year 1982, by 50 percent in fiscal year 1983, and by 56 percent in fiscal year 1984.

The reconciliation act reauthorized CETA through fiscal year 1982. The act provides that, if the Congress fails to enact a new reauthorization by September 10, 1982, the fiscal year 1982 authorization of appropriations limits will apply to fiscal year 1983.

The reconciliation act modified the individual CETA programs in the following manner:

Public Service Employment—Title II-D

This structural PSE program was eliminated. The CBO current policy baseline for fiscal year 1982 budget authority was $2,671 million.

**CBO Baseline and Effect
of Congressional Action During Calendar 1981
(in millions of dollars and percentages)
Account No. 16-0174-504**

Category	FY1982		FY1983		FY1984	
	Dollar Level	Percent Change	Dollar Level	Percent Change	Dollar Level	Percent Change
CBO Baseline						
Budget						
authority	8,354	—	9,088	—	9,716	—
Outlays	8,338	—	8,959	—	9,588	—
Reconciliation Act						
Budget						
authority	3,906	−53	4,286	−53	4,100	−58
Outlays	4,931	−41	4,471	−50	4,269	−55
Final FY 1982 Expenditures After All Changes						
Budget						
authority	3,037	−64	—	—	—	—
Outlays	4,276	−49	—	—	—	—

General Training Programs

The reconciliation act set an authorization of appropriations limit of $1,430 million for job training programs. This compares to a CBO current policy fiscal year 1982 baseline figure for budget authority of $2,291 million—a 38 percent reduction.

Youth Programs

The reconciliation act set an authorization limit of $576 million for the youth employment and training program (YETP). This represents a 39 percent reduction below CBO's 1982 current policy baseline for budget authority of $947 million.

The summer youth employment program (SYEP) was reauthorized at $628 million, a 27 percent reduction from CBO's current budget authority policy baseline for 1982 of $865 million.

The job corps authorization of appropriations limit was increased to $628 million. This represents a 4 percent rise above CBO's fiscal year 1982 budget authority baseline of $607 million.

The young adult conservation corps (YACC) was not reauthorized by the reconciliation act, thus preventing the passage of an appropriation for fiscal year 1982. CBO's budget authority baseline for this program for fiscal year 1982 was $154 million.

The reconciliation act sought to increase the flexibility of the organizations administering CETA's youth programs (prime sponsors). State and local prime sponsors were given greater authority over the allocation of youth employment and training funds. The reconciliation act allowed prime sponsors to transfer up to 20 percent of their funds between youth employment and training programs and summer youth programs.

Greater allocations were made for local prime sponsors; the percentage of youth employment and training funds going to local government prime sponsors rose from 75 to 85 percent. At the same time the share of funds going to the Labor Department's discretionary programs was reduced from 16 to 6 percent. Youth community conservation and improvement project (YCCIP) funds reallocated by the secretary of labor can now be used for youth employment and training programs (YETP).

National Programs and Private-Sector Initiatives

The reconciliation act set a $494 million authorization limit on CETA titles III and VII. This represents a 5 percent reduction in fiscal year 1982 from CBO's current policy baseline of $522 million for budget authority.

Appropriations and Other Changes

For fiscal year 1982, the programs under CETA received their budget authority from a continuing resolution. The continuing resolution reduced budget authority (and CBO's estimate of outlays) for this account by an additional $869 million for fiscal year 1982. This means that after receiving its appropriation, CETA's budget authority for fiscal year 1982 was reduced by 64 percent from what it would have been under current policy. For the same period CETA's outlays are estimated to have dropped by 51 percent below current policy levels.

The magnitude of the additional appropriations process reductions varied by type of CETA program. The greatest reductions occurred in the training programs and the smallest reductions occurred in the national and private-sector programs.

General Training Programs

The continuing resolution reduced budget authority for titles II-A, II-B, and II-C by an additional $278 million. This had the effect of reducing fiscal year 1982 budget authority by 50 percent below current policy levels.

Youth Programs

The youth programs under title IV received an additional $407 million reduction in budget authority with the passage of the continuing resolution. This had the effect of lowering budget authority by 41 percent below fiscal year 1982 current policy levels for these programs.

The largest continuing resolution reduction was applied to the youth employment and training program (YETP), which had its fiscal year 1982 budget authority reduced by an additional $384 million. Compared to CBO's fiscal year 1982 current policy estimate, this program had its budget authority reduced by 80 percent.

The continuing resolution raised the fiscal year 1982 budget authority for the summer youth employment program (SYEP) by $19 million above the authorization of appropriation limit contained in the reconciliation act. However, the budget authority for this program still declined by 25 percent below CBO's fiscal year 1982 current policy level.

The job corps had its budget authority cut by an additional $42 million by the continuing resolution. However, since the reconciliation act raised the authorization of appropriation limit for the job corps by $21 million, this continuing resolution reduction only caused a 3 percent drop in the program's budget authority below CBO's fiscal year 1982 current policy level.

National and Private-Sector Programs

The continuing resolution increased the level of fiscal year 1982 budget authority by $28 million above the authorization of appropriation limit set by the reconciliation act. Overall, however, these programs had their fiscal year 1982 budget authority cut by 36 percent from the current policy level.

Administrative Regulations

Only minor changes in administrative regulations have been made for the remaining programs under CETA. The Department of Labor has attempted to lighten the administrative burden of CETA prime sponsors by deleting several items that in the past had to be included in a master plan filed with the federal government.

The Labor Department issued its final regulations for the private-sector initiative program (title VII) in October 1981. These regulations delete the economic development initiative bonus set-aside requirement, under which 10 percent of the program's funding was to be used for bonuses for prime sponsors who attempted to coordinate activities with federal economic development agencies. The rule reinstates the previously required formula distributing 95 percent of title VII funds to prime sponsors.

Assessment

The budget reductions of the last year were directed not only against CETA's public service employment programs, but also against its training and youth programs. The Reagan administration appears to want to continue this pattern.

In his fiscal year 1983 budget, President Reagan calls for the creation of a new training and employment block grant. This grant would absorb four CETA programs: employment and training services (titles II-A, II-B, and II-C), the youth employment and training program (YETP, title IV), the summer youth employment program (SYEP, title IV), and the private-sector programs (title VII). Under the administration's proposal, fiscal year 1983 budget funding for the new block grant would be set at $1.8 billion in budget authority and $1.496 billion in outlays. This would mean a 43 percent reduction in budget authority (-$1,334 milllion) and a 60 percent cut in outlays (-$1,974 million) below the Congressional Budget Office's fiscal year 1983 current policy estimate for these programs.

The administration is also recommending large reductions in CETA's other programs. The president's budget calls for a fiscal year 1983 reduction of 27 percent in budget authority and 34 percent in outlays from CBO's fiscal year 1983 current policy estimate for the job corps. Under the president's budget, CETA's national programs (title VIII) are to be transformed into a new special targeted program. But this new program will be funded at a lower level, with budget authority dropping by 27 percent and outlays by 21 percent below CBO's fiscal year 1983 current policy levels.

SOCIAL SERVICES BLOCK GRANT

Program Description

Most of the services to be provided by the social services block grant were funded through title XX of the Social Security Act before the reconciliation act. Title XX authorized federal reimbursement for a wide variety of social services such as child day care, counseling, information and referral, legal services, protective services for children and adults, homemaker and other in-home services. Welfare recipients were categorically eligible for assistance. Other eligibility criteria were determined by states within a maximum income limit of 115 percent of median income. Funds were distributed according to the states' relative population size. The federal matching share for most services was 75 percent. Family planning was matched at a 90 percent federal rate and certain child day care services were 100 percent federally funded. In fiscal year 1981, Congress appropriated $2.398 billion in new budget authority for the combined predecessor programs.

Reconciliation Act Changes

The reconciliation act merges the title XX social services program with two other small title XX programs: grants for training of state and local social service workers and child day care services. Under the block grant, states will receive shares of the total appropriation to support the services listed above. More generally, programs must serve the following purposes: (1) help social service clients achieve ''economic self-support'' and ''self-sufficiency''; (2) prevent or remedy neglect, abuse, or exploitation of children and adults; (3) prevent or reduce inappropriate institutional care; and (4) secure referral or admission for institutional care when most appropriate.

The reconciliation act authorizes the appropriation of $2.4 billion in fiscal year 1982, $2.45 billion in fiscal year 1983, $2.5 billion in fiscal year 1984, $2.6 billion in fiscal year 1985, and $2.7 billion in fiscal year 1986 and any succeeding fiscal years. The act reduced budget authority from the CBO baseline by $698.7 million in fiscal year 1982, $755.3 million in fiscal year 1983, and $811.5 million in fiscal year 1984. The cuts represent decreases of 23, 24, and 25 percent in each respective year.

In addition to budgetary changes described above, the reconciliation act sets out a new application procedure, distribution formula, and other program requirements as outlined below.

Programs Consolidated into Block Grant

Program	Fiscal 1981 budget authority (millions)	Type of grant	Type of recipient	Authorizing statute
Social services	$2,204	Formula	State agency	Social Security Act
Day care service	200	Formula	State agency	Social Security Act
State and local training	75	Formula	State agency	Social Security Act

Distribution Formula

As in the title XX social services program, annual allotments are proportional to each state's share of the national population, as determined by the secretary of HHS. Territories must receive allotments from the authorized spending levels equal to their percentage share of the funds available in fiscal year 1981. States no longer have to match federal funds with state funds.

Application Process

Before spending funds, a state must provide an annual report on how it intends to use them, including information on the types of activities supported and the characteristics of individuals served. Reports must be made available for public review and comment during development.

Phasing

States were to have taken over administration of the block grants by October 1, 1981, or as soon as possible. (The act makes no other transition provisions.)

Transferability

Up to 10 percent of a state's allotment may be transferred for use under other block grants that support health services or low-income energy assistance.

Audit Requirements

Activity reports and independent audits are required every two years. State reports must reconcile actual and intended use of funds. States deter-

**CBO Baseline and Effect
of Congressional Action During Calendar 1981
(in millions of dollars and percentages)
Account No. 75-1634-506**

Category	FY1982		FY1983		FY1984	
	Dollar Level	Percent Change	Dollar Level	Percent Change	Dollar Level	Percent Change
CBO Baseline						
Budget authority	3,099	—	3,205	—	3,312	—
Outlays	3,086	—	3,198	—	3,304	—
Reconciliation Act						
Budget authority	2,400	−23	2,450	−24	2,500	−25
Outlays	2,387	−23	2,443	−24	2,492	−25
Final FY 1982 Expenditures After All Changes						
Budget authority	2,400	−23	—	—	—	—
Outlays	2,387	−23	—	—	—	—

mine the form, content, and frequency of the reports, but must make reports available to the state legislature and the secretary of HHS thirty days after completion. States must repay amounts found not spent according to law, or the secretary may offset such amounts against state allotments.

Other Requirements and Provisions

The requirement that at least 50 percent of funds allocated be used for welfare recipients is removed; also removed is the requirement that services be limited to families with incomes below 115 percent of the state's median income. The reconciliation act includes eight limitations on states' uses of allotted funds. Payments may not be used for (1) construction or capital expenditures (unless waived by the secretary), (2) wages as a social service (except to certain welfare recipient employees, as currently authorized), (3) free-standing medical care (unless waived by the secretary), (4) institutionally provided social services, (5) public education, (6) cash payments as a service, (7) subsistence payments, or (8) child day-care services that do not meet state and local standards.

States must spend allotted funds within two years; there is no reallocation provision. States may use funds to purchase technical assistance from public and private entities, and to support state administrative expenses. States will receive quarterly allotments of their annual payments through quarterly grant awards.

Appropriations Process Changes

In fiscal year 1982, the block grant operates under a continuing resolution. For states that took over block grant administration on October 1, 1981, grant awards are made equal to one-quarter of the amount that would be allotted to states if the continuing resolution applied to the entire fiscal year. No programmatic or funding level changes were made.

Administrative Regulations

The regulations that apply to the health block grants (described in "Introduction to Health Block Grants") also apply to social services block grant with the following exceptions. Certain statutory provisions applicable to a state's basic block grant allotment may not apply to funds transferred for use in that block grant. No state hearings are required on uses of funds received under this block grant.

The reconciliation act prohibits states from using block grant funds to provide room and board and medical care unless they are an "integral but subordinate" part of state-authorized social services. The HHS regulations specifically state that room and board shall not be considered an "integral but subordinate" part of service if provided in a foster family home.

Assessment

Apart from the budget cut of almost 25 percent in fiscal year 1982, the social services block grant is essentially the same as the title XX predecessor programs. Some planning requirements were dropped and eligibility for social services provided through the block grant was broadened.

States played a large role in administering the program prior to the reconciliation act, and all fifty states took control on October 1, 1981. Moreover, by February 1982, twenty states had transferred funds from other block grants to help absorb the cuts made in funding for social services, according to the National Governors' Association.

COMMUNITY SERVICES BLOCK GRANT

Program Description

The Community Services Administration (CSA), abolished by the reconciliation act, ran some of the programs that originated as part of the "war on poverty" during the 1960s. It provided financial assistance to local organizations that coordinated and delivered a wide variety of social services to low-income individuals. A statutory formula for allocating funds to states was authorized, based on each state's relative number of unemployed persons, welfare recipients, and related children living in families below the poverty line. However, allocations were generally based on historical patterns rather than a strict reapplication of the formula each year. In general, CSA programs required a 20 percent nonfederal share, although this had been waived in certain circumstances.

In fiscal year 1980, there were 893 community action agencies (CAAs) serving 2,212 of the 3,141 counties in the nation. Counties served by such agencies contained 75 percent of the nation's total population and 86 percent of the nation's poor. In 1981 the Community Services Administration received $524 million in new budget authority.

Reconciliation Act Changes

The block grant provides funds to states for community-based programs that offer health, nutrition, housing, and employment services to improve the standard of living of low-income persons. The reconciliation act transferred administrative responsibility for CSA's grants to state governments. (The Office of Community Affairs was established is HHS to carry out the secretary's responsibilities.)

The reconciliation act authorized the appropriation of $389.4 million in each fiscal year from 1982 through 1986. The act reduced budget authority by $196.7 million in fiscal year 1982, $235.3 million in fiscal year 1983, and $273 million in fiscal year 1984, as estimated by the Congressional Budget Office. The reductions are 34 percent, 38 percent, and 42 percent below the current policy baseline in those years. Estimated outlay reductions are 21 percent in fiscal year 1982, 37 percent in fiscal year 1983, and 39 percent in fiscal year 1984.

In addition to these budgetary changes, the reconciliation act sets out a new application procedure and changes program requirements as outlined below.

CBO Baseline and Effect
of Congressional Action During Calendar 1981
(in millions of dollars and percentages)
Account No. 81-0500-506

Category	FY1982 Dollar Level	FY1982 Percent Change	FY1983 Dollar Level	FY1983 Percent Change	FY1984 Dollar Level	FY1984 Percent Change
CBO Baseline						
Budget						
authority	586	—	625	—	662	—
Outlays	569	—	606	—	645	—
Reconciliation Act						
Budget						
authority	389	−34	389	−38	389	−41
Outlays	451	−21	386	−37	395	−39
Final FY 1982 Expenditures After All Changes						
Budget						
authority	348	−41	—	—	—	—
Outlays	441	−22	—	—	—	—

Distribution Formula

Annual allotments are based on each state's relative share of fiscal year 1981 funds for community action programs; no state may receive less than 0.25 percent of the total funds appropriated. Territories will receive 0.5 percent of the funds appropriated each year. The secretary of HHS may reserve amounts from state allotments for direct funding of Indian tribes. Up to 9 percent of the funds appropriated may be reserved by the secretary to fund discretionary federal activities. The secretary may withhold funds if a state does not comply with provisions of the law.

Application Process

To receive the block grant allotment, a state must apply each year. The application must contain a certification by the governor that the state will comply with ten program and administrative requirements. They are (1) use of funds for authorized activities, (2) limits on administrative expenses (described below), (3) assurance that community action agencies' boards of directors are appropriately composed, (4) special consideration for previously funded grantees in designating local agencies, (5) limits on funds transferred for use under other block grants (described below), (6) prohibitions on political and election assistance activities, (7) coordination of community antipoverty and energy crisis intervention programs, (8) establishment of needed fiscal control and accounting procedures, (9) cooperation with federal audits and investigations, and (10) allocation of funds to existing community action agencies (described below).

States must also furnish the secretary of HHS with an annual plan that describes how application assurances will be carried out, but the secretary may not prescribe how states will comply with application assurances. The plan must be made public, and, after the first fiscal year for which funds are received, the state legislature must hold public hearings on the proposed use of funds. States must also furnish an annual report on proposed use of funds. Beginning in fiscal year 1983, the annual report must describe how funds have been used to meet the goals, objectives, and needs described in the preceding year's report.

Phasing

States could have taken over administration of the block grant beginning October 1, 1981; they must have taken over administration by October 1, 1982 in order to receive funds beyond fiscal year 1982.

Transferability

Up to 5 percent of a state allotment may be transferred to services under the older Americans, head start, or low-income energy assistance programs.

Audit Requirements

Biennial independent audits are required; they must be submitted to the state legislature and the secretary of HHS within thirty days of the completion of the audit. States must repay amounts found not expended according to law, or the secretary may offset such amounts against state allotments.

Other Requirements and Provisions

At least 90 percent of the fiscal year 1982 state funds must be grants to officially existing community service agency grantees or organizations serving migrant and seasonal farmworkers. In fiscal year 1983 and in subsequent years, states must distribute at least 90 percent of the funds to local government subdivisions of the state, nonprofit private community organizations, or migrant farmworker organizations.

States may not use funds for construction or capital expenditures, unless permitted by the secretary. No more than 5 percent of a state allotment may be used for state administrative expenses. States must spend allotted funds within two years.

Discrimination on the basis of race, color, national origin, age, handicap, or sex is prohibited.

Appropriations Process Changes

Because the Labor, Health and Human Services, and Education Appropriations Act had not been enacted by April 1982, funding for this account was being provided under a continuing resolution. Under this resolution, budget authority was reduced from $389 million to $348 million, a cut of 11 percent below the reconciliation act limit.

Administrative Regulations

The regulations that apply to the health block grants (described in "Introduction to Health Block Grants") also apply to the community services block grant with the following exceptions. On October 1, 1981, HHS issued a ruling that current regulations governing programs replaced by block grants are to remain in effect during the transition period, including CSA regulations published on August 31, 1981, which made the following changes:

1. Termination of all requirements under the grantee program management system.
2. Repeal of grantee personnel regulations. CAAs are now responsible for grantee personnel management, except for affirmative action requirements.
3. Repeal of most regulations affecting community food programs. CAAs are now responsible for complying with statutory requirements on community participation without direction from the federal government.

No rules concerning this block grant are currently under regulatory review by HHS.

Assessment

The reconciliation act and subsequent appropriations action made sharp cuts in funding for the community services block grant—in fiscal year 1982 the program was reduced 41 percent below the CBO baseline in budget authority and 54 percent in outlays.

States have been reluctant to assume responsibility for the community services block grant because they have had no relationship with community action agencies; the Community Services Administration had provided aid directly to the CAAs. In addition, many CAAs are uncertain what new procedures and requirements states will implement when administrative control is transferred. As a result, many CAAs have been reluctant to break their relationship with HHS and have urged states to postpone assuming control until fiscal year 1983.

The distribution formula ensures that states will receive the same proportion of total aid appropriated in the future as they received in 1981. However, as state populations and especially low-income populations change, the existing distribution formula will become more and more unrealistic. Congress is unlikely to change the formula in the second session of the 97th Congress; other issues will probably dominate the legislative agenda.

The Reagan administration's fiscal year 1983 budget proposals call for funding of $100 million, a sharp reduction from the level authorized for 1982 in the continuing resolution.

MEDICAID

Program Description

The medicaid program provides medical services to low-income persons, particularly the aged, blind, disabled, and members of families with dependent children. Of these four groups, the medical requirements of the elderly are the most costly, making up 37 percent of total program expenditures in fiscal year 1981. The aged represent 15 percent of program participants.

Medicaid costs are shared by the federal and state governments; the federal government finances approximately 56 percent of total medicaid benefits. The rate at which the federal government subsidizes benefits varies by state, based on the state's per-capita income relative to the national average. The federal government also finances 50 percent of state administrative costs. In fiscal year 1981, the medicaid program served nearly 22.5 million individuals at a total cost of $30.4 billion. The federal share of these costs was $17.1 billion.

Eligibility Criteria and Benefit Levels

States are allowed wide discretion in determining eligiblity for medicaid. All states provide medicaid coverage to the "categorically needy"—that is, persons who receive cash assistance under one of two programs, aid to families with dependent children (AFDC) or supplemental security income (SSI). Some states include as categorically needy those individuals who receive state supplemental SSI benefits and those individuals who would be eligible for cash assistance if they were not residing in a medical institution.

States may also provide medicaid coverage to the "medically needy." The medically needy are those individuals who would be eligible for AFDC or SSI except that their income or resources are above the eligibility criteria for these programs. As of January 1, 1982, thirty-four states and jurisdictions provided medicaid coverage to the medically needy. If a state has a medically needy program, federal law requires that all four eligible groups participate and receive comparable benefits.

Federal law determines the medical benefits covered under medicaid for the categorically needy. Included are: (1) inpatient and outpatient hospital services; (2) laboratory and X-ray services; (3) skilled nursing facilities for those over age twenty-one; (4) early screening diagnosis and treatment for those under twenty-one; (5) family planning services and supplies; and (6) physicians' services. Within these categories, however, states control the nature and duration of medical services provided. States have the option of covering additional medical services including drugs, eyeglasses, intermediate care facilities, and some psychiatric services. Because states have discretion over the range and scope of benefits, the medicaid program varies significantly from state to state.

Medicaid is an appropriated entitlement. Individuals who meet the eligibility criteria are entitled to benefits under the law. An appropriation is necessary before funds can be expended but a person can sue if benefits are not forthcoming. The appropriations process does not, therefore, control the level of spending for this program. To the extent possible, federal control is exerted through the authorizing legislation. However, state discretion over program eligibility and benefits makes federal control of medicaid expenditures very difficult.

Reconciliation Act Changes

The reconciliation act achieved savings in federal medicaid expenditures in two ways. First, it reduced the proportion of total program costs financed by the federal government. Second, it increased state discretion in the medicaid program, thereby reducing total program costs. The net effect was to reduce federal expenditures by approximately 5 percent per year from fiscal year 1982 through fiscal year 1984.

Reduce Federal Matching Payments

Nearly 50 percent of the budget authority savings achieved by reconciliation resulted from reducing the federal matching payments. The reconciliation act requires that the federal match to states be reduced by 3 percent in fiscal year 1982, by 4 percent in fiscal year 1983, and by 4.5 percent in fiscal year 1984. A state can lower the reductions by one percentage point per year for each of the following conditions that it meets: (1) a qualified hospital cost review program; (2) a state unemployment rate of 150 percent or more of the national average; and (3) a fraud and abuse recovery rate equal to 1 percent of the federal payment.

A state is also eligible for a dollar-for-dollar offset in the reductions if the federal portion of a state's medicaid funding falls below a targeted amount. The targeted amount for fiscal year 1982 is 109 percent of the 1981 federal payment. The targets for fiscal years 1983 and 1984 will be set by the secretary of health and human services (HHS) based on the increase in the medical care category of the consumer price index (CPI).

**CBO Baseline and Effect
of Congressional Action During Calendar 1981
(in millions of dollars and percentages)
Account No. 75-0512-551**

Category	FY1982		FY1983		FY1984	
	Dollar Level	Percent Change	Dollar Level	Percent Change	Dollar Level	Percent Change
CBO Baseline						
Budget						
authority	18,515	—	20,101	—	21,692	—
Outlays	18,016	—	19,714	—	21,327	—
Reconciliation Act						
Budget						
authority	17,343	−6	19,191	−5	20,919	−4
Outlays	17,072	−5	18,834	−4	20,313	−5
Final FY 1982 Expenditures After All Changes						
Budget						
authority	17,624	−5	—	—	—	—
Outlays	17,297	−4	—	—	—	—

Control Reimbursement Rates

The reconciliation act increased state discretion over the rate at which hospitals would be reimbursed for providing medicaid services. The act replaced the requirement that states pay the reasonable cost of inpatient hospital service with a requirement that states use reimbursement rates that "are reasonable and adequate to meet the costs that must be incurred by efficiently and economically operated facilities." The rates must be sufficient to ensure that medicaid patients have "reasonable access" to inpatient facilities. In other words, a sufficient number of facilities must be willing to provide a sufficient level of services at the state-determined reimbursement rates. The act further required that states consider special circumstances of hospitals that serve a disproportionate level of low-income families when setting reimbursement rates for inpatient services. (A similar provision of the fiscal year 1980 reconciliation act changed reimbursement practices for long-term-care facilities.)

Modify Freedom of Choice

State discretion over the medicaid program was increased by four provisions of the reconciliation act that limited the "freedom of choice" of program participants. The new provisions allow states to arrange for laboratory services and medical devices through competitive bidding; restrict the physicians or facilities available to recipients who overutilize services; limit participation in medicaid by a provider whose services are not considered medically necessary or of good quality; and devise and implement a case management system that requires recipients to use only certain providers.

Redefine Medically Needy

As explained earlier, states have the option of providing medicaid services to the medically needy. The reconciliation act increased state discretion over the medically needy, not only by allowing states to determine which groups are medically needy but also by allowing states to choose which medical services will be provided. States are no longer required to offer the same services to each medically needy group.

Extend Medicaid Coverage

Reconciliation also allows states to offer, under secretarial waiver, a variety of home- and community-based services if these services can keep a person from being institutionalized. This provision does not expand eligibility for the medicaid program, but simply extends the range of benefits available to eligible individuals. The cost of maintaining a person at home may not exceed the cost of maintaining him or her in an institution.

Modify Medicaid and Medicare Legislation

The reconciliation act made a series of small changes in provisions relating both to medicaid and medicare. They included (1) elimination of hospital occupancy test; (2) elimination from program participation of anyone involved in fraud, and assessment of a dollar penalty; (3) provision of reimbursement for closing or converting an underutilized hospital; (4) prohibition of payment for medically ineffective drugs; (5) prohibition of payment to a health care provider who received but did not return an overpayment; (6) requirement that the secretary of HHS assess the effectiveness of professional standards review organizations (PSROs); and (7) allowing states to contract with PSROs for review of medicaid services.

Administrative Regulations

On September 30, 1981 and on October 1, 1981, the Department of Health and Human Services issued regulations implementing provisions of the reconciliation act. The regulations stressed that states will be given discretionary authority both in implementing the provisions of the reconciliation act and in administering the program.

Appropriations and Other Changes

As described earlier, the appropriations process merely provides the level of funding necessary to cover the benefits required by the authorizing legislation. Hence, to meet the mandated level of service for fiscal year 1982, $17.6 billion was included in the continuing resolution for this program. (Funding is being provided under the continuing resolution because the Labor, Health and Human Services, and Education Appropriations Act has not yet been enacted.)

Assessment

Federal policy makers have two routes to budgetary savings in the medicaid program. First, they can make the program smaller by restricting eligibility or reducing benefits. Second, they can attempt to deliver services more cheaply by lowering reimbursement rates to health care providers, restructuring medical markets, or directly decreasing the federal share of expenses.

The Reagan administration used both of these routes. It made the program smaller by reducing the number of AFDC program participants and by allowing states to offer smaller and less generous programs for the medically needy. It tried to make the program cheaper by allowing states to tighten hospital reimbursement rates and by directly lowering the federal share of expenses. It has not yet attempted to restructure medical markets, although federal policy makers continue to study free-market alternatives to current practices.

Health experts have pointed to several potential consequences of the changes in the medicaid program. For example, individuals who have lost all or part of their previous coverage under medicaid face several choices: (1) pay for the services themselves, thereby increasing personal medical expenses; (2) rely on "charity care," which must be paid for by private health care users; (3) attempt to regain medicaid benefits, perhaps by again qualifying for AFDC; or (4) forgo medical services.

Similarly, health care providers face several choices. In states that lower reimbursement rates, hospitals may (1) accept lower fees for medicaid patients; (2) devote their time to more lucrative nonmedicaid patients, or (3) continue to accept medicaid patients but provide them with less expensive or lower quality service.

Some commentators believe that hospitals in low-income areas may feel substantial economic pressures. Other knowledgeable observers of health care speculate about the possibility of intensifying the "two-class" medical care system that has emerged in the United States. Finally, it is not yet clear whether the waiver for community services will actually decrease the use of nursing homes or instead simply increase the use of community facilities. For example, some health care experts have raised the possibility that state governments may use the waiver to substitute medicaid funds for those cut under title XX, which provided similar community services.

The fiscal impact of changes in the medicaid program on state governments is not immediately clear. By lowering the federal share of medicaid expenses, the reconciliation act shifted federal costs to the states. At the same time, the act attempted to reduce state costs by increasing state discretion in regard to reimbursement rates and other program activities. The net fiscal impact of these two actions is likely to vary by state, depending on each state's reaction to its increasing discretionary authority.

The fiscal year 1983 budget requests $12.9 billion in budget authority for this account. This is $4.7 billion less than the amount appropriated for fiscal year 1982. Three proposed changes account for this reduction: (1) removal of administrative expenses from this account; (2) further reductions in the AFDC and SSI programs; and (3) actual program reductions.

The Reagan budget attributes $2 billion of the proposed reduction to program changes. Approximately $600 million of this amount is obtained by a 3 percent reduction in the federal match for optional health services provided to the categorically needy and for all services provided to the medically needy. The remaining savings are obtained by requiring copayment from program participants for services rendered. Copayments of $1 and $2 would be required of categorically needy and medically needy respectively for inpatient hospital service. Copayments of $1 and $1.50 respectively would be required per visit for all other services.

MEDICARE

Program Description

Medicare is a federal entitlement program that provides basic health insurance coverage to most aged and certain disabled persons. Medicare has two components. The first (part A) is *universal hospital insurance,* which is paid from a trust fund that is primarily supported by a payroll tax of 2.6 percent levied and divided in a manner similar to social security taxes. The second component (part B) is the *supplementary medical insurance* (SMI) program, which covers the cost of physicians' services and certain other medical care expenses. While the SMI is voluntary, a person's enrollment is assumed—indeed, a person has to specify that he or she does not want to enroll in part B. As a consequence, 98 percent of those eligible have chosen to participate by paying the $11 monthly premium, which is deducted from the participant's paycheck. This premium covers about 25 percent of the program's cost; the balance is borne largely by general revenues.

Because medicare is an entitlement program, the cost of the program in any given year is determined by the interaction of the eligibility rules and the economy. The only way to control spending in this program is to alter the eligibility rules. In fiscal year 1981, the medicare program served 27.9 million persons at a cost of $43 billion.

Reconciliation Act Changes

Reconciliation achieved its savings in the hospital insurance fund by requiring part A beneficiaries to pay the first $256 of hospital costs in fiscal year 1982 instead of the $228 formerly required. The increased deductible is expected to save the hospital insurance trust fund $185 million in 1982.

Reconciliation also achieved savings by reducing reimbursement rates to hospitals and home health agencies. Medicare's reimbursements for routine operating costs for hospitals were reduced from 112 percent to 108 percent of the mean costs of comparable groups of hospitals. Reimbursements for home health agencies were reduced from the 80th to the 75th percentile of the average cost per visit.

Finally, the reconciliation act eliminated medicare coverage for new options that had not yet become effective (for example, payments for alcohol detoxification centers).

In the supplemental medical insurance program (SMI), savings of $206 million in fiscal year 1982, $305 million in fiscal year 1983, and $340 million in fiscal year 1984 were achieved. Most of this saving ($175 million in fiscal year 1982) was made through two changes to the part B deductible.

**CBO Baseline and Effect
of Congressional Action During Calendar 1981
(in millions of dollars and percentages)
Account No. 20-8004&5-551**

Category	FY1982 Dollar Level	FY1982 Percent Change	FY1983 Dollar Level	FY1983 Percent Change	FY1984 Dollar Level	FY1984 Percent Change
CBO Baseline						
Budget authority	56,339	—	63,070	—	70,517	—
Outlays	48,127	—	55,069	—	62,993	—
Reconciliation Act						
Budget authority	56,152	0	62,828	0	70,302	0
Outlays	46,743	−3	54,090	−2	61,852	−2
Final FY 1982 Expenditures After All Changes						
Budget authority	56,162	0	—	—	—	—
Outlays	46,571	−3	—	—	—	—

The deductible was increased from $60 to $75, and the laws that permitted beneficiaries of the previous year to determine if they met the annual part B deductible for the current year was repealed.

The reconciliation act made several other changes in the SMI program, but each of them is expected to have only a minor cost-saving effect. One change, which is not expected to have any cost-saving effects but received a lot of attention, was made in the renal disease program. Under reconciliation, medicare will continue to pay for renal services until regular payments are obtained from the beneficiary's private group health plan. This change is intended to make medicare the secondary payer when a medicare beneficiary has private coverage through an employer's group health plan.

Appropriations and Other Changes

The universal hospital insurance part A of medicare is funded essentially through the 2.6 percent payroll tax. Hence no appropriation action has been necessary. However, the supplemental insurance program (part B) is only partly funded through the receipts from the premium payments. The balance of the estimated program costs (approximately three-quarters) is financed through an annual appropriation. In fiscal year 1982, $9.6 billion was appropriated.

Assessment

Medicare outlays have increased 45 percent from 1979 to 1981 alone. Because medicare is an entitlement program, its expenditures are determined by the interaction of entitlement rules and economic and demographic trends. The medicare program is expected to continue to grow rapidly as a result of the aging population and the declining relative proportion of persons in the workforce.

This growing and seemingly uncontrollable aspect of the medicare program made it the object of administration attempts to reduce the federal budget. In an attempt to achieve some control over the program, changes in the entitlement rules were made in the Omnibus Reconciliation Act of 1981. The rule changes were estimated to reduce outlays for medicare by 3 percent in fiscal year 1982.

The 1983 budget proposal illustrates the continuing effort to contain this program. The budget proposed to reduce medicare expenditures by nearly $2.5 billion from fiscal year 1983's current services budget. To achieve these further reductions, the budget specified a number of legislative proposals. The proposals were designed to reduce health care cost by improving efficency and to reduce reimbursements to providers. Specifically, the budget proposal included a 2 percent reduction in medicare hospital reimbursement, the institution of a copayment for home health services, and a mandate for employers of the working aged to provide private primary insurance coverage. These and other proposed changes were intended to reduce medicare program costs while maintaining basic insurance protection.

Reducing the hospital reimbursement rate without also cutting the cost of medical care will either reduce services for medicare patients or shift the burden of payment for these services, or both. Part of the burden will fall on the elderly themselves through the increased deductible. The remaining portion will likely fall on state and local governments, since many of the hospitals serving medicare patients are publicly owned and operated.

INTRODUCTION TO HEALTH BLOCK GRANTS

The reconciliation act consolidated twenty-one categorical grants, administered by the Department of Health and Human Resources, into four block grants: (1) primary care; (2) preventive health; (3) alcohol, drug abuse, and mental health; and (4) maternal and child health. The block grants are not so far-reaching as those proposed by President Reagan, but they do transfer control of many programs to the states. While states will have considerably more responsibility for and control of the programs included in the block grants, not all federal control will lapse. This section describes the programs included in the grants, the changes in funding levels, and the federal controls remaining over state expenditure of block grant funds.

Features included in each block grant are as follows:

- Distribution formulas for the new grants in most cases are principally based on the proportionate shares received by states in fiscal year 1981 for the programs consolidated. (The primary care block grant formula depends on fiscal year 1982 shares.) State populations and low-income populations are also factors in some grants.

- Spending limitations are included in the authorizing language of each block grant. States may not use allocated funds to:
  1. provide inpatient services,
  2. make cash payments to intended recipients of health services,
  3. purchase or improve land or buildings, or purchase major medical equipment,
  4. satisfy any matching requirements, or
  5. provide financial assistance to any entity other than a public or non-profit private entity.

- Applications, annual reports, and audits are required for each state so that HHS can monitor spending. Public hearings on the use of block grant funds are also required.

- Broad provisions against discrimination are included in each block grant.

- All block grants except maternal and child health provide that the Department of Health and Human Services may make some of a state's allocation available for Indian tribes or tribal organizations in that state.

- The secretary of HHS may withhold funds from states that do not use block grant funds in compliance with the law.

In October 1981 HHS issued regulations concerning the seven block grants (including health) under its jurisdiction. Secretary Richard Schweiker set the tone in an August letter to governors which stated, ''I have decided that where the law provides this department policy discretion, I will pass that discretion through to the states.'' In all, HHS regulations take up 11 pages in the October 1 *Federal Register,* replacing 318 pages of regulations governing the categorical programs.

The reconciliation act requires each state to make an annual submission with respect to each block grant prior to receiving funds. Regulations require no particular format for submission, stating only that each state must ensure that its application meets the provisions of the statute. Application will consist of specified assurances or a description of the intended uses of the funds or both.

Public comment is required before the plan is approved, but each state can decide how it obtains comment. Public hearings on the use and distribution of funds are to be conducted by the state legislature, with the manner at each state's discretion. Conflicts may arise due to the fact that Secretary Schweiker in his August letter waived the hearings in the first year for HHS grants.

States will be exempt from administrative requirements in 45 CFR 74 (based on the OMB circular A−102, ''Uniform Administrative Requirements for Grants to State and Local Governments,'' and A−87, ''Cost Principles''); the states' own laws and procedures governing expenditures will apply. Statutes place primary responsibility for conducting audits on the use of block grants with the state; any additional audits will be built on the work of the state.

In addition to these provisions, each block grant has requirements peculiar to it. Each block grant is described in greater detail in the following sections.

PRIMARY CARE BLOCK GRANT

Program Description

Before the reconciliation act, the community health centers program supported the planning, development, and operation of community health centers, which provide a wide range of outpatient health services to medically underserved populations (as defined by law). Under the reconciliation act, the health centers program will be supported by block grants and administered by state health agencies.

The transfer of administrative control will not take place until fiscal year 1983; until then, regional offices of the Health Services Administration (HSA) will manage the program under previous law. The HSA requires centers to fulfill a variety of requirements. For example, health centers must show how their services are coordinated with state and locally provided health services, and centers must file annual expenditure reports with the regional office at the end of each budget period. In 1980, 872 centers across the country served over five million people. In fiscal year 1981, the program obligated $338 million and was provided new budget authority of $324 million.

Reconciliation Act Changs

The reconciliation act authorized appropriations for the community health center program under the new block grant format in 1983 and 1984. The existing program is authorized under a different act in fiscal year 1982 at a level of $248 million. Congress must appropriate budget authority annually to maintain program funding levels.

The reconciliation act authorized the appropriation of $302.5 million in fiscal year 1983 and $327 million in fiscal year 1984 for the community health service program. (The fiscal year 1982 authorization level of $282 million was authorized in an earlier act.) The act therefore reduced budget authority by an estimated $70 million in both fiscal years 1983 and 1984, which represents cuts of budget authority of 19 and 17 percent respectively.

In addition to the budgetary changes described above, the reconciliation act established new programmatic requirements and guidelines for phasing in state control, protecting previous grant recipients, and matching federal funds with state funds.

Program Consolidated into Block Grant

Program	Fiscal 1981 budget authority (millions)	Type of grant	Type of recipient	Authorizing statute
Community health center program	$324	Project	State & local gov'ts, non-profit & public organizations	Public Health Service Act, sec. 330

Phasing

Control of funds appropriated for the primary care block grant will not shift to the states until fiscal year 1983. In that year states will receive allotments, once their grant applications are approved by the secretary of HHS.

Hold-Harmless Restrictions

In fiscal year 1983, each community health center that was funded in fiscal year 1982 must get a grant no smaller than the one it received in fiscal year 1982, provided the center meets the legal definition of a center and applies to the state for a grant. In fiscal year 1984, states must ensure that medically underserved populations formerly served by community health centers—if still medically underserved—continue to receive health care.

In more general terms, states also must not disrupt established provider-patient relationships "to the extent practicable." To implement this requirement, the state's application must establish evaluation criteria for community health centers and an independent review procedure for existing community health centers that receive reduced funding from the state.

Other Restrictions and Requirements

In fiscal year 1983, states must provide matching funds equal to 20 percent of their block grant allotment. In fiscal year 1984, the matching requirement increases to 33 percent. The state requirement can be fulfilled by provision of in-kind services to community health centers. In addition, a small separate planning grant program was established. States can apply for grants of up to $150,000. The funding level authorized in the reconciliation act for fiscal year 1982 is $2.5 million.

Beginning in fiscal year 1984, state legislatures must conduct public hearings before block grant funds may be allotted.

CBO Baseline and Effect
of Congressional Action During Calendar 1981
(in millions of dollars and percentages)
Account No. 75-0350-551

Category	FY1982 Dollar Level	FY1982 Percent Change	FY1983 Dollar Level	FY1983 Percent Change	FY1984 Dollar Level	FY1984 Percent Change
CBO Baseline						
Budget authority	352	—	372	—	395	—
Outlays	NA	—	NA	—	NA	—
Reconciliation Act						
Budget authority	282	−20	302	−19	327	−17
Outlays	NA	NA	NA	NA	NA	NA
Final FY 1982 Expenditures After All Changes						
Budget authority	248	−30	—	—	—	—
Outlays	NA	NA	—	—	—	—

States will receive apportionments of their annual allotments through letters of credit.

Appropriations Process Changes

Because the Labor, Health, and Human Services and Education Appropriations Act has not been enacted, funding for this program is being provided under a continuing resolution. Under this resolution, budget authority was reduced from $282 million to $248 million. The total cut from the CBO baseline to appropriations limit was $104 million, or 30 percent.

Administrative Regulations

The HHS block regulations (see page 239) apply to the primary care block grant with the following exceptions. Amounts that are obligated will not be available for succeeding fiscal years unless the secretary determines that states acted in accordance with the requirements of the act or with good cause. Unlike other block grants, states cannot use portions of their primary care block grant allocations to meet administrative costs.

The regulations of this block grant are not currently under review by HHS.

Assessment

The reconciliation act did little to directly change the way community health centers operate, except to turn administrative responsibility over to the states and reduce funding levels below the CBO baseline. (In absolute terms, the program will grow 31 percent from 1982 to 1984, assuming Congress appropriates the full amount authorized under the reconciliation act.) States cannot substantially change the allocation of funds among health centers in 1983 because of the hold-harmless restrictions. States may make changes in health center administration as they assume control of the block grant, but the act makes no new programmatic requirements.

The distribution formula ensures that states will receive the same proportion of total aid in the future as they received in 1981, but as state populations and especially medically underserved populations change, the existing distribution formula will become more and more unrealistic. Congress is unlikely to change the formula in the second session of the 97th Congress; other issues will probably dominate the legislative agenda.

Although states are not given flexible control over the program, additional burdens are placed on them. First, the states much match a fixed share of their allotted funds. Previously, matching requirements were determined on a case-by-case basis. Second, the reconciliation act requires states to establish evaluation criteria and independent review procedures. Finally, state legislatures must hold public hearings beginning in 1984 on uses of the block grant funds. Although the costs incurred under the last two requirements can be used to satisfy the matching requirement, potentially significant administrative costs could be imposed on states without providing the additional flexibility that is part of the rationale for the block grant approach.

The Reagan administration's 1983 budget proposals call for the primary care block grant to be merged with three other programs: black lung clinics, migrant workers' health, and family planning. While details of the proposal are not firm, it appears that the administration intends to keep the October 1, 1982 startup date, but eliminate the states' option of accepting responsibility for the grant or leaving the program under federal control. The 1983 budget proposals call for budget authority of $417 million in fiscal year 1983, which would provide $115 million above the amount authorized by the reconciliation act to fund the three additional programs. The proposed 1983 level represents a decrease under the total authorized ($166 million) for these three additional programs in fiscal year 1982.

MATERNAL AND CHILD HEALTH SERVICES

Program Description

The reconciliation act brings seven federally run categorical programs under state administration by 1983. The crippled children's services program accounts for 84 percent of the budget authority appropriated in 1981 for all seven programs. The accompanying table outlines the programs included in the block grant.

The crippled children's services program provided financial support to states for medical and related services to crippled children under the age of twenty-one, and special projects of regional and national interest. The program provided formula grants to state health agencies for services (which states had to match dollar for dollar), and project grants for special projects (which had no matching requirement). Half of the appropriated funds were allocated to each grant type.

Other programs consolidated into the block grant provided services such as maternity counseling, referral to voluntary genetic testing and counseling programs, and aid for cities developing comprehensive programs to prevent lead-based-paint poisoning. Of the six smaller programs consolidated, only one—SSI disabled children's services—provided formula grants.

In fiscal year 1981, Congress appropriated $455 million in budget authority for the predecessor programs combined.

Reconciliation Act Changes

The block grant created from several categorical grant programs will provide similar services and meet objectives similar to the old programs'. The block grant will seek to reduce infant mortality and the incidence of preventable disease and handicapping conditions among children, provide rehabilitative services for blind and disabled children under the age of sixteen, and furnish treatment and care for crippled children.

The reconciliation act authorized the appropriation of $373 million in fiscal year 1982 and each fiscal year thereafter. It reduced the CBO baseline for budget authority by $122 million in fiscal year 1982, $151 million in fiscal year 1983, and $182 million in fiscal year 1984. The reductions are 25, 29, and 33 percent below current policy budget authority levels, respectively.

In addition to the budgetary changes described above, the reconciliation act established new programmatic procedures and requirements for the phasing in of state control, the protection of previous grant recipients, and the required match of state to federal funds.

Programs Consolidated into Block Grant

Program	Fiscal 1981 budget authority (millions of dollars)	Type of grant	Type of recipient	Authorizing statute
Maternal and child health care—crippled children	357	Formula & project	State health agencies	Social Security Act, V
Hemophilia treatment	3	Project	State and local gov't, non-profit orgs.	Public Health Service Act, sec. 1131
Sudden infant death syndrome	3	Project	Any public or nonprofit org.	PHS, sec. 1121
Lead-based-paint poisoning prevention	10	Project	Local agencies, nonprofit orgs.	PHS, sec. 316
Genetic diseases testing and counseling	13	Project	State and local gov'ts, public & nonprofit organizations	PHS, sec. 1101
Adolescent pregnancy prevention and services	10	Project	State & local gov't, public & nonprofit organizations	Health Services and Centers Act, title IV
SSI disabled children's services	30	Formula	States	Social Security Act, sec. 1615 (c)

CBO Baseline and Effect
of Congressional Action During Calendar 1981
(in millions of dollars and percentages)
Account No. 75-0350-551

Category	FY1982		FY1983		FY1984	
	Dollar Level	Percent Change	Dollar Level	Percent Change	Dollar Level	Percent Change
CBO Baseline						
Budget authority	495	—	524	—	555	—
Outlays	NA	—	NA	—	NA	—
Reconciliation Act						
Budget authority	373	−25	373	−29	373	−33
Outlays	NA	NA	NA	NA	NA	NA
Final FY 1982 Expenditures After All Changes						
Budget authority	348	−30	—	—	—	—
Outlays	NA	NA	—	—	—	—

Phasing

States could take over administration beginning October 1, 1981; in order to continue receiving funds, states must have taken control by October 1, 1982. Transfer of control may occur at quarterly intervals through fiscal year 1982, as state applications are approved by HHS (as defined in title XVII of the reconciliation act).

Hold-Harmless Restrictions

A reasonable proportion of funding, based on previous funding patterns in each state, must be used for each of several purposes: reducing infant mortality, reducing preventable diseases and handicapping conditions, increasing maternity care, immunization, and increasing assessments of and services to low-income children.

The act sets aside 15 percent in fiscal 1982 and 10 to 15 percent in other years for research, demonstration and training projects of national or regional significance, hemophilia centers, and genetic disease counseling and screening projects.

Other Restrictions and Requirements

State health agencies are required to operate under a number of restrictions imposed by the reconciliation act. First, states must must match every four federal dollars with three state dollars. Second, no transfer to other block grants can be made. Third, states may not cancel grants or contracts entered into after enactment of block grant legislation unless three months' notice is given. States will receive quarterly apportionments of their annual allotments through   letters of credit.

Appropriations Process Changes

Because the Labor, Health and Human Services, and Education Appropriations Act has not been enacted, funding for this program is being provided under a continuing resolution. Under this resolution, budget authority was reduced from $373 million to $347 million, a reduction of $26 million from the CBO baseline. Therefore, actions of the 97th Congress reduced this program by a total of $148 million from the CBO baseline.

Administrative Regulations

The regulations that apply to the HHS block grants (see page 239) also apply to the maternal and child health care block grant.

Assessment

In creating this block grant, Congress abolished the program structure of the crippled children's service program. States may model their programs on the previous federal program or develop entirely new structures. The regulations do not provide guidelines for states to act in accord with congressional intent; the burden of compliance falls on the states. Thus, as with some of the other block grants, the reconciliation act does increase the flexibility of administration, and also imposes the responsibility for complying with congressional intent on state governments.

The distribution formula ensures that states will receive the same proportion of total aid appropriated in the future as they received in 1981, but as state populations change, especially medically underserved populations, the existing formula will become more and more unrealistic. Congress is unlikely to change the formula in the second session of the 97th Congress; other issues will probably dominate the legislative agenda.

The 1983 Reagan budget proposals would establish a new block grant to consolidate the maternal and child health services block grant; the women's, infants', and children's nutrition program; and the commodity supplemental food program. The services for the women's, infants', and children's block grant would be administered by HHS and would receive funding of $1 billion, which represents a cut from the CBO baseline of $45 million.

PREVENTIVE HEALTH BLOCK GRANT

Program Description

Before the reconciliation act, eight small programs, authorized by the Public Health Services Act, had funded a broad variety of health-related programs administered mainly by state agencies. The accompanying table outlines the programs included in the block grant. All the services provided related to preventive medicine, but program activities varied. Health incentive formula grants provided unrestricted aid to supplement and support medical services provided by state health authorities. The rodent control or urban rat program funded state or local public agency efforts to eliminate infestation in urban areas. The emergency medical services program provided assistance for the development of comprehensive regional emergency medical services systems. The rape prevention program had been authorized in 1981, but was never funded. Only one of the eight programs (health incentive grants) provided aid through formula grants.

In fiscal year 1981, Congress appropriated $93 million in budget authority for the combined predecessor programs. No single program accounted for more than 30 percent of the baseline estimate.

Reconciliation Act Changes

The reconciliation act consolidated these eight programs into a block grant, established new programmatic requirements and guidelines, and authorized the block grant through 1984. Grants administered by the Department of Health and Human Services were to be turned over to state control, on state request, in fiscal year 1982.

The reconciliation act authorized the appropriation of $95 million in fiscal year 1982, of $96.5 million in fiscal year 1983, and of $98.5 million in fiscal year 1984. It reduced the budget authority anticipated in the CBO baseline by $33 million in fiscal year 1982, $39 million in fiscal year 1983, and $45 million in fiscal year 1984. The cuts represent decreases of 26 percent, 29 percent, and 31 percent in each year.

In addition to the budgetary changes described above, the reconciliation act established new programmatic procedures and requirements for phasing in state control, protecting previous grant recipients, and transferring funds to other block grants.

Programs Consolidated into Block Grant

Program	Fiscal 1980 budget authority (millions)	Type of grant	Type of recipient	Authorizing statute
Emergency medical services	$30	Project	State & local govt's, public & nonprofit organizations	Public Health Service Act, sec.1202-1204
Health incentive grants	9	Formula	State health authorities	PHS, sec. 314(d)
Hyper-tension control	20	Project	State health authorities	PHS, sec. 317(a)(1)
Rodent control	13	Project	State & public agencies	PHS, sec. 317(a)(2)
Fluori-dation	5	Project	States, any public or non-profit supply-ing water	PHS, sec. 317(a)(2)
Health education —risk reduction	16	Project	State health agencies	PHS, sec. 1703(a)
Home health services	NA	Project	State & local public & non-profit orgs.	PHS, sec. 339
Rape prevention and crisis services	NA	NA	NA	Health Services and Centers Amendments of '78 sec. 401, 402

Phasing

No specific provisions are included, so the general block grant provisions (title XVII of the reconciliation act) apply. These provisions allow states to take over after applications have been approved by HHS. Such applications must have been made before October 1, 1982 or thirty days before the start of any other quarter of the federal fiscal year, so that the states may receive block grant funds at the start of a quarter.

**CBO Baseline and Effect
of Congressional Action During Calendar 1981
(in millions of dollars and percentages)
Account No. 75-0943-551**

Category	FY1982 Dollar Level	FY1982 Percent Change	FY1983 Dollar Level	FY1983 Percent Change	FY1984 Dollar Level	FY1984 Percent Change
CBO Baseline						
Budget authority	128	—	135	—	143	—
Outlays	NA	—	NA	—	NA	—
Reconciliation Act						
Budget authority	95	−26	96	−29	98	−31
Outlays	NA	NA	NA	NA	NA	—
Final FY 1982 Expenditures After All Changes						
Budget authority	82	−36	—	—	—	—
Outlays	NA	NA	—	—	—	—

Hold-Harmless Restrictions

For emergency medical service systems that received funding during fiscal year 1981, funding must be provided at least through fiscal year 1982, although no minimum funding level is specified. The secretary of HHS may allow exceptions.

For hypertension programs, states must provide 75 percent of fiscal year 1981 funding in their fiscal year 1982 program, 70 percent in fiscal year 1983, and 60 percent in fiscal year 1984.

For fiscal years 1982, 1983, and 1984, $3 million is set aside from the total allotment to fund rape prevention and crisis service programs. The $3 million is distributed according to the population of each state.

Other Restrictions and Requirements

States must operate the block grant under a number of special provisions included in the reconciliation act. No matching requirement is made, but block grant funds must supplement, rather than supplant, state and local spending. A state may transfer up to 7 percent of its allocation to other health block grants: up to 93 percent of the transfer is allowed during the first three fiscal quarters, and the remainder in the last quarter. No more than 10 percent of block grant funds can be used for state administration costs. Finally, states will receive apportionments of their annual allotments through quarterly letters of credit.

Appropriations Process Changes

Because the Labor, Health and Human Services, and Education Appropriations Act has not been enacted, funding for this program is being provided under a continuing resolution. Under this resolution, budget authority was reduced from $95 million to $82 million, a cut of $13 million, or 13 percent below the reconciliation act limit. The total cut from the CBO baseline to the appropriation limit was $46 million or 36 percent.

Administrative Regulations

HHS block grant regulations apply to the preventive health and health services block grant. Section 1742(a) of the reconciliation act requires an annual report on the proposed use of funds under this block grant. HHS interprets this section as identifying information that a state must include in its annual application about its intended use of the funds.

Assessment

Legislation reduced funds available for preventive health services by nearly 36 percent in fiscal year 1982. Because of the sharp cuts and the small size of the block grant, some states have expressed concern that the resources required to administer the program in accord with congressional intent are greater than the funds provided by Congress.

Although the distribution formula ensures that states will receive the same proportion of total aid in the future that they received in 1981, the existing distribution formula will become more and more unrealistic as state populations and especially medically underserved populations change. Congress is unlikely to change the formula in the second session of the 97th Congress; other issues will probably dominate the legislative agenda.

The Reagan 1983 budget proposed funding for the preventive care block grant of $82 million, the same level as authorized under the continuing resolution for fiscal year 1982.

ALCOHOL, DRUG ABUSE, AND MENTAL HEALTH

Program Description

This block grant consolidates programs designed to meet three different objectives. The largest program, mental health services, provided grants to support community mental health centers. The other four programs suported activities with two related goals: the prevention of drug abuse and alcoholism and the rehabilitation of drug abusers and alcoholics. The programs are summarized in the accompanying table.

The grants to mental health centers included separate grants for planning community mental health center programs, initial operations of mental health centers, consultation and education services, and programs in financial distress. The Alcohol, Drug Abuse, and Mental Health Administration of the Department of Health and Human Services (HHS) had established specific application and expenditure guidelines for each type of grant. For example, the period of support provided each grant varied from a single year for planning grants to eight years for staff support. Matching requirements also differed for each grant.

In 1981, the budget authority provided for the separate grants totaled $541 million.

Reconciliation Act Changes

The reconciliation act consolidated five categorical grant programs and established program expenditure requirements. The reconciliation act authorized the appropriation of $491 million in fiscal year 1982, $511 million in fiscal year 1983, and $532 million in fiscal year 1984. It reduced budget authority contained in the CBO baseline by $200 million in fiscal year 1982, $220 million in fiscal year 1983, and $243 million in fiscal year 1984. These cuts represent reductions of 29 percent in fiscal year 1982, 30 percent in fiscal year 1983, and 31 percent in fiscal year 1984. Because the block grant requires appropriation, further cuts could be imposed during the appropriations process.

In addition to the budgetary changes described above, the reconciliation act established new programmatic procedures and requirements for the phasing in of state control, the protection of previous grant recipients, and the transfer of funds to other block grants.

Programs Consolidated into Block Grant

Program	Fiscal 1981 budget authority (millions)	Type of grant	Type of recipient	Authorizing statute
Mental health services	$278	Project	Community health centers	Community Mental Health Centers Act
Drug abuse grants	172	Project & formula	State drug abuse centers	Drug Abuse Prevention Treatment, & Rehab. Act
Alcoholism grants	91	Project & formula	State agencies and other organizations	Comp. Alcoholism Prevention, Treatment, & Rehab

Phasing

States were able to take over administration on October 1, 1981, but in order to continue receiving funds states must have taken over by October 1, 1982. Transfer of control may occur at quarterly intervals through fiscal year 1982 as state applications are approved by HHS (as defined under title XVII of the reconciliation act).

Hold-Harmless Restrictions

In fiscal year 1982, states must spend the same overall proportions of the block grant funds on mental health, drug abuse, and alcohol services as under fiscal year 1981 mental health and fiscal year 1980 drug and alcohol categorical programs.

In fiscal year 1983, 95 percent of funds must be so divided, and in fiscal year 1984, 85 percent must be so divided.

States must make grants to all community mental health centers that received grants in fiscal year 1981, unless the secretary of HHS agrees to discontinue funding.

Within the alcohol and drug abuse section, at least 35 percent must go to alcohol abuse programs; 35 percent must go to drug abuse programs; and at least 20 percent must go to prevention and early intervention programs.

**CBO Baseline and Effect
of Congressional Action During Calendar 1981
(in millions of dollars and percentages)
Account No. 75-1361-551**

Category	FY1982		FY1983		FY1984	
	Dollar Level	Percent Change	Dollar Level	Percent Change	Dollar Level	Percent Change
CBO Baseline						
Budget authority	691	—	731	—	775	—
Outlays	NA	—	NA	—	NA	—
Reconciliation Act						
Budget authority	491	−29	511	−30	532	−31
Outlays	NA	NA	NA	NA	NA	NA
Final FY 1982 Expenditures After All Changes						
Budget authority	432	−37	—	—	—	—
Outlays	NA	NA	NA	NA	NA	NA

Other Restrictions and Requirements

States must operate the block grant under a number of special provisions included in the reconciliation act. A state may transfer up to 7 percent of its allocation to other health block grants: up to 3 percent is allowed during the first three fiscal quarters and the remainder in the last quarter. No more than 10 percent of block grant funds may be spent on administration costs. No matching requirement is made, but block grant funds must supplement rather than supplant state and local spending.

States must implement arrangements to locate jobs for mental health workers adversely affected by state actions to emphasize outpatient services. But no more than 1 percent of the total allotment may be spent on this retraining.

Finally, the act requires state-funded community mental health clinics to provide: (1) outpatient services for the mentally ill, (2) 24-hour-a-day emergency services, (3) day treatment or other partial hospitalization services, (4) screening for patients being considered for admission to state mental health facilities, and (5) consultation and education services.

Appropriations Process Changes

Because the Labor, Health and Human Services, and Education Appropriations Act has not been enacted, funding for this program is being provided under a continuing resolution. Under this resolution, budget authority was reduced from $491 million to $432 million, a cut of $59 million, or 12 percent below the reconciliation act limit. The total cut from the CBO baseline to the appropriations limit was $259 million, or 37 percent.

Administrative Regulations

The regulations that apply to HHS block grants also apply to the alcohol, drug abuse, and mental health block grant with the following exception. The reconciliation act requires each state to submit an annual report describing the rationale for the proposed use of funds and, beginning in 1983, the uses of block grant funds. The HHS regulations modify this section so that states are not required to report on uses of funds; under the regulations, the information required in the act refers only to the descriptions of proposed uses.

Assessment

The 97th Congress made larger cuts in the alcohol and drug abuse block grant than in any other health block grant. Funding was reduced by 37 percent from the CBO baseline.

In combination with the large budget cuts, the alcohol and drug abuse block grant imposes stricter spending requirements than the other block grants. States have little leeway to shift funds among different types of programs. However, for the final recipients of funds, state administrations could force many programmatic changes if federal program requirements are not continued. For example, the community mental health center program can change dramatically if the many separate grant categories described above are consolidated under state management.

The distribution formula ensures that states will receive the same proportion of total aid approved in the future as they received in 1981, but, as described in the other health block grants, the formula may not reflect the relative needs of the states as time passes and populations shift.

The Reagan 1983 budget proposes funding for the alcohol and drug abuse block grant of $432 million, the same level authorized under the continuing resolution for fiscal year 1982.

TRADE ADJUSTMENT ASSISTANCE PROGRAM

Program Description

Trade adjustment assistance (TAA) is a federal program designed to assist workers who are totally or partly unemployed because of foreign competition. The largest component of the program is cash assistance, which accounted for nearly $1.5 billion of total program cost in fiscal year 1981. The program also provides funds for employment training, job search, and relocation expenses. In fiscal year 1981, these activities were funded at $4.9 million, $0.2 million, and $1.8 million respectively.

Eligibility Criteria and Benefit Levels

To be eligible for trade adjustment assistance, a worker must meet two criteria. First, the worker's firm must be certified by the secretary of labor. Certification is granted to firms that (1) experience significant employment loss; (2) suffer an absolute decline in sales, and (3) demonstrate an important causal link between increasing imports and the firm's decline. Second, the worker must apply for assistance within a specified length of time and must have been employed during twenty-six of the fifty-two weeks preceding layoff.

Benefit levels are standard throughout the nation. Prior to reconciliation, the maximum benefit was 70 percent of the worker's gross weekly wage, up to the average weekly manufacturing wage. In general, federal benefit payments under TAA were less than the maximum because payments were reduced by the amount of unemployment compensation received, by 50 percent of any part-time earnings, as well as by certain training allowances. Eligible workers could receive cash assistance for up to fifty-two weeks. Older workers and workers in training could qualify for another twenty-six weeks of benefits.

The cash assistance component of TAA is an appropriated entitlement. Eligible workers are entitled to receive benefits, with funding provided through annual appropriations legislation. An eligible individual can sue for cash assistance if it is not provided due to funding shortages. Therefore, this component of TAA spending cannot be controlled through the appropriations process. The remaining elements of the program are not entitlements. The size of these benefits is strictly limited to the amount provided in the appropriations legislation. Traditionally, a portion of discretionary funds available to the secretary of labor under the CETA program has been allocated for employment search and relocation activities. Funding for employment services was provided by federal grants to states.

CBO Baseline and Effect
of Congressional Action During Calendar 1981
(in millions of dollars and percentages)
Account No. 16-0326-603

Category	FY1982 Dollar Level	FY1982 Percent Change	FY1983 Dollar Level	FY1983 Percent Change	FY1984 Dollar Level	FY1984 Percent Change
CBO Baseline						
Budget authority	1,828	—	1,286	—	867	—
Outlays	1,828	—	1,286	—	867	—
Reconciliation Act						
Budget authority	268	−85	232	−82	173	−80
Outlays	268	−85	232	−82	173	−80
Final FY 1982 Expenditures After All Changes						
Budget authority	306	−83	—	—	—	—
Outlays	342	−81	—	—	—	—

Note: This budget account consists of the cash allowance component of TAA, unemployment compensation for ex-servicemen and laid-off federal employees, disaster relief, and unemployment compensation for workers in Redwood National Park. Reconciliation only affected the TAA cash allowance.

Reconciliation Act Changes

The reconciliation act sought to control federal spending on TAA by restricting the entitlement portion of the program. The act restricted eligibility and reduced benefits. It also tried to reduce the program's emphasis on cash assistance and to encourage employment search and relocation. The changes imposed by the reconciliation act have significant effects on program costs, with budget authority and outlays falling below CBO's current policy baseline levels by 85 percent in fiscal year 1982, 82 percent in fiscal year 1983, and 80 percent in fiscal year 1984.

Restrict Eligibility

The reconciliation act tightened the certification criteria for firms by requiring that import competition be a "substantial cause" rather than an "important contribution" to the firm's decline. A "substantial cause" is defined as a cause that is important and no less so than any other cause.

Restrict Benefits

TAA cash assistance will no longer be provided in addition to unemployment compensation. Payment of TAA is restricted to the time after unemployment benefits are exhausted. In addition, the act limits the combined time during which a worker can receive unemployment compensation or TAA cash assistance to a maximum of fifty-two weeks. Finally, the act restricts eligibility for cash assistance to the week beginning sixty days after the certification is requested. This final provision helps eliminate payment of lump-sum benefits by delaying eligibility for payments by two months.

Change Program Focus

In three separate actions, the reconciliation act sought to shift the focus of TAA to new employment opportunities. First, the reconciliation act increased the maximum amounts payable for job search activities and for relocation expenses to $600 each. In addition, the act authorized the secretary of labor to require a participant to accept employment training or to extend the employment search beyond the local area by the eighth week of program participation. Finally, the act required the secretary of labor to develop an employability plan with participants and required the secretary to pay training costs under the plan.

Appropriations and Other Changes

Funding for TAA is currently provided under a continuing resolution. This resolution contains $238 million for the cash assistance portion of the TAA program, a reduction of $30 million from the $268 million estimated by the reconciliation act.

Administrative Regulations

No regulations implementing the reconciliation act had been forthcoming by the end of calendar year 1981.

Assessment

At the time of the reconciliation act, the TAA program had grown rapidly and uncontrollably. The cost of the program exploded with the onset of the 1979 recession. In fiscal year 1979, the program cost $269 million. In fiscal year 1980, the program had grown to $1.7 billion, but declined slightly to $1.5 billion in fiscal year 1981. In addition to the uncontrollable growth, the program had been criticized for providing lucrative benefits that discouraged workers from looking for new employment.

The reconciliation act specifically dealt with these two issues. Both program costs and benefits were significantly reduced. However, these reductions may increase the costs of other government programs. For example, families that lose income as a result of the changes may become eligible for the food stamp program. In addition, some persons who lose benefits may resort to state general assistance sooner than they would in the absence of these reductions. It is unlikely, however, that these additional costs will fully offset the reductions in the TAA program and, therefore, savings will undoubtedly be realized. These reductions may, however, shift some of the burden of supporting the unemployed to the states.

The fiscal year 1983 Reagan budget proposed the complete elimination of TAA cash assistance as of July 1, 1982, except for those workers already enrolled in approved training.

UNEMPLOYMENT COMPENSATION TRUST FUND

Program Description

The federal-state unemployment compensation system supports both regular and extended benefit programs. The regular program provides cash assistance to qualified unemployed workers for up to twenty-six weeks. During periods of high unemployment, the extended benefits program continues the compensation for up to thirteen weeks after the regular benefits have been exhausted. State payroll taxes finance the regular benefits and 50 percent of the extended benefits. Federal payroll taxes finance the remaining 50 percent of the extended benefits. In fiscal year 1981, 8.8 million persons benefited from the unemployment compensation system; $13.5 billion was provided in regular benefits, and $2.1 billion was provided in extended benefits.

Eligibility Criteria and Benefit Levels

Because major provisions of the unemployment compensation system are determined by state law, specific eligibility and benefit levels vary. This section will describe the broad federal program guidelines but will not attempt to describe specific state criteria.

To be eligible for unemployment compensation, a worker must meet three criteria. First, the person must be a "covered" employee. Covered employees are those subject to state and federal payroll taxes. Second, a worker must meet state-determined minimum wage and length of employment requirements. Third, the worker must continually demonstrate ability and availability to work. Ability to work is defined by physical and mental capacity. Availability to work is determined by registering for work at local employment agencies and, in most states, by actively pursuing employment opportunities. Under this final criterion, an individual cannot refuse "suitable" work and remain eligible for unemployment compensation.

Before the reconciliation act, an individual worker was eligible for extended benefits when the state's covered unemployment rate for the previous thirteen weeks was at least 4 percent and was 20 percent higher than the rate during the same thirteen-week period in the two previous years. If the 20 percent requirement was not met, states had the option of providing extended benefits when the covered unemployment rate reached 5 percent. In addition, extended benefits were provided in all states when the national covered unemployment rate reached 4.5 percent. At present, extended benefits are provided in thirty-one states, the Virgin Islands, and Puerto Rico.

The amount of compensation is a fraction of the worker's full-time weekly earnings. Compensation varies widely from state to state in both the amount and the duration of benefits. The weekly compensation for minimum-wage earners in 1981 ranged from $67 per week in ten states to $90 per week in New Jersey. The maximum weekly compensation ranged from $105 in Missouri to $223 in Ohio. In addition, the duration of benefits in relation to time worked varied widely among states, but most states provide up to twenty-six weeks of regular benefits.

Activities of the unemployment compensation system flow through the unemployment trust fund, consisting of trust funds of the individual states and the federal government. Although there is only one trust fund, the financial position of each state and of the federal government is accounted for separately. Both the state and federal payroll taxes are paid into the fund. Regular and extended benefits are paid from the fund. When the cost of a state's benefits exceed the revenues from its payroll tax, the state can borrow federal funds. Prior to reconciliation, loans to the states were interest free.

The trust fund is authorized to operate by title III of the Social Security Act and by chapter 23 of the Internal Revenue Code. No appropriation is required. The bulk of spending from the trust fund is uncontrollable because eligible individuals are entitled to benefits that are set by state law and heavily influenced by the economy.

Reconciliation Changes

The reconciliation act sought to control spending from the unemployment insurance trust fund by restricting eligibility for the extended benefits program and by discouraging state borrowing of federal funds. The effect of these provisions was minimal, reducing expenditures below the CBO baseline by 1 percent in fiscal year 1981, 4 percent in fiscal year 1982, and 1 percent in fiscal years 1983 and 1984.

In four separate actions, the reconciliation act sought to reduce eligibility for the extended benefits program. First, the act raised state covered unemployment trigger levels from 4 percent (plus 20) to 5 percent (plus 20) and raised optional state trigger levels from 5 to 6 percent. Second, the act deleted the national covered unemployment trigger. Third, the act required the exclusion of extended benefit recipients from the calculation of covered unemployment for the purposes of the state triggers. Finally, the act required that a worker have been employed for twenty weeks or have earned an equivalent amount in wages in order to be eligible for extended benefits.

The reconciliation act also discouraged state borrowing of federal funds by charging interest on loans to states granted between April 1, 1982, and December 31, 1987. The rate of interest charged will be the rate paid by the

CBO Baseline and Effect
of Congressional Action During Calendar 1981
(in millions of dollars and percentages)
Account No. 20-8042-603

Category	FY1982 Dollar Level	FY1982 Percent Change	FY1983 Dollar Level	FY1983 Percent Change	FY1984 Dollar Level	FY1984 Percent Change
CBO Baseline						
Budget authority	24,089	—	23,842	—	23,386	—
Outlays	19,736	—	17,854	—	17,629	—
Reconciliation Act						
Budget authority	23,889	−1	23,442	−2	23,286	0
Outlays	18,950	−4	17,632	−1	17,405	−1
Final FY 1982 Expenditures After All Changes						
Budget authority	21,257	−12	—	—	—	—
Outlays	18,287	−7	—	—	—	—

federal government on balances of the state's unemployment trust fund, but no higher than 10 percent. To mitigate difficulties faced by particularly hard-pressed states, the act limited the current penalty imposed on states for failing to repay these loans if states take certain steps to improve the solvency of their trust funds.

Appropriations and Other Changes

No appropriations action is required for this program.

Administrative Regulations

No regulations implementing the reconciliation act had been published by the end of calendar year 1981.

Assessment

The federal government has little direct control over the unemployment compensation system. Expenditures from the trust fund are subject to the unemployment rate, with the magnitude of the expenditures determined primarily by state eligibility criteria and benefit levels. For this reason, the reconciliation act imposed minimal direct reductions on the unemployment compensation system. The final impact of these reductions will vary from state to state, depending on the financial solvency of each state system.

The major problem facing the trust fund at the time of the reconciliation act was uncertain financial solvency. States that have experienced prolonged unemployment have borrowed heavily from federal revenues and have been unable or unwilling to repay the loans. Although the act required that interest be charged on these loans, it also recognized that some state systems are hard pressed and lightened penalties for nonpayment. States may change their unemployment compensation systems to encourage financial solvency, but the response is not immediately clear. The effects of these changes on local workers and industries will depend on the reform measures that are instituted.

The provisions of the reconciliation act that tightened eligiblity criteria for the extended benefit program should reduce payments and thereby improve the financial position of state unemployment systems.

The Reagan budget for fiscal year 1983 includes a legislative proposal to reduce expenditures from the trust fund by $6 million, by rounding weekly benefit amounts to the next lower dollar, to become effective with initial claims beginning July 1, 1983.

ASSISTED HOUSING

Program Description

Assisted housing is made up of two separate but related programs, the public housing program and the section 8 housing program.

The *public housing program* provides housing to low-income families. This program is operated by local public housing agencies (PHAs), which engage in or assist in the development and operation of public housing projects. The projects may be newly constructed, existing, rehabilitated, or leased. The federal government makes annual contributions to the agencies for the PHA-owned or leased housing. The federal government also provides funds to Indian housing authorities for public housing projects. In practice, the effect of new budget allocations is to subsidize construction of new apartments for the poor. (For a discussion of the program of subsidies for maintaining and operating public housing, see "Public Housing Operating Subsidies.")

Most federal housing assistance to low- and moderate-income people is provided through the *section 8 program,* which has two major components: (1) subsidies for tenants in newly constructed housing, including substantially rehabilitated units, and (2) subsidies for tenants in private-market rental housing. Under the new construction program, the government guarantees the owner of a housing project that it will pay a portion of the rent for a section 8 recipient. The payment goes to the project. Under the existing housing program, eligible families are responsible for finding acceptable housing (that is, up to HUD minimum property standards and below a specific "fair market rent") and they receive a rent subsidy directly.

Federal funds for both programs are allocated to localities in accordance with a formula reflecting population, extent of poverty, amount of substandard housing, and the rental vacancy rate.

Neither public housing nor the section 8 program is an entitlement program. Both programs require an annual appropriation, and when all new funds are obligated, HUD may not enter into more commitments. In general, outlay savings from assisted housing occur very slowly. This happens because entering into housing contracts implies a commitment ranging from fifteen to forty years, a commitment that must be backed with budget authority at the onset of the contract. Outlays are simply the money paid out for the current year, which reflects some new commitments but mostly those from earlier years. Additionally, because new construction may take as long as two to five years to begin, many reductions in budget authority do not translate into   outlay savings for several years.

**CBO Baseline and Effect
of Congressional Action During Calendar 1981
(in millions of dollars and percentages)
Account No. 86-0139-604**

	FY1982		FY1983		FY1984	
Category	Dollar Level	Percent Change	Dollar Level	Percent Change	Dollar Level	Percent Change
CBO Baseline						
Budget authority	28,637	—	31,708	—	33,476	—
Outlays	6,981	—	8,270	—	9,566	—
Reconciliation Act						
Budget authority	17,080	−40	18,045	−43	17,967	−46
Outlays	6,865	−2	7,935	−4	8,845	−8
Final FY 1982 Expenditures After All Changes						
Budget authority	16,367	−43	—	—	—	—
Outlays	6,860	−2	—	—	—	—

Reconciliation Act Changes

For fiscal year 1982, the reconciliation act provided subsidies for a total of 153,000 additional housing units, which was a little more than half of the 280,000 units funded in fiscal year 1981. The impact of the lower level of housing is to reduce budget authority to about $17 billion in fiscal year 1982. The CBO estimate assumes equivalent reductions in fiscal years 1983 and 1984 although the reconciliation act does not specify figures for these years. Outlay savings are estimated at $116 million in fiscal year 1982.

Besides reducing the number of units provided in fiscal year 1982, the reconciliation act made a number of structural changes in the program. Although these do not change the basic nature of the program, three are significant: changes in rents, changes in program mix, and changes in eligibility rules.

Rents

The maximum level of tenant contribution toward rent was raised. Previously, a tenant was expected to pay rent equal to 25 percent of his or her adjusted income. In fiscal year 1982, the tenant proportion of rent was increased to 26 percent, and it will be increased by one percentage point per fiscal year until it reaches 30 percent of income. More specifically, the new law sets the rent for section 8 and public housing at the highest of three figures: (1) 26 percent (rising to 30 percent in four years) of the family's monthly adjusted income, (2) 10 percent of the family's monthly gross income, or (3) that part of a family's welfare payments specifically designated to meet housing costs in those states which adjust welfare to cover housing.

Program Mix

The mix between new and existing housing was not dramatically changed, with 55 percent of subsidies being used for new units, while the remaining 45 percent is to be used to support existing housing. However, within this national figure, the secretary is directed to accommodate local preferences as much as possible. Because of the difference in prices for new and existing housing, this pattern of subsidies implies that about 55 percent of units will be existing while about 45 percent will be new.

Eligibility

The overall income eligibility standard was left at 80 percent of median income but the discretion of the secretary to admit higher-income tenants was limited. In addition, nationally, only 10 percent of the occupants in existing housing as of October 1, 1981, could have incomes between 50 percent and 80 percent of the median income. The remaining tenants must have earned less than 50 percent of the median. Over time, only 5 percent nationally may be occupied by people whose incomes fall between 50 percent and 80 percent of the median. However, with regard to individual projects, the act eliminates the requirement that new housing projects rent at least 30 percent of their units to families who earn less than 50 percent of the median income.

Other changes were made in the assisted housing program that seem likely to be less significant. For example, the secretary is required to assure that new section 8 units be modest in design. The secretary is allowed to keep up to 15 percent of annual contract contributions for unforeseen needs and services for the handicapped or for minority enterprises. Under certain conditions, section 8 may now be used in mobile homes and for single-room apartments. Public housing authorities may retain part of the funds they recover from money wrongfully paid as a result of fraud and abuse.

Appropriations Process Changes

Additional cuts were made in subsidized housing during the appropriations process. Budget authority was cut an additional 4 percent, or $713 million, for a total reduction of 43 percent from the CBO baseline for fiscal year 1982.

Regulatory and Administrative Changes

A number of regulations have appeared, but these do not seem likely to alter the basic operation of assisted housing.

Assessment

The large cuts in assisted housing reflect the controversial nature of the program. It has been controversial for three reasons. First, per-unit subsidies are very high, especially for newly constructed units. Second, because the programs are not entitlements, relatively few eligible people actually receive assistance—only about 10 percent of eligible families receive a subsidy, although this rises to about 30 percent for the very poor. Finally, there is a substantial tension between the goal of stimulating new construction and the goal of income assistance to the poor. This tension is reflected politically by conflict between proponents of new construction, especially the construction industry, and proponents of voucher systems, which offer the possibility of lowering program costs and increasing the number of people served.

In determining its position with regard to assisted housing programs, the Reagan administration has consistently selected the less costly options. For example, it emphasizes an income assistance goal for the section 8 program, thus justifying large reductions in new construction and, in the fiscal year 1983 budget, moving to convert the program to a voucher. In other words, the administration would end new section 8 construction altogether, replacing it with a direct rent subsidy. In public housing, the administration emphasizes a supply goal, which it feels has been met relatively well, rather than the income maintenance goal. Accordingly, it has increased rents among public housing tenants and suggested cutting public housing operating subsidies.

Aside from the voucher proposal in the 1983 budget, it seems clear that the largest change wrought in assisted housing programs by the administration is the large reduction in the number of additional units to be supported by the 1982 budget. At the same time, results from this cut will be difficult to measure, for the following reasons:

● *Time delays in capital construction.* The cuts affect construction projects that are still some distance "in the pipeline" and effects will not be observable for perhaps as long as two years.

• *Problems of measuring what does not happen.* The effect of reductions is that additional units will simply not be supported while currently supported units remain unaffected. It may be difficult to measure this "nonevent."

More readily discernible will be the effects of higher rents. Tenants will have to pay a greater proportion of their income in rent, forcing them to reallocate their budgets. But again, this effect will only emerge slowly as rent increases are phased in over time.

Finally, some authorities on assisted housing expect local managers of public housing and landlords of section 8 apartments to react to the new emphasis on self-sufficiency by keeping out costly or unreliable tenants. This might occur despite the shift in eligibility rules favoring low-income tenants. For example, managers may try to exclude so-called multiproblem families from assisted housing. Again, however, this shift—if it occurs at all—will probably be observable only over time.

For fiscal year 1983, the Reagan administration proposes converting section 8 into a voucher subsidizing rents, as mentioned previously. By eliminating all new construction (including public housing) and by shortening the length of contracts with landlords, the administration would achieve sufficient savings to bring about a net reduction in budget authority of $5.2 billion. Outlays, largely driven by previous decisions, are estimated at $7.4 billion.

PUBLIC HOUSING OPERATING SUBSIDIES

Program Description

In addition to supporting the capital costs of public housing, the federal government pays operating subsidies to local public housing authorities (PHAs) to bridge the gap between operating costs and the rent received from tenants. Each tenant's rent is set at a percentage of the household income. Public housing operating subsidies are paid to approximately 2,700 public housing agencies, which administer nearly 97 percent of all public housing units. Subsidies typically account for 40 percent to 50 percent of the operating incomes of the local housing authority.

The mechanism used by the Department of Housing and Urban Development (HUD) to establish the subsidy rate is the performance funding system, which estimates the operating costs of well-run projects. The system relates operating expenses to tenant and project characteristics in the more successful projects. The operating subsidy provided by HUD is the difference between the estimated cost for a well-run project of its type and a project's actual income from tenants.

Operating subsidies are an appropriated account. That is, if Congress wishes to decrease expenditures in this area, it need only appropriate less money. Moreover, because the funds in this account are for operating rather than capital expenses, many reductions in budget authority translate rapidly into lower outlays. This is one of the few housing programs where such immediate reductions can be made.

Reconciliation Act Changes

Although the administration requested cuts in operating subsidies, Congress increased funding above the CBO baseline. Budget authority was increased by 21 percent in fiscal years 1982, 1983, and 1984, while outlays are slated to increase 13 percent in fiscal year 1982 and 21 percent in the following two years.

Although rent increases were instituted under the aegis of the assisted housing programs (see "Assisted Housing"), the increase in rents for tenants in public housing was a major change affecting operating subsidies.

CBO Baseline and Effect
of Congressional Action During Calendar 1981
(in millions of dollars and percentages)
Account No. 86-0163-604

Category	FY1982		FY1983		FY1984	
	Dollar Level	Percent Change	Dollar Level	Percent Change	Dollar Level	Percent Change
CBO Baseline						
Budget						
authority	1,240	—	1,451	—	1,708	—
Outlays	1,071	—	1,350	—	1,585	—
Reconciliation Act						
Budget						
authority	1,500	+21	1,756	+21	2,067	+21
Outlays	1,206	+13	1,634	+21	1,918	+21
Final FY 1982 Expenditures						
* After All Changes*						
Budget						
authority	1,156	−7	—	—	—	—
Outlays	1,034	−17	—	—	—	—

Appropriations Process Changes

During the appropriations process, Congress retreated somewhat from the increases called for in the reconciliation act. Outlays were left untouched, but budget authority was scaled down by $344 million, or 23 percent of the amount envisioned under reconciliation. The net changes from the CBO baseline were a 7 percent reduction in budget authority for fiscal year 1982 and a 13 percent increase in outlays.

Administration and Regulation

No regulatory action has yet taken place for this program; changes during the budget process affected only funding levels, not the program's basic structure or operation.

Assessment

Funding of operating subsidies has generally fallen below the levels suggested by the performance funding system for two reasons. First, operating subsidies are a convenient target for budget balancers since immediate cuts can be made in outlays as well as budget authority, unlike the public housing or section 8 programs. Second, the results of underfunding can temporarily be hidden through deferred maintenance. Over a longer period, however, underfunding results in substantial deterioration in the physical quality of public housing. This problem is made worse by a flaw in the performance funding system itself, namely, failure to make adequate allowance for rising utility costs. Some program experts believe that deep cuts in operating subsidies could lead to some scandal involving heating, maintenance, or security, as housing authorities try to balance their books without sufficient federal subsidies.

Awareness of these problems made Congress reluctant to cut subsidies dramatically, rejecting the administration's proposals. However, Congress did agree to raise rents for tenants of public housing, thus decreasing somewhat the growing pressure on operating subsidies.

In summation, the operating subsidy program is one of the few housing programs where one can anticipate observable short-term consequences of budgetary action, rather than simply the absence of construction activity. Expert opinion is that the net effects of budgetary action in the operating subsidies program, in combination with rent increases in public housing, will be continued deferral of maintenance (with limited capital improvements in those projects which benefit from a small, separate program of modernization), increased efforts by housing agencies to collect rents, and continuing efforts by agencies to cut operating costs, possibly creating some deleterious situations if subsidies take deep cuts in the future.

In fiscal year 1983, the Reagan administration is requesting $1.1 billion in budget authority and a similar amount in outlays for operating subsidies, a reduction of 22 percent in budget authority and 12 percent in outlays from the current CBO baseline. According to the administration, these reductions are to be achieved by raising rents and through reducing energy consumption levels 15 to 20 percent below 1981 levels in response to "intensive efforts now underway to modernize public housing and make it more energy efficient." Additionally, the administration proposes to issue regulations to allow housing agencies to collect delinquent rents and evict disruptive tenants more easily.

SPECIAL MILK PROGRAM

Program Description

Under previous law, the special milk program subsidized half-pints of milk sold in public and private nonprofit schools and child care institutions. The subsidy covered the full cost of milk for needy children who qualified for free lunches under the national school lunch program and also covered part of the cost for other students. The program is administered by the Food and Nutrition Service of the Department of Agriculture. The department provides funds to state education agencies, which pass them on to local schools and institutions. In fiscal year 1981, $119 million was appropriated for this account.

The basic authorizing legislation for the special milk program is found in the Child Nutrition Act of 1966. Funds are provided through the Agriculture, Rural Development and Related Agency Appropriations Bill on an annual basis.

Reconciliation Act Changes

The reconciliation act amended the Child Nutrition Act to significantly reduce the number of institutions eligible for federal subsidies under the special milk program. This change, in addition to marginally tightening the income eligibility requirement for free milk, reduced budget authority and outlays by an estimated $100 million in each year, beginning in fiscal year 1982. This represents a program reduction of approximately 76 percent.

Eliminate Overlap with Federally Subsidized Meals

The reconciliation act eliminated the special milk program for those schools and institutions participating in the national school lunch, school breakfast, commodity only, or child care food programs.

Eliminate Subsidies to Private Schools

The reconciliation act discontinued the special milk program for private schools whose average annual tuition is greater than $1,500 per child.

Restrict Income Eligibility

The reconciliation act also restricted the income eligibility requirements for free milk. Under the new act, free milk is available only to children whose family income is less than 130 percent of the poverty level. The pre-

CBO Baseline and Effect
of Congressional Action During Calendar 1981
(in millions of dollars and percentages)
Account No. 12-3502-605

Category	FY1982		FY1983		FY1984	
	Dollar Level	Percent Change	Dollar Level	Percent Change	Dollar Level	Percent Change
CBO Baseline						
Budget authority	125	—	130	—	134	—
Outlays	124	—	130	—	134	—
Reconciliation Act						
Budget authority	30	−76	31	−76	32	−76
Outlays	21	−83	32	−75	33	−75
Final FY 1982 Expenditures After All Changes						
Budget authority	28	−78	—	—	—	—
Outlays	27	−78	—	—	—	—

vious income limit was 125 percent of the poverty level plus an $80 monthly income deduction. After fiscal year 1983, the income eligibility limits will be the same as those for the food stamp program (see next section).

Appropriations and Other Changes

The Agriculture, Rural Development and Related Agency Appropriations Act provided $28 million for the special milk program in fiscal year 1982. This is a modest reduction from the budget authority allowed under reconciliation.

Administrative Regulations

On October 20, 1981, the Department of Agriculture published changes in the rules for the special milk program. These rules simply restated provisions of the law.

Assessment

The special milk program is one of several federal programs designed to encourage the consumption of milk by children. The child nutrition programs subsidize meals that include milk; the special milk program subsidized milk apart from or in addition to the federally subsidized meals. Special milk, therefore, did not duplicate a service provided under the child nutrition programs.

The trend toward reducing the special milk program was established before reconciliation. P.L. 95-627, enacted November 10, 1978, made the service of free milk optional. Two years later, P.L. 96-499 reduced the subsidy for milk served to children from middle- and upper-income households. The state and local impact of changes due to reconciliation will depend on whether the schools will try to replace the program with local funds.

The administration's fiscal year 1983 budget called for the elimination of this program July 1, 1982.

FOOD STAMPS

Program Description

Food stamps is a federal program designed to increase the food-purchasing power of low-income households. The program is administered at the federal level by the Department of Agriculture and at the state and local levels by welfare agencies. The welfare agencies determine eligibility and process benefits based on nationally uniform eligibility criteria and benefit levels. Eligible households receive coupons that are redeemable for food at most stores.

States participate in the food stamp program at their own discretion. In fiscal year 1981, all fifty states, the District of Columbia, Puerto Rico, Guam, and the Virgin Islands participated in the program. The federal government paid the full cost of the benefits, its own administrative costs, and a portion of the state and local administrative costs. In fiscal year 1981, federal spending on the food stamp program totaled $11.8 billion, providing $10.7 billion in benefits.

Eligibility Criteria and Benefit Levels

For a household to be eligible for food stamps, its "countable" income must be less than the poverty level. Not all income is "countable." Countable income is gross income less certain exemptions and deductions. Exemptions are extended primarily for noncash forms of assistance (i.e., housing subsidies). Deductions take various forms: every household receives a standard deduction; other deductions attempt to offset circumstances that reduce food-purchasing power; the remaining deductions are work incentives. Because of the exemptions and deductions, a household with an income substantially above the poverty level may still meet the eligibility guidelines for food stamps.

Once income eligibility is ascertained, the monthly benefit level of food stamps can be determined. The Department of Agriculture estimates the cost of a nutritionally adequate diet called the thrifty food plan. A household's food stamp allotment is determined by subtracting 30 percent of its "countable" income from the cost of the thrifty food plan. The rationale for this method is that 30 percent of a household's countable income should be reserved for food. Food needs above 30 percent of income should be provided by food coupons.

The (food stamp program) is an appropriated entitlement, so eligible households are entitled to receive food stamps, with program costs funded by an appropriation. This program has some unique funding provisions, however. An entitlement generally provides legal recourse to individuals if benefits are not provided due to funding shortages. This is not true of food stamps. In an attempt to control the cost of the food stamp program, Congress enacted the Food Stamp Act of 1977 which (1) placed a "cap" on annual appropriation levels; (2) required that benefits be reduced if necessary to stay within the caps; and (3) made benefit levels strictly subject to the availability of appropriations. These provisions have not been effective in exercising fiscal control because Congress has always provided additional funds if needed to maintain benefit levels.

Reconciliation Act Changes

Because the Food Stamp Act of 1977 had not been effective in controlling the program costs, the reconciliation act contained provisions to restrict eligibility and benefits. These program changes reflected three objectives: (1) tightening program administration; (2) reducing indexing provisions; and (3) restricting program eligibility. CBO estimated that the changes imposed by the reconciliation act would reduce the program below the CBO baseline by 14 percent in fiscal year 1982, by 17 percent in fiscal year 1983, and by 18 percent in fiscal year 1984.

1. Program Administration

The reconciliation act took three steps to tighten program administration. CBO estimated the savings from these provisions to be $499 million, $568 million, and $807 million in fiscal years 1982, 1983, and 1984 respectively.

Prorated First Month Benefits. The greatest savings achieved by administrative changes involve prorating the first month of benefits to newly enrolled households. Rather than receiving a full month's allotment of benefits, newly enrolled households will receive food stamps based on the date of application.

Prior Month Accounting and Monthly Reporting. Beginning October 1, 1983, income eligibility and benefit levels will be based on the prior month's income rather than projected future income. Households will also be required to regularly report income and other relevant household information.

Improved Recovery of Overissued Benefits. If any member of a household receives more benefits than he or she is entitled to, the government will get back the improper ("overissued") benefits from all recipients in that household. States will be required to collect overissued benefits in nonfraud cases.

**CBO Baseline and Effect
of Congressional Action During Calendar 1981
(in millions of dollars and percentages)
Account No. 12-3505-605**

Category	FY1982 Dollar Level	FY1982 Percent Change	FY1983 Dollar Level	FY1983 Percent Change	FY1984 Dollar Level	FY1984 Percent Change
CBO Baseline						
Budget						
authority	12,304	—	12,599	—	12,947	—
Outlays	12,298	—	12,598	—	12,946	—
Reconciliation Act						
Budget						
authority	10,596	−14	10,503	−17	10,563	−18
Outlays	10,590	−14	10,502	−17	10,562	−18
Final FY 1982 Expenditures After All Changes						
Budget						
authority	10,280	−16	—	—	—	—
Outlays	10,407	−15	—	—	—	—

2. Indexing Provisions

Nearly 50 percent of the fiscal year 1982 savings achieved by reconciliation results from reducing or repealing indexation provisions. CBO estimated the savings from these provisions to be $817 million, $887 million, and $883 million in fiscal years 1982, 1983, and 1984 respectively.

Inflation Indexing. Prior to reconciliation, food stamps were indexed to annual inflation rates in four ways: (1) the standard deduction was adjusted each January for changes in the consumer price index (CPI); (2) certain other deductions were adjusted each January; (3) the poverty level was adjusted each July; and (4) the thrifty food plan was adjusted for changes in food prices each January. Several provisions in the reconciliation act changed indexing guidelines affecting both the calculation of "countable" income and the determination of benefit levels. Reconciliation also delayed the indexation of deductions and provided that homeownership be factored out of the CPI for future inflation adjustments. In addition, benefit levels were reduced in real terms by delaying the annual food-price adjustment of the thrifty food plan by one quarter each fiscal year for three years.

Repeal of Liberalization in Indexing Rules. Beginning in January 1982, the index used to inflate benefits and deductions was to have been a more up-to-date estimate of changes in the cost of living. Reconciliation repealed this provision.

3. Program Eligibility

Six provisions of the reconciliation act restricted eligibility, lowered program participation, or both. CBO estimated the savings from these provisions at $342 million, $591 million, and $654 million in fiscal years 1982, 1983, and 1984 respectively.

Block Grant. The largest estimated savings in the program eligibility category are associated with the provision that converted Puerto Rico's food stamp program into a block grant, with funding anticipated at $825 million per year.

Lower Income Eligibility. As discussed above, households with gross income considerably above the poverty level were eligible for food stamps, because some income is not counted. Reconciliation restricted eligibility to those households with gross income equal to 130 percent of the poverty level. The elderly and disabled are exempt from this limit.

Change in Definition of Household. The act required that all people living in the same household apply as a single unit regardless of whether they prepared or purchased food together.

Eligibility of Strikers. The reconciliation act denied eligibility for households with members on strike unless the household was eligible for food stamps before the strike. Benefits may not be increased because of income lost during a strike.

Lowered "Earned Income" Deduction. Prior to reconciliation, 20 percent of a household's "earned income" was deducted from gross income as a work incentive. Reconciliation lowered the deduction to 18 percent.

No Funding for Outreach. Reconciliation eliminated federal sponsorship of programs designed to inform households of the food stamp program.

Appropriations and Other Changes

Although the reconciliation act amended provisions of the Food Stamp Act of 1977, it did not extend the authority to appropriate funds, which expired at the end of fiscal year 1981. In November 1981, Congress authorized the appropriation of $11.3 billion for fiscal year 1982. This single-year authorization represented a compromise between the two houses, which failed to reach agreement on a four-year authorization bill. Congress appropriated $10.3 billion for the food stamp program for fiscal year 1982. The appropriations amount is below both the reconciliation target and the authorization level. Language in the conference report of the appropriations bill suggests that the appropriated amount may fall short of program needs in fiscal year 1982.

Administrative Regulations

On September 4, 1981, the Department of Agriculture published the final rules needed to bring the food stamp program in line with the reconciliation act. The rules simply restated provisions of the act. In the semiannual regulatory agenda published on October 27, 1981, the department announced which major rules would be considered or changed within the following six-month period. Provisions relating to the reconciliation act were: (1) prior month accounting and monthly reporting; (2) the specification of household composition; (3) income eligibility standards; (4) initial month benefits; (5) deductions; and (6) outreach efforts. No new rules had been issued on these provisions by the end of calendar year 1981.

Assessment

The cost of the food stamp program more than doubled from fiscal year 1977 to 1981. Soaring costs were attributable to (1) the increasing number of participants; (2) the effect of inflation and indexation on benefit levels and deductions, and (3) general economic conditions.

Because of the rapid growth in program costs, restrictions on this program have been proposed in recent years. The final Carter budget, for example, proposed both a cap on some deductions and a repeal of the liberalized indexation rules. Because the reconciliation act delayed rather than eliminated some indexation provisions, the real effects of these changes on program participants are likely to be small.

Reductions in program eligibility had also been proposed before reconciliation. Provisions of the Food Stamp Act of 1977 restricted income eligibility of program participants. Reconciliation, however, went significantly beyond the 1977 act and substantially reduced eligibility for some groups. The people who will be hardest hit by these reductions are the working poor.

It has been estimated that nearly every recipient of food stamps will be affected by the reconciliation act. Because the cuts are broadly based, the effect on any particular group is minimized. Even though reconciliation imposed large dollar reductions that affected nearly every participant, the impact of these reductions on state and local governments is negligible.

The new Reagan budget proposes additional program reductions in the food stamp program. The budget authority request for fiscal year 1983 is $1.8 billion less than the amount that would be required under current legislation. The bulk of these savings results from two proposals. The first proposal changes the percentage of a household's countable income reserved for food consumption from 30 to 35 percent. The second proposal eliminates all deductions from earnings in determining benefit levels. Other proposed cuts will further restrict program eligibility and limit benefit payments.

CHILD NUTRITION

Program Description

The child nutrition programs provide free and subsidized meals and snacks to children in schools, day care centers, and summer programs. The school lunch program, the oldest and largest of these programs, originated during the 1930s as a way to increase employment and dispose of agricultural surpluses. The National School Lunch Act of 1946 set up the basic framework of today's system, which was greatly expanded by the amendments of 1970. Through these changes, school lunch became an entitlement, and uniform federal eligibility standards were established for the subsidized aspects of the program.

During fiscal year 1980, over 27 million children from 94,000 schools participated in the school lunch program. The program makes grants to states, which administer them through their education agencies. These agencies then allocate the funds to local school districts. Federal standards for the nutritional content of meals must be met in order for a school to participate. Children from families below a certain income level receive free food, other children get lunches at a reduced price, and even those paying "full price" get some subsidy. For fiscal year 1981, the school lunch program received 69 percent of the total budget authority of $3.5 billion for child nutrition programs.

The school breakfast program is designed to provide morning meals in areas where children tend to be undernourished, although any school in the lunch program may participate. About 3.3 million students in 35,000 schools take part, and the program received 9 percent of child nutrition funding in 1981.

A third component of child nutrition programs is the summer food program. It provides meals and snacks for children in schools and nonprofit institutions (such as summer camps) in areas where poor economic conditions exist. This program received 4 percent of fiscal year 1981 budget authority.

The final major child nutrition program provides funding for meals and snacks served to children in child and day care centers. About 9 percent of 1981 budget authority was devoted to this program. Another 8 percent is spent on commodities which are divided among all four programs. The remaining child nutrition funds go for a variety of support services, such as state administrative expenses and nutrition studies.

Child nutrition programs are funded through a complicated mixture of several types of subsidies. School lunches may qualify for as many as five subsidies: (1) a cash subsidy available to all; (2) a special subsidy given to those who qualify for a reduced-price lunch; (3) a further subsidy for those receiving free meals; (4) a commodity subsidy provided by the federal government in the form of lower-cost foodstuffs; and (5) an additional subsidy of 2.5 cents per meal to those districts where 60 percent of lunches are served free or at a reduced price. In exchange for these subsidies, school districts had to agree to provide free and reduced-price lunches to all those who met federal eligibility rules, and they could not charge more than 20 cents for the reduced-price lunch. The federal cash subsidies were all indexed for inflation twice a year by using the "Food Away From Home" component of the Consumer Price Index.

The school breakfast program has a two-tier system of subsidies. Like the lunch program, there is a basic subsidy for all meals, plus additional subsidies for those served free or at a reduced price. However, the amount of subsidy is not uniform nationwide; schools in areas of "severe need" (roughly defined as those where 40 percent of lunches are provided free or at a reduced price) receive considerably higher amounts per meal than do other schools.

The summer food program provides free meals to children in summer programs and uses a uniform subsidy schedule. Only areas where one-third of the students would qualify for free or reduced-price lunches are eligible.

Subsidies for the child care food program followed the same guidelines as those of the school lunch and breakfast programs. However, if enough children came from families with incomes below 195 percent of the poverty line, all meals would be subsidized at the free or reduced-price level.

Total funding for the child nutrition programs had grown rapidly over the last decade as subsidy rates were raised and eligibility standards were loosened. Budget authority for fiscal year 1981 was $3.5 billion and outlays were $3.4 billion.

Reconciliation Act Changes

The reconciliation act made major reductions in child nutrition programs. Both budget authority and outlays were reduced by approximately $1.4 billion in fiscal year 1982, $1.5 billion in fiscal year 1983, and $1.6 billion in fiscal year 1984. Since this program is an entitlement, these savings were made by changing basic provisions of the authorizing legislation. Some of the major changes included a reduction in federal subsidies for school breakfasts and lunches, tightened eligibility standards for free and reduced-price meals, stricter fraud standards, and changes in both the summer food and child care food programs. Each of these changes is outlined below.

CBO Baseline and Effect
of Congressional Action During Calendar 1981
(in millions of dollars and percentages)
Account No. 12-3539-605

Category	FY1982 Dollar Level	FY1982 Percent Change	FY1983 Dollar Level	FY1983 Percent Change	FY1984 Dollar Level	FY1984 Percent Change
CBO Baseline						
Budget authority	4,110	—	4,468	—	4,878	—
Outlays	4,032	—	4,439	—	4,847	—
Reconciliation Act						
Budget authority	2,712	−34	2,988	−33	3,298	−32
Outlays	2,662	−34	2,968	−33	3,276	−32
Final FY 1982 Expenditures After All Changes						
Budget authority	2,847	−31	—	—	—	—
Outlays	2,662	−34	—	—	—	—

Reductions in Federal Subsidies

Each of the five federal subsidies for the school lunch program was changed. The cash subsidy was reduced from 17.75 cents per meal to 10.5 cents per meal, and the special subsidy for reduced-price meals was cut from 71.5 cents per meal to 58.75 cents per meal, but the subsidy for free meals was raised from 91.5 cents per meal to 98.75 cents per meal. The commodity subsidy had been 14.75 cents per meal and would have been increased automatically to 16.75 cents per meal on October 1, 1981; reconciliation reduced this level to 11 cents per meal. The added subsidy for districts serving 60 percent or more of their lunches free or at a reduced price was pared from 2.5 cents per meal to 2 cents per meal.

As a result of these changes, free meals now receive a subsidy of 120.25 cents per meal, down from the previous law's figure of 124 cents per meal. The subsidy for reduced-price meals was changed from 104 cents per meal to 80.25 cents per meal. Full-price lunches will now be subsidized at 21.5 cents per meal instead of 32.5 cents per meal. These figures do not include the added subsidy for districts in poor areas.

In addition, the allowable charge for reduced-price lunches was raised from 20 cents to 40 cents. Subsidies will be indexed for inflation only once per year.

School breakfast subsidies were also cut. For most schools, the subsidy levels would have been 16.25 cents per meal for full-price breakfasts, 46.5 cents per meal for reduced-price breakfasts, and 57 cents per meal for free breakfasts. After reconciliation, these levels are 8.25 cents per meal, 28.5 cents per meal, and 57 cents per meal, respectively. Those districts qualifying as in "severe need" would have received subsidies of 68.5 cents for each free meal and 63.5 cents for each reduced-price meal; reconciliation cut the latter figure to 38.5 cents per meal. As with school lunches, these rates will be changed annually for inflation.

Tightened Eligibility Standards

Income eligibility standards for free meals have been reduced from 125 percent of the federal poverty line plus an $80 dollar per month standard deduction to 130 percent of the poverty line. This means that for a family of four the yearly income limit in fiscal year 1982 has been reduced from $11,520 to $10,990.

The maximum income limit for reduced-price meals has been changed from 195 percent of the poverty level plus a standard deduction, to 185 percent of the poverty level with no standard deduction. This means that the yearly income limit for a family of four in fiscal year 1982 has been lowered from $17,440 to $15,630.

Stricter Fraud Standards

Schools and institutions are required to verify the information from free and reduced-price meal applications according to Department of Agriculture regulations. In addition, the applications now require social security numbers of all adult household members whose children are receiving free and reduced-cost meals. Also, the applications contain only the income guidelines for reduced-price meals while the public announcements contain both free and reduced-price meals information. This is to increase the probability that people who are eligible for the free lunch will sign up for the reduced-price lunch.

Summer Food Service Program Limited

Eligibility for the summer food service program has been limited to public or nonprofit school food authorities; local, municipal, or county governments (provided they operate the program directly); and residential summer camps in areas in which at least half the children are eligible for free or reduced-price meals. Previously, other nonprofit service institutions had been eligible.

Reductions in the Child Care Food Program Subsidies

Participation has been restricted and eligibility standards tightened for the child care food program. The reimbursement levels for administrative costs to the same groups were reduced by 10 percent on January 1, 1982.

Reimbursement rates for the costs of food per meal have been lowered to the new levels for the school lunch and breakfast programs. The "tiering system," under which day care centers could receive payment based on percentages of needy children, has been eliminated. As of January 1, 1982, institutions are reimbursed only if their children meet the national school lunch guidelines for free or reduced-price meals. The age limit for receiving reimbursements has been lowered to twelve years, except for children of migrant workers where it remains fifteen years. No age limit exists for children of the handicapped.

Other Changes

The food service equipment subsidy and the nutrition education program subsidy have been terminated. Several provisions are aimed at reducing state planning requirements and accounting paperwork provisions.

Appropriations Changes

The child nutrition program is an appropriated entitlement. In practice, the program is largely free from control by the appropriations committees. This pattern was borne out again for fiscal year 1982, when only marginal changes were made. The estimated outlay level remained unchanged, and a small change in budget authority probably reflects a reestimate of the costs of the programs.

Administrative Regulations

Several new regulations were issued in the fall of 1981 which affect the child nutrition programs. Most of these regulations simply implemented the changes ordered by the reconciliation act. A few others are designed to give more administrative freedom to the states. For example, states no longer must submit estimates of the total number of children eligible for free or reduced-price meals, and the requirement that the states submit a master program plan in order to participate in the child care food program has been waived.

Changes in nutrition standards were also proposed in early September, partly as a way to offset reductions in federal subsidies. These included the infamous definition of catsup as a vegetable, along with changes in the size of allowable portions. The storm of controversy that resulted led the Department of Agriculture to withdraw the proposals for further study.

Assessment

The child nutrition programs were a major target of administration cost-cutters in 1981. It was widely perceived that a subsidy was inappropriate for the meals of many children, particularly those from middle- or upper-class families. Many districts were criticized by budget-cutters for wasting food, and these critics suggested that lower subsidies would result in better food utilization. Although the administration did not get the full reductions it sought, most of the proposed changes were made.

Cuts in the child nutrition programs were among the most widely publicized and disputed provisions of the reconciliation act. The reduction in eligibility for free and reduced-price lunches will put an increased burden on many low-income families. The lower subsidy for each meal will mean higher costs for the schools, and critics claim this will cause fewer children to participate in the programs. Caught between higher costs and lower levels of participation, many schools may drop the program entirely. Similar effects may be noted as a result of the cuts in the other aspects of the program.

It should be pointed out that subsidies for the neediest children were cut far less than others. In the school lunch program, the subsidy for free meals was cut by only 3 percent, while the subsidy for reduced-price lunches was decreased by 23 percent and that for full-price meals by 34 percent. The subsidy for the neediest children in the school breakfast program was not cut at all. So, there is some justification for the administration's contention that a "safety net" remains in this program.

The Reagan administration has proposed further cuts for fiscal year 1983. The summer food service program would be eliminated, and funding would be decreased for the school breakfast and child care food programs. If adopted, these changes would reduce both budget authority and outlays by about 15 percent from baseline levels. Furthermore, the administration has suggested child nutrition could be one of the programs turned back to the states as part of the "new federalism."

SUPPLEMENTAL SECURITY INCOME

Program Description

Supplemental security income (SSI) is a federally administered program that provides cash assistance to the aged, blind, and disabled. Federal eligibility standards and benefit levels are uniform throughout the nation. A person is eligible if he or she is (1) sixty-five years of age or older; (2) has corrected vision of 20/200 or less; or (3) has physical or mental impairment prohibiting employment. Benefits are based on income, living arrangements, and marital status. As of July 1981, the SSI program provided a maximum benefit of $265 per month for an eligible individual and $397 per month for an eligible couple.

Some states supplement the federal SSI benefits. A state supplement is required under federal law for states in which benefits would have been reduced when the state-administered program was replaced by the SSI program in 1974. Some states have also elected to supplement benefits for some or all of their program recipients. States may choose to have the state supplemental benefits administered by the federal government.

In fiscal year 1981, the federal program provided assistance to approximately 3.7 million people at a cost of $7.2 billion. Federally administered state supplemental benefits totaled $1.8 billion and served an additional 448,000 people. The level of state-administered supplemental aid is $200 million.

SSI is an appropriated entitlement. Individuals who meet the eligibility criteria are entitled to benefits, with funding provided by an appropriations act. Eligible individuals have legal recourse if benefits are not provided due to funding shortages. A special provision of the Labor, Health and Human Services, and Education Appropriations Act allows the Department of Health and Human Services to borrow against future appropriations to meet benefit payments. This means that benefits will not be curtailed if the appropriated amount falls short of program needs, but it also means that program costs are not controllable in the appropriations process.

Reconciliation Act Changes

To reduce federal spending, the reconciliation act tightened certain eligibility and payment procedures in the basic SSI authorization act. However, in a separate action, the reconciliation act eliminated the minimum social security benefit for some individuals, causing them to become eligible for SSI. CBO estimated that the net effect of the two actions will be to increase

CBO Baseline and Effect
of Congressional Action During Calendar 1981
(in millions of dollars and percentages)
Account No. 75-0406-609

Category	FY1982 Dollar Level	FY1982 Percent Change	FY1983 Dollar Level	FY1983 Percent Change	FY1984 Dollar Level	FY1984 Percent Change
CBO Baseline						
Budget						
authority	7,799	—	9,174	—	8,411	—
Outlays	7,833	—	9,184	—	8,405	—
Reconciliation Act						
Budget						
authority	7,949	+2	9,416	+3	8,746	+4
Outlays	7,983	+2	9,426	+3	8,740	+4
Final FY 1982 Expenditures						
After All Changes						
Budget						
authority	7,779	0	—	—	—	—
Outlays	7,813	0	—	—	—	—

SSI budget authority and outlays by 2 percent in fiscal year 1982, 3 percent in fiscal year 1983, and 4 percent in fiscal year 1984.

Retrospective Accounting

Income calculations for determining eligibility for the SSI program will be based on an applicant's actual past income rather than projected future income. CBO estimates that this change will lower budget authority and outlays by $30 million in fiscal year 1982, $60 million in fiscal year 1983, and $60 million in fiscal year 1984.

Payments for Vocational Services Provided by States

Until the reconciliation act, advance payments were made to the states for their vocational education for SSI recipients. Under the reconciliation act, the states would only receive payments after an SSI recipient had been in a vocational educational program for a year. CBO surveyed the states and determined that under these new requirements the states would stop running vocational rehabilitation programs for SSI recipients. CBO estimated that this would lower SSI budget authority and outlay levels by $20 million in fiscal year 1982, $18 million in fiscal year 1983, and $15 million in fiscal year 1984.

Elimination of the Social Security Minimum Benefit

Without the minimum benefit, many social security recipients would meet the income test to qualify for the SSI program. CBO estimates that this would cause SSI budget authority and outlays to increase by $200 million in fiscal year 1982, $320 million in fiscal year 1983, and $410 million in fiscal year 1984.

Appropriations and Other Changes

The provision of the reconciliation act that eliminated the social security minimum benefit was amended after the reconcilation act. Under the new legislation, the minimum benefit is eliminated only for new retirees and is kept in place for those currently receiving social security. The new legislation saved the SSI program $185 million in fiscal year 1982, $287 million in fiscal year 1983, and $362 million in fiscal year 1984 from the amounts estimated under the reconciliation act.

Funding for the SSI program is currently being provided under a continuing resolution. Under this resolution, funding is provided at the level requested by the administration in September 1981. Estimated funding requirements have increased slightly since the September estimate, and these additional program costs will be met by borrowing against future appropriations.

Assessment

Although the reconciliation act imposed only modest reductions in the SSI program, one program change is likely to have a significant impact. Changes in the vocational education program will undoubtedly reduce the number of disabled individuals who are eligible for federally sponsored job training and are thus given a chance to enter the job market. This change is also likely to increase the fiscal strain on state rehabilitation agencies, which are already experiencing financial difficulty due to the loss of other federal support. The total fiscal impact of the vocational education amendment on state governments will depend upon whether they choose to support this program with state funds.

The 1983 Reagan budget proposes additional cuts in the SSI program. The proposed changes would reduce benefit levels and restrict program entry. The administration estimated the savings from these proposals at $78 million in fiscal year 1982 and $256 million in fiscal year 1983.

AID TO FAMILIES WITH DEPENDENT CHILDREN

Program Description

The primary purpose of the aid to families with dependent children (AFDC) program is to support needy children in single-parent households. Nearly all AFDC assistance goes to female-headed households, with above average participation occurring in large cities. In addition to the basic program, twenty-three states, the District of Columbia, and Guam provide cash assistance to two-parent households if the father is unemployed. The two-parent program is a relatively minor part of the AFDC program, accounting for less than 6 percent of the AFDC households in fiscal year 1981.

Although AFDC is a federal program, it varies widely from state to state. Each state determines income eligibility and benefit levels. Before reconciliation, federal law did require certain work incentives for program participants. In general, however, states were allowed almost total discretion in determining the amount of support provided through AFDC. In July 1981, the maximum AFDC benefit payment for a family of three ranged from $96 per month in Mississippi to $571 per month in Alaska.

AFDC program costs are shared by federal, state, and local governments. The federal government funds about 54 percent of AFDC benefits, states fund about 40 percent, and localities fund about 6 percent. The rate at which the federal government subsidizes benefit payments varies by state and is based in part on the state's per-capita income relative to the national average. The federal government also subsidizes state administrative costs, training costs, child support enforcement, etc.

In fiscal year 1981, AFDC benefits supported a monthly average of 11.1 million people. The total cost of the program was $14.2 billion, of which $7.7 billion was provided by the federal government.

Eligibility Criteria and Benefit Levels

A household that has dependent children and is otherwise eligible can receive aid if its "countable" monthly income falls below the state's need standard. Each state has its own standard of need. In all states but three, the standard of need is below the federal poverty level. As stated earlier, prior to reconciliation, program recipients who entered the work force received work incentives. "Countable income" for working participants was determined by disregarding from gross earnings the following amounts: (1) $30 of monthly earnings, (2) 30 percent of the remaining monthly earnings, (3) work expenses, and (4) tax deductions. As a consequence, in some states

297

employed AFDC recipients could earn more than twice the state need standard before losing eligibility for AFDC support.

The level of AFDC cash assistance is calculated by subtracting "countable" monthly income from the maximum benefit level. The maximum benefit level is determined by each state and can be equal to or less than the state need standard. In twenty-four states, the maximum benefit level falls short of the state need standard.

AFDC is an appropriated entitlement. Households that meet the eligibility criteria are entitled to benefits under the law. Although an appropriation is necessary, an eligible individual can sue if benefits are not provided due to funding shortages. In addition, a special provision of the Labor, Health and Human Services, and Education Appropriations Act allows the Department of Health and Human Services (HHS) to borrow against future appropriations to meet benefit payments. Therefore, federal AFDC expenditures are not controllable in the appropriations process.

Reconciliation Act Changes

The reconciliation act sought to control federal spending on AFDC not only by reducing federal requirements but also by limiting state discretion. CBO estimated that these proposals would save the federal government $1.1 billion in fiscal year 1982. Total savings provided by the reconciliation act would include not only the federal savings detailed in the CBO estimate but also sizable savings to state and local governments. HHS estimated that state and local government savings for fiscal year 1982 would come to $800 million. Program changes implemented by the reconciliation act reflected six objectives: (1) require work for benefits, (2) change treatment of earnings, (3) change calculation of income, (4) impose categorical eligibility restrictions, (5) tighten program administration, and (6) reduce administrative costs.

1. Require Work for Benefits

The reconciliation act contained three provisions that allow states to permit or require AFDC participants to work in exchange for benefits. Although these are potentially the most radical program changes, CBO estimated no savings from these provisions in fiscal year 1982 and estimated savings of $20 million in fiscal 1983 and $41 million in fiscal year 1984.

2. Change Treatment of Earnings

In three separate actions, the reconciliation act changed the treatment of earnings for employed AFDC recipients. In all cases, the act reduced the

CBO Baseline and Effect
of Congressional Action During Calendar 1981
(in millions of dollars and percentages)
Account No. 75-0412-609

Category	FY1982		FY1983		FY1984	
	Dollar Level	Percent Change	Dollar Level	Percent Change	Dollar Level	Percent Change
CBO Baseline						
Budget authority	6,568	—	8,956	—	9,209	—
Outlays	8,588	—	8,956	—	9,209	—
Reconciliation Act						
Budget authority	5,410	−18	7,558	−16	7,749	−16
Outlays	7,430	−13	7,558	−16	7,749	−16
Final FY 1982 Expenditures After All Changes						
Budget authority	5,461	−17	—	—	—	—
Outlays	7,483	−13	—	—	—	—

disregards allowed for employed AFDC recipients, thereby tightening eligibility criteria for the working poor. CBO estimated the combined savings from these three proposals at $425 million, $433 million, and $441 million in fiscal years 1982, 1983, and 1984 respectively.

Limit Earnings Disregards. The reconciliation act allows deductions for earned income ($30 per month plus one-third of the remaining amount) during the first four months of employment only. Prior law set no time restriction.

Limit Work Expense Disregards. Under prior federal law, no limit was set on the amount of work expenses that could be disregarded from gross income. State practices in this area varied widely. Reconciliation placed a cap on child care disregards at $160 per child per month and a cap on other work-related disregards at $75 per month. Reconciliation also required that these disregards be deducted from earnings before the work incentive was applied, thereby reducing the amount of that deduction.

Earned Income Tax Credit. Low-income families are eligible for tax credits or rebates through the earned income tax credit (EITC). Reconciliation required that in determining income eligibility states assume that eligible parents received advance payments of the EITC regardless of whether or not they had applied for it.

3. Change Calculation of Income

In six separate actions, the reconciliation act modified the way income and resources are calculated for eligibility purposes. In all cases, the eligibility criteria were tightened, thereby reducing the number of people eligible for AFDC benefits. CBO estimated the combined savings from these proposals at $244 million, $251 million, and $255 million in fiscal years 1982, 1983, and 1984 respectively.

Limit Resources. Although federal law provided no resource limit for participation in the AFDC program, federal regulation had set the resource limit at $2,000 per person. States could exclude a dwelling, personal effects, an automobile, and income-producing property when determining a household's resources. The reconciliation act tightened the resource requirement by limiting resources to $1,000 per household. States can exclude a house and one motor vehicle from consideration, or they can restrict the resource limit even further.

Treat Federal Benefits as Income. Although the Food Stamp Act had prohibited state and federal benefit programs from considering food stamps as income, some states did take the availability of food stamps into account when setting AFDC benefit levels. The reconciliation act explicitly allows states to consider food stamps and housing subsidies as income.

Limit Gross Income Eligibility. Under prior law, gross income was not a determinant of AFDC eligibility. Reconciliation limited AFDC benefits to households with a gross income of 150 percent of the state need standard.

Treatment of Lump-Sum Income. Reconciliation changed the treatment of lump-sum payments. Under prior law, lump-sum income was treated as "countable" income in the month received and unspent amounts included in resources in following months. The new law requires that the lump sum be divided by the monthly state need standard and be considered income for the calculated number of months.

Inclusion of a Step-Parent's Income. Under prior law, the Supreme Court had determined that a step-parent's income could not be considered available except in a limited number of situations. Reconciliation requires a portion of a step-parent's income to be treated as available for support of the AFDC stepchild.

Inclusion of Income of Alien's Sponsor. For purposes of AFDC eligibility, a specified portion of the income of an alien's sponsor is considered to be available for support of the alien for three years after the alien's entry into the United States.

4. Restrict Categorical Eligibility

The reconciliation act also placed categorical restrictions on AFDC eligibility. Each of these provisions eliminates certain groups from participation in the AFDC program. CBO estimated the federal savings from these provisions at $121 million, $126 million, and $130 million in fiscal years 1982, 1983, and 1984 respectively.

Prohibit Payment to Strikers. Prior law stipulated that states that participated in the two-parent assistance program for the unemployed could deny benefits to a household if the unemployment had resulted from a strike. The reconciliation act specifically prohibits AFDC eligibility for the household of a striker.

Eliminate Payment for Children Over Eighteen. Prior law allowed participation of a child in the AFDC program up to age twenty if the child was a student. Reconciliation ends a child's eligibility at age eighteen but allows state discretion in extending AFDC support through age eighteen if the child is still in high school.

Restrict Eligibility for Pregnant Women. In cases in which a woman has no children, reconciliation precludes a pregnant woman from receiving AFDC benefits until the sixth month of pregnancy.

Unemployed Parent. Reconciliation limits the participation of two-parent households to those in which the *principal* earner is unemployed.

5. Tighten Program Administration

In keeping with the Reagan administration's desire for tighter program administration, the reconciliation act included two mechanisms for stricter administrative control and five measures for stricter enforcement of child support collection. CBO estimated the federal savings from these proposals at $247 million, $440 million, and $458 million in fiscal years 1982, 1983, and 1984 respectively.

Retrospective Accounting and Monthly Reporting. Under prior law, states could choose whether to base monthly benefits on actual income in the previous month or on estimated future income. Reconciliation requires states to base benefits on the prior month's income. Reconciliation further requires monthly reporting by recipients of relevant household information if savings anticipated from this provision are estimated to be greater than the cost of administering the provision.

Recover Overpayments/Pay Underpayments. Although federal law did not stipulate a mechanism for dealing with incorrect payments, federal regulation allowed states to recoup overpayments and most states had a recovery program. The reconciliation act specifically requires states to recover AFDC overpayments and correct underpayments.

Child Support Enforcement. Five provisions of the reconciliation act contain measures to encourage payment of child support. One provision imposes a fee for support collected on behalf of non-AFDC households.

6. Reduce Administrative Costs

Finally, the reconciliation act included two measures to reduce federal administrative costs. CBO estimated the federal savings from these provisions at $121 million, $128 million, and $135 million in fiscal years 1982, 1983, and 1984 respectively.

Eliminate Payments Under $10. Under prior law, most states made payments to AFDC participants regardless of the size of the benefit. Reconciliation instructs the states not to pay   benefits of less than $10.

Reduce Federal Contribution for Training Costs. Under previous law, the federal government subsidized 75 percent of state and local training costs. Reconciliation reduced this subsidy to 50 percent.

Administrative Regulations

On September 21, 1981, HHS published interim rules designed to allow implementation of the reconciliation act by October 1, 1981. Because of the short time between enactment of the reconciliation bill and the desired implementation date, the entire rules procedure was considered too time consuming and inefficient. The published interim rules restated provisions of the reconciliation act.

Appropriations Process Changes

Funding for AFDC is currently being provided under a continuing resolution. The funding level specified in the continuing resolution was the administration's estimate of program costs as of September 1981. This funding level is likely to fall short of program expenses. However, because the program can borrow against future appropriations, no program cuts are anticipated.

Assessment

Beginning in the early 1970s, federal law placed greater restrictions on the AFDC program. The resulting hodgepodge of federal and state regulations produced relative inequities not only among states but among participants in the same state. These inequities, together with the growing national antiwelfare sentiment, made reform of the AFDC program inevitable. Many reform proposals adopted in the reconciliation act were not new. One proposal had been made by the Ford administration; six proposals had been made by the Carter administration.

The impact of these program changes must be assessed in terms of two distinct audiences: the state and local governments responsible for administering the program and the program participants. First, state and local governments appear likely to save money from these changes. Although the reconciliation act provided a mechanism for delaying the implementation of the new policies, the majority of states implemented the changes immediately. This might suggest that state and local governments were anxious to reap the savings from the reconciliation act at a time when they were experiencing financial hardship.

The second impact of these program changes is, of course, on program participants. Shortly after passage of the reconciliation act, the Department of Health and Human Services estimated that 18 percent of AFDC families and 19 percent of AFDC children would either be dropped from the program or receive lower benefits as a result of the law.

By far the largest dollar impact of the reconciliation act was on the employed participants. One primary focus of the reconciliation act was on reducing the number of working poor eligible for AFDC assistance. The total fiscal impact of dropping these participants from the rolls is difficult to measure. In states where there is no medically needy program, former AFDC recipients will lose medicaid coverage, reducing both federal and state costs. The working poor who retain their jobs despite the loss of AFDC benefits will not qualify for state general assistance in most states. Therefore, state financial requirements should not increase for these former participants. The loss of AFDC benefits will reduce household income and increase the use of food stamps, a federally funded program. Finally, it is too early to tell whether the reduction or loss of AFDC and medicaid benefits will act as a disincentive to work and force households back to total financial dependence on welfare. This outcome would increase both federal and state costs.

The fiscal year 1983 Reagan budget included additional cuts in the AFDC program for fiscal year 1982. By fiscal year 1983, these proposed reductions would save the federal government an estimated $1.2 billion of the amount required under current legislation. These proposals strengthen the work requirements and increase the amount of income considered "countable."

LOW-INCOME ENERGY ASSISTANCE BLOCK GRANT

Program Description

The Home Energy Assistance Act of 1980 authorized direct grants to off-set the rising energy costs of eligible households (owners and renters) and of assisted housing projects. States administered the program, but had to have plans approved by the Office of Family Assistance in the Department of Health and Human Services (HHS) before funds could be disbursed. States received 100 percent reimbursement for funds distributed to low-income households; 7.5 percent of the reimbursement could be used for state administrative costs. In 1981, Congress appropriated $1.85 billion to make such reimbursements. Outlays totaled $1.73 billion in fiscal year 1981.

Reconciliation Act Changes

The reconciliation act shifted administrative responsibility for the energy assistance program to the states and sets minimum standards for control and reporting of the use of funds. The secretary of HHS "may not prescribe the manner in which states will comply," so that states will have maximum control over the block grant. In addition, the reconciliation act authorized the appropriation of $1.9 billion for each of fiscal years 1982, 1983, and 1984. The act thereby reduced the budget authority levels contained in the CBO baseline by $372 million in fiscal year 1982, $672 million in fiscal year 1983, and $992 million in fiscal year 1984. The cuts represent decreases of 17, 26, and 35 percent respectively. Estimated outlay reductions are the same as budget authority reductions.

The act further specified administrative and procedural changes for the block grant as discussed below.

Distribution Formula

Appropriated funds will be apportioned to each state based on its relative share of fiscal year 1981 funds available under the old program. If a state violates provisions of the act, the secretary of HHS may withhold funds. A state may carry over to the second year up to 25 percent of its allocation. Between 0.1 and 0.5 percent of appropriated funds must be allotted to the territories. The secretary may reserve amounts from states' allotments for direct funding of Indian tribes. At state option, the secretary can make direct payments to supplemental security income recipients.

**CBO Baseline and Effect
of Congressional Action During Calendar 1981
(in millions of dollars and percentages)
Account No. 75-0420-609**

| | FY1982 | | FY1983 | | FY1984 | |
Category	Dollar Level	Percent Change	Dollar Level	Percent Change	Dollar Level	Percent Change
CBO Baseline						
Budget						
authority	2,247	—	2,547	—	2,867	—
Outlays	2,247	—	2,547	—	2,867	—
Reconciliation Act						
Budget						
authority	1,875	−17	1,875	−26	1,875	−35
Outlays	1,875	−17	1,875	−26	1,875	−35
Final FY 1982 Expenditures After All Changes						
Budget						
authority	1,752[a]	−22	—	—	—	—
Outlays	1,752	−22	—	—	—	—

a. A supplemental appropriation in 1982 restored budget authority to $1,875 million.

Application Process

To receive an allotment, a state must apply each year to the secretary of HHS. The application must include a certification by the governor that the state will comply with thirteen program and administrative requirements. They are: (1) use of funds in accordance with the act, (2) payments only to eligible households, (3) conduct of outreach activities, (4) coordination of related federal and state programs, (5) provision of the highest assistance levels to the lowest income persons, (6) special consideration for previously funded grantees in designating local agencies, (7) establishment of procedures for paying home energy suppliers, (8) assurance that homeowners and renters will be treated equitably, (9) limitation of administrative expenses (described below), (10) establishment of needed fiscal control and accounting procedures, (11) cooperation with federal investigations, (12) provision for public participation in developing the state plan, and (13) provision of fair housing procedures for adversely affected individuals. The secretary may waive assurance requirements in order to promote program objectives, but may not prescribe how states will comply with assurances. After the first year for which funds are received, states must hold public hearings on the proposed use of funds.

Phasing

States were to take over administration of the block grant by October 1, 1981 or as soon as possible. (The act makes no other provisions.)

Transferability

States may transfer up to 10 percent of their allotments to health, social services, and community services block grants.

Audit Requirements

Independent audits are required annually of each state. States must repay amounts found not to have been expended according to law, or the secretary may offset such amounts against state allotments. These unused amounts may be reallocated by the secretary for use by all states in the next fiscal year.

Other Requirements and Provisions

States may make payments directly to eligible households or to suppliers of home energy. States may also use funds to provide tax credits to firms supplying home energy to low-income households at reduced rates; credits may not exceed revenues lost due to rate reductions.

Up to 15 percent of allocated funds may be used by a state for low-cost residential weatherization or other energy-related home repairs for low-income households. Other than for weatherization and repairs, no funds may be used for construction or capital expenditures.

States must have reasonable reserves of funds for energy crisis intervention based on data from previous years. No more than 10 percent of a state's allotment may be used for program planning and administration.

Discrimination on the basis of race, color, national origin, handicap, or sex is prohibited.

Assistance provided under this block grant is not to be considered as income for any other purpose under state or federal law.

Appropriations Process Changes

Because the Labor, Health and Human Services, and Education Appropriations Act has not been passed, funding for this block grant is being provided under a continuing resolution. This resolution reduced authorized spending to $1.8 billion in fiscal year 1982, but a supplemental appropriation returned the funding level to $1.9 billion as authorized by the reconciliation act.

Administrative Regulations

HHS block grant regulations apply to this program, which are discussed on page 239.

Assessment

Although the reconciliation act reduced program funding by nearly 20 percent, the block grant is virtually identical to the energy assistance program it replaced. States have been given greater control over transferring of funds and at least twenty-seven states have shifted part of the funds allocated under the block grant to other block grants. While states have greater control over administration of the grant, they also are responsible for fulfilling the congressional intent of the thirteen administrative and program requirements of the act.

The distribution formula ensures that states will receive the same proportion of total aid appropriated in the future as they received in 1981. However, as described in the block grants, the formula might not reflect states' relative needs as time passes and populations shift.

The 1983 Reagan budget proposes merging the low-income energy assistance block grant with the AFDC emergency assistance program. This expanded block grant would give the states the ability to use funds for non-energy-related crises as well as energy assistance. The budget proposal calls for substantial cuts in the program—budget authority would fall from $1.9 billion in 1982 to $1.3 billion in fiscal year 1983.

REFUGEE ASSISTANCE

Program Description

The refugee assistance program fully reimburses states for cash assistance, medical assistance, and social services to refugees for up to three years after their arrival in the United States. Most of those served by this program are Cuban and Haitian refugees who came to the United States in 1980 and 1981. A relatively small and declining amount of the program's expenditures are for a program that is specifically directed at those Cuban refugees who arrived between 1962 and 1968. In fiscal year 1981 all the programs funded under this account received an appropriation of $902 million, resulting in outlays of $726 million.

In fiscal year 1981, 59 percent of expenditures were for state and volunteer assistance to refugees. The other 31 percent was for reimbursement of the state share of federal income and medical assistance and social services assistance. Expenditures for this last category, therefore, were driven by the number of refugees and the degree to which they required such programs as aid to families with dependent children (AFDC) and medicaid.

Reconciliation Act Changes

The reconciliation act lowered the program's authorization of appropriations limit to $583 million, causing an 11 percent drop in the program's budget authority for fiscal year 1982 from CBO's current policy level. This drop implies a 4 percent decline in outlays. The figures in the accompanying table assume that this authorization of appropriations limit will continue in place in fiscal years 1983 and 1984. This, however, will require further congressional action.

Appropriations and Other Changes

The program is currently funded under the November 1981 continuing resolution, which further reduced its fiscal year 1982 budget authority level by $23 million. Thus, at the end of the first session of the 97th Congress, budget authority for the program had been cut by 14 percent below CBO's current policy level. This led to an outlay reduction of 9 percent below fiscal year 1982 current policy outlays.

The continuing resolution combined six refugee assistance line-items into a single category of refugee assistance and two entrance assistance line-items into a single category of operating costs. The object of this change was to

CBO Baseline and Effect
of Congressional Action During Calendar 1981
(in millions of dollars and percentages)
Account No. 75-0473-609

Category	FY1982 Dollar Level	FY1982 Percent Change	FY1983 Dollar Level	FY1983 Percent Change	FY1984 Dollar Level	FY1984 Percent Change
CBO Baseline						
Budget authority	652	—	636	—	530	—
Outlays	675	—	646	—	594	—
Reconciliation Act						
Budget authority	583	−11	569	−11	474	−11
Outlays	648	−4	578	−11	531	−11
Final FY 1982 Expenditures After All Changes						
Budget authority	560	−14	—	—	—	—
Outlays	613	−9	—	—	—	—

give the Department of Health and Human Services greater flexibility to respond to the needs of refugees. The Reagan administration seeks to increase its flexibility by requesting in its fiscal year 1983 budget that these two new categories be combined into a single line-item.

Administrative Regulations

On December 11, 1981 the Social Security Administration and the Department of Health and Human Services issued a proposed rule in the *Federal Register* modifying the conditions of providing cash and medical assistance in the refugee resettlement program (RRP) and the Cuban-Haitian entrant program (CHEP). This new rule would shorten the special assistance to the states in connection with the RRP from thirty-six to eighteen months. This would lead to a decline in the level of federal reimbursements for refugee cash and medical assistance.

The federal government will continue to reimburse states and localities for their share of income and medical costs for the second eighteen months through general aid disbursements. In determining refugee eligibility for refugee cash assistance during this period, states would apply their AFDC need standard, excluding one-third of the applicant's income or other applicable disregards.

During this second eighteen-month period, states have the option of providing support for refugees through their general assistance programs (GA) rather than through federal income maintenance and medical programs. The states would be reimbursed for their general assistance program refugee costs. Because general assistance payments average roughly half the level of AFDC payments, states that adopt this option would lower their and the federal government's costs by providing lower levels of benefits to refugees.

The stated objectives of the rule are to reduce the likelihood of unnecessary welfare dependence resulting from extended periods of special support, and to reduce the degree of special treatment offered to refugees, which would lead to unequal treatment of various low-income groups. A major objective, however, is to limit the program's expenditures by shifting its recipients from federal entitlements to state programs with lower benefit levels.

Assessment

As indicated, the refugee assistance program is in large measure an appropriated entitlement. Its costs are driven by the number of refugees and their need and ability to take advantage of income maintenance and health programs.

During 1981 the Reagan administration proposed, and the Congress enacted, cuts in the program under the assumption that the administration's announced curtailment of immigration from Cuba and Haiti would lead to a decline in the refugee population. Unfortunately for those seeking program savings, the decline in the economy increased the use of income maintenance and health services by refugees. Thus, in its fiscal year 1983 budget the administration has projected a 19 percent increase in fiscal year 1982 budget authority and a 69 percent increase in fiscal year 1982 outlays beyond CBO's current policy levels. This is a classic example of how changes in the economy can eliminate expected savings. The administration's new regulations appear to be an attempt to reduce the chances that this will pose a future problem by giving the states the opportunity to shift refugees in need of assistance to general assistance programs, where benefit levels are much lower than those of the equivalent federal programs.

PART 3

Initial Assessment of Effects

Initial Effects
of the Fiscal Year 1982 Reductions
in Federal Domestic Spending

By Richard P. Nathan, Philip M. Dearborn,
Clifford A. Goldman, and Associates

President Reagan moved quickly on domestic issues in his first year in office. In mid-February 1981, he proposed a series of major changes in domestic policy in the form of revisions to the federal budget for fiscal year 1982. The most surprising fact was not so much that these major proposals were set forth so quickly, but that so much of the Reagan program was enacted five months later in the Omnibus Budget Reconciliation Act of 1981.

In the spring of 1981, as it became increasingly apparent that important, if not historic, changes were likely to be made, the Princeton Urban and Regional Research Center began work on the design of a study on how such changes would affect state and local governments and the people they serve. The result of the planning process was the initiation of this field network evaluation study, supported by the Ford Foundation, based on field evaluations in a representative sample of fourteen states as well as one major city in each of the fourteen states, thirteen suburban jurisdictions, and thirteen rural towns.

This report presents *preliminary* observations on the effects of the fiscal year 1982 domestic budget cuts and related policy changes in part of the sample: the fourteen state governments and fourteen major cities (see table 3.1). These observations were made for the period between October 1 and December 31, 1981—the first quarter of federal fiscal year 1982. A report on observations from the full sample for the full fiscal year will be issued in 1983, along with other reports and special analyses.

TABLE 3.1
States and Large Cities in Sample

States and cities	Region	1980 Population (in thousands)
Arizona	West	2,718
Phoenix		765
California	West	23,669
Los Angeles		2,966
Florida	South	9,740
Orlando		128
Illinois	N. Central	11,418
Chicago		3,005
Massachusetts	Northeast	5,737
Boston		563
Mississippi	South	2,521
Jackson		203
Missouri	N. Central	4,917
St. Louis		453
New Jersey	Northeast	7,364
Newark		329
New York	Northeast	17,557
Rochester		242
Ohio	N. Central	10,797
Cleveland		574
Oklahoma	South	3,025
Tulsa		361
South Dakota	N. Central	690
Sioux Falls		81
Texas	South	14,228
Houston		1,594
Washington	West	4,130
Seattle		494

The Study

This study focuses on what has been happening in state and local government as a result of policy changes made in Washington. Most of the money saved by the fiscal year 1982 budget reductions was saved in programs administered by state and local governments. Different state or local governments will respond to federal policy changes in different ways, depending on such factors as the government's fiscal situation, demographic conditions, and the political outlook of its decision makers. The challenge for researchers who want to study the effects of federal policy changes is first to identify them and second to account for the influence of variations in the characteristics and conditions of state and local governments.

This is a formidable task. The American federal system is not tidy. Its great diversity and dynamism present a substantial challenge to researchers. There are nearly forty thousand "general-purpose" governments in the United States—counties, cities, towns, townships—and another forty thousand units that the Census Bureau classifies as "special-purpose governments," including fifteen thousand independent school districts.

In this complex policy setting, no existing set of uniform data can be used for the nation as a whole to answer questions about the services reduced as a result of the Reagan administration's domestic policy changes, and the groups affected by those changes. Federal budget data do not provide the needed information on the state and local programs and activities affected. Census data on state and local government expenditures provide only limited information on the response of states, localities, and nonprofit organizations to national policy changes. Likewise, budget documents and financial reports from state and local governments do not provide detailed, comparable information on the services and groups affected by national policy changes.

We have used a field network evaluation approach as a way of collecting data and conducting analyses on a uniform basis.[1] The field evaluations are being conducted by academic economists and political scientists, referred to in this report as associates. All of the field research associates are residents of the areas they are studying and participate on a part-time basis in this research. Many of them have participated in earlier field evaluation studies going back to 1972.[2] The field associates interview state, local, and inter-

1. For a description and discussion of the field network evaluation methodology, see Richard P. Nathan, "The Methodology for Field Network Evaluation Studies," in Walter Williams et al., *Studying Implementation: Methodological and Administrative Issues* (Chatham, N.J.: Chatham House, 1982).

2. Earlier field network evaluation studies were conducted, beginning in 1972, of the general revenue sharing program, the community development block grant program, and the public service employment component of the Comprehensive

est-group officials and collect and analyze the records and reports of the individual agencies affected by changes in federal policy. They report on the situations in the jurisdictions they are studying, using a reporting format developed jointly by the associates and the central staff. This format ensures a high degree of uniformity in the types of information that the associates gather and in the analyses they conduct.

This report contains three appendixes. The first lists the field associates for this study, their affiliation, and the jurisdictions they are studying. Appendix B consists of a set of comments by field research associates excerpted from the transcript of a conference on the field research held at Princeton University on March 15, 1982. Appendix C is the report form for the field research for this study.[3]

When the field associates completed their reports on the first three months of federal fiscal year 1982, they began collecting more detailed data for the entire fiscal year for the full sample of fifty-four jurisdictions. For this purpose, associates use "major program change forms" (see appendix C). These forms call for information on the dollar effects of the 1981 cuts and policy changes, and for analyses of their fiscal, employment, programmatic, incidence, institutional, and administrative effects presented in a standardized way.

Major Findings

This report covers the findings from the first stage of the study. It provides a framework for considering the fiscal year 1982 changes and highlights some of the early and emerging points about their effects. Five points stand out:

● *First, the cuts that were made in federal domestic spending in fiscal year 1982 affected poor people—especially the "working poor"—more than they affected the treasuries of state and local governments.* Although there were exceptions, state and local governments as a rule did not replace lost federal aid for the poor with their own revenues. We refer to this behavior as *ratifying* the federal cuts—that is, allowing such benefits and programs to be reduced. (By "ratify," we do not imply that the jurisdictions necessarily approved of or willingly endorsed the cuts, but simply that they passed them on without using their own money to make up for them.)

Employment and Training Act (CETA). The work began, and most of the research was conducted, under the auspices of The Brookings Institution.

3. The report form has two parts. The first is for baseline data and was completed for state governments and major cities at the end of the first quarter of the federal fiscal year 1982; these are the data used in this report.

- *Second, other fiscal problems—the worsening recession, legal limits on spending and revenues, and the effects of earlier tax cuts—were of more immediate importance to most state and local governments than were the federal aid cuts.* The state and local governments were preoccupied with these problems and were largely unable to replace lost federal funds, even if they wanted to. They frequently adopted various coping and delaying strategies to put off dealing with the fiscal year 1982 cuts for as long as they possibly could.

- *Third, the block grants, which tended to have high public visibility in the first year of the Reagan administration, did not result in the announced 25 percent cuts in spending in the early period, although there are indications that over time the cuts will have greater effects on spending and programs, and will produce important institutional changes.* The early budgetary effects of the block grants tended to be muted for a variety of reasons. Their impact on political processes and institutions will take time to materialize.

- *Fourth, nonprofit organizations (particularly community-based organizations) appear to have been among the major victims of the cuts made in 1981.* While there is some early evidence of greater and compensatory efforts on the part of philanthropic organizations such as the United Way, local nonprofit organizations lost CETA workers and experienced funding cuts under the new block grant and other programs. Some of them went out of existence.

- *Fifth, the rapid pace of the process for making budget cuts in 1981 and its constantly shifting character created confusion and uncertainty among state and local government officials.* Under these conditions, the responses of state and local governments were generally hurried and short-term accommodations, and they do not necessarily foreshadow the ultimate effects. It is possible that, as the Reagan administration has claimed, its program will stimulate longer-run increases in the efficiency of the domestic public sector. These and other institutional effects of the Reagan program will be a major focus of the research in the future.

In elaborating on and explaining these findings, this report first reviews the overall setting for state and local governments of the fiscal year 1982 budget cuts and domestic policy changes. The section that follows this review describes the effects of the changes in five major program areas.

THE EFFECTS OF THE 1982 CUTS ON GOVERNMENTS

This section considers the size of the cuts in federal domestic spending made in fiscal year 1982, the fiscal condition of state and local governments in 1981, the way these governments have treated federal grants-in-aid in the past, and some of the strategies available to them for coping with federal aid cuts.

Cuts in Federal Domestic Spending

As part 1 of this volume makes clear, estimates of the size of the 1982 cutbacks in federal domestic spending can vary widely. An estimate based on changes in budget authority will differ from one focusing on shifts in outlays, and different assumptions about the baseline will produce different estimates of how the Reagan budget differs from what otherwise would have been the levels of federal spending. Estimates of total reductions in the 232 federal budget accounts affected by the reconciliation act range from a high of $51 billion in budget authority and $33 billion in outlays to a low of $37 billion in budget authority and $15 billion in outlays (see chapter 4).[4] These cuts amount to between 10 percent and 7 percent of current policy budget authority for all spending in fiscal year 1982 aside from defense spending and interest on the national debt, and between 7 percent and 3 percent of all outlays.

We believe estimates in the lower range should be used in assessing the outlay cuts in 1982, as they affected state and local governments, though readers can refer to the data in part 1 and draw their own conclusions. Even when we use the lower estimates, the cuts constitute an important change in direction, coming at the end of a long period of growth in domestic spending and activism in domestic affairs on the part of the federal government. They do not, however, constitute a deep penetration into the 1982 base of federal spending for domestic purposes.

This conclusion is somewhat at variance with the popular view. We think this is because there is a strong tendency for public officials to overstate the size of the cuts. This tendency is not hard to explain. Conservatives tend to exaggerate the fiscal year 1982 cuts because they supported them and want to take credit for them. Liberals also tend to exaggerate the size of the cuts, but for different reasons. They want to create public concern about their impact and build up political support for resisting further cuts.

State and Local Fiscal and Budgetary Conditions

As the Reagan domestic program began to unfold in late summer of 1981, many of the state and local governments in the sample were preoccupied with their own fiscal problems. Especially debilitating was the impact of the recession, which was growing deeper during that period. As a result of the recession and of their dependence on income and sales taxes, several states in the sample were collecting far less in tax revenues than they had

---

4. The $51 billion figure can be found in table 1.9 of chapter 4.

budgeted for fiscal 1982 (which started for most of them on July 1, 1981).

In Ohio, for example, officials were faced with a severe drop in revenues caused by the recession. The field associate reported:

With a predicted general fund deficit of over $1 billion for the biennium 1981-1983, the shortfall in federal aid, while not unimportant, is not the prime mover in the state's reckoning of its current fiscal crisis.

The capsule below describes the way fiscal pressure overwhelmed the federal budget cuts in the state of Washington.

Washington State Fiscal Reversal

The recession had a severe and much greater than expected impact in Washington State. In July 1981, state officials, especially those with the Department of Social and Health Services, prepared plans to replace portions of the federal cuts with state funds. By October, however, the recession had overwhelmed almost all of the plans for substituting state funds for federal aid in programs hard hit by the federal cuts.

Washington's economy was especially vulnerable. Tight monetary policies and high interest rates reduced nationwide demand for new housing, all but halting activity in the state's timber and construction industries. Revenues from the sales tax (the state's major source of revenue) were drastically affected by the slowdown in construction-related purchases. A statewide unemployment rate of 12 percent contributed to the revenue shortfall. The revenue estimates for the state's biennial budget (July 1, 1981 to June 30, 1983) had to be revised three times. In seven months, the original estimates used to plan the state's budget were adjusted downward by $1 billion. The shortfall created serious cash-flow problems that forced the state to borrow on future revenues to meet current expenditures. Between September 1981 and spring 1982, Moody's and Standard & Poor's each reduced the state's bond rating twice. The Washington associate observed:

Prior to October, a good deal of attention had been given to the federal cuts on an agency-by-agency and a statewide basis. All of that was quickly cast aside, as were the plans to replace cuts in federal grants, when the state's fiscal problems exploded so forcefully onto the scene.

In October 1981, Florida budget officials lowered their estimate of revenues for the fiscal year that had started July 1 by $55 million, and expected a further reduction of $100 million. Mississippi officials found that their forecast of revenues from the personal income tax was between 30 percent and 50 percent too high.

As soon as state officials saw the revenues dropping below estimates, they began to reduce expenditures and draw on general fund surpluses. Some states were able to raise taxes to maintain the balanced budgets that their constitutions mandated. Other states had previously enacted tax reductions that governors and legislators were reluctant to reverse for political reasons.

In South Dakota:

Despite the decline in relative tax take, political leaders seek to avoid new taxes at all costs. This is the position taken by Republican Gov. William Janklow.

Officials in Texas had a similar attitude. The associate in that state reported:

Texas will not suffer fiscally as a result of the Reagan program. Although Texas receives a substantial portion of revenue from the federal government, the state has exhibited a willingness to ratify any federal movement to fiscal conservatism. A federal shortfall will simply result in a reduction in services.

Overall, most of the jurisdictions in the sample faced strained economic conditions. In some states and cities, decision makers may have wanted to use their own revenue sources to make up for the cuts in federal grants, but were unable to do so because they faced fiscal problems caused by tax limitations. The Massachusetts story illustrates this point.

Massachusetts Tax Limit Problems

Massachusetts and Boston were preoccupied with fiscal problems caused in part by self-imposed tax limits that overshadowed any immediate effects of federal spending cuts. Proposition 2 1/2, approved by voters in November 1980, restricts the amount of property tax revenue collected by cities and towns to 2.5 percent of the full market value of property. The property tax is the only broad-based tax that localities in Massachusetts are allowed to impose, and more than 80 percent of all revenue raised by local governments within the state comes from the property tax. Localities taxing above the 2.5 percent rate must reduce their tax revenues by 15 percent per year until they reach the maximum rate. Cities and towns already below the maximum rate cannot increase taxes by more than 2.5 percent per year. The result of Proposition 2 1/2 was that local governments were expected to collect an estimated $486 million less from property taxes in 1982 than they had in 1981.

This property tax limit did not directly affect state revenues, but it did put pressure on the state to help replace lost local revenues. Eventually, the state came up with $286 million in new local aid. To raise this additional aid, the state made large cuts in state services and employment. The Massachusetts associate observed that the search for new local aid by the state took precedence over any fiscal response to the federal cuts: "While state officials had access to reasonably good information on the Reagan program, the publicity and political energy focused on the fallout from Proposition 2 1/2. Straining to find as much money as possible for local aid, state legislators were in no mood to take a serious look at the potential losses from the federal cuts."

Proposition 2 1/2 had a greater impact in Boston. The city was already under extreme fiscal stress, which was compounded by Proposition 2 1/2. Before the tax limit, Boston's tax rate was approximately 10 percent of the city's assessed property values. The limit meant a loss of $77.8 million in property tax revenues to the city. Anticipating the effects of the cuts, the city laid off approximately 1,850 city-funded workers in its 1981 fiscal year. Between July 1981 and January 1982, another 1,000 workers were laid off. The bulk of the cuts—82 percent—came in police, fire, health, and hospital services. As a result of the city's fiscal problems, Moody's and Standard & Poor's suspended Boston's bond rating. "Virtually all capital projects have been stopped, some in midstream." The associates noted that Proposition 2 1/2 and its fiscal impact precluded efforts to replace federal spending cuts: "Proposition 2 1/2 was the main preoccupation of most city officials; its financial impact dwarfed the impact of the federal cuts. . . . The situation might have been different had there been city funds to offset the federal cuts."

In California, the associate reported:

The first announcement of Reagan's proposed cuts coincided with the depletion of the post-Proposition 13 state surplus and the consideration of the fiscal year 1981−82 state budget with a projected deficit of $355 million. Therefore, state officials were already faced with tough decisions.

In some governments, the federal cuts were not replaced for political or ideological reasons. Retrenchment was the politically popular theme; few politicians opposed it.

In Houston, the associate reported:

There's no question that the city has the financial capacity to deal with most of these pressures. However, Houston still remains a low-tax, basic-service city, which makes it politically difficult to expand services, implement new programs, or raise taxes.

Likewise, for Tulsa, the associates reported:

Major public officials not only accept but also support the Reagan budget reductions. This staunchly conservative city feels the federal government has long been too large.

And in Arizona:

The prevailing retrenchment climate and the local media support the Reagan program cuts in this state.

State and Local Treatment of Federal Grants

Although federal grants-in-aid to states and localities grew steadily from the mid-sixties through the seventies, state and local governments tend not to regard federal aid dollars "just like any other dollars." Often federal dollars come encumbered with their own bureaucracies and purposes. Public agencies and outside interest groups at the state and local levels seek to have these dollars used for new and "innovative" purposes. Generalist officials as a result tend to be wary of federal dollars, and see them as a secondary and generally unreliable source of funds—"secondary" because of the claims made against them and "unreliable" because of the possibility—indeed, often the likelihood—that the federal government will change its mind and reduce funding for a particular program or change the rules for its use. This possibility of federal aid cuts or major rules changes make state and local officials cautious about "getting hooked" on federal aid for regular and continuing operating functions.

These generalizations do not apply to all federal grants and recipient governments. General revenue sharing funds, for example, are very flexible. Most local governments treat them "just like any other dollar." In addition, fiscally hard-pressed jurisdictions are more likely to use federal aid for basic services such as police, fire, streets, and sanitation, and thus absorb these resources into their own fiscal bloodstream as a substitute for their own local revenues.[5]

Even for governments that resist becoming dependent on federal aid, there are some federal aid programs that as a practical matter make it very hard to do so. For example, operating grants for mass transit systems involve functions that have to be continued with or without federal aid. Therefore, a cut in federal aid for mass transit operations does require compensatory action—a cut in service, an increase in fares, or replacement with state or local funds. Each alternative is politically difficult to implement. Similarly, a reduction in the percentage of medicaid costs for which the federal government reimburses state or local governments does not, by itself, limit the entitlement of recipients to health services or the obligation of the state and local governments to pay their bills. Difficult legislative action is needed in this case to change eligibility rules, reduce services, or raise replacement funds.

To summarize, although there are exceptions, most state and local officials under most conditions do not want to become dependent on federal money for basic services. They tend to appropriate federal aid funds only if

5. For a more extensive discussion, see James W. Fossett, *Federal Grants and American Cities: The Politics of Dependence* (Washington, D.C.: The Brookings Institution, forthcoming).

and when they receive them. If federal aid funds for a particular activity are cut, the jurisdiction simply curtails the activity by spending less on it. This approach avoids unbalanced budgets, as well as the need to take the politically difficult actions of raising new revenues or cutting services. Most of the federal aid cuts in 1982 were of the type that could relatively easily be ratified by states and localities—i.e., passed along to the ultimate recipients.

Delaying the Effects of the Cuts

Even where federal cuts had a direct effect on state and local budgets, the operation of the federal, state, and local fiscal systems offered several ways of easing the initial effects of the cuts.

Many jurisdictions had unspent balances in federal grants accounts that could be carried forward to offset budget cuts. In Ohio, the associate reported:

> Within individual programs, the immediate impact of the reductions in new federal revenue has been partly offset by the availability of carryover balances from prior-year allocations.

From Missouri, the report was as follows:

> Preventive health programs and mental health programs had a momentary carryover "windfall" effect, which is being spread over a two- to three-year funding period to cushion the funding cuts while additional state and local funding can be developed.

For Jackson, Miss., the associate reported:

> When possible, agencies have juggled funds or used carryover to put off the impact until fiscal year 1983. In other cases, forward funding means the impact of fiscal year 1982 changes will come in fiscal year 1983. For these reasons, planning was concentrated on fiscal year 1983. Fiscal year 1982 is a year of reaction and patchwork.

In one functional area—education—the impact of cuts in federal aid was delayed because these grants are forward funded—that is, appropriated in one year for use in the following year. The effects of the 1982 federal cuts were delayed until the 1983 school year; little or no immediate adjustment was required.

Another coping strategy was possible where federal welfare cuts actually created savings for some state and local governments. This occurred because they were required to spend less in matching funds for AFDC and medicaid after newly ineligible families were removed from the rolls and other changes were made in those programs. Here, a general pattern of response was noted. These "savings" were widely used to replace cuts in social services and to permit delays in making program changes in this area (i.e., under the title XX program).

Another reason the impact of the federal cuts was delayed was the overlapping of fiscal years. If the applicable federal cut in title XX, for example, was 25 percent in federal fiscal year 1982 (beginning October 1981), the loss to a state with the typical July-to-June fiscal year began in its second quarter, and hence was three-fourths of 25 percent for the full state fiscal year.

Block grants require comment here. Most of the states in our sample picked up most of the block grants, but they also tended to defer making changes in funding arrangements. This was possible because, under some of the new block grants, states received as much money or more than they had under the old categorical programs, even though the new block grants cut funding on an annual basis by an average of 25 percent. This effect can be seen, for example, in the alcohol, drug abuse, and mental health block grant and the community services block grant. The grant year for the categorical grants that were merged into these block programs had begun for many states in the middle or latter part of fiscal 1981, so that categorical funding at the previous level was available well into federal fiscal year 1982. The full amount of the new block grant funding, covering the same programs, became available on October 1, 1982. Thus, there was an unintended windfall created by the overlap of the old programs and the new block grant. This meant in some cases that more funds were available in 1982 than would have been available if the new block grant had not been implemented.

Cuts in federal grants for capital purposes, such as highways, wastewater treatment plants, and mass transit, also have a delayed effect, due to the long lead time between the time a grant is made and the time funds are actually spent. Committed funds already in the federal aid pipeline for capital grants were for the most part unaffected by fiscal year 1982 budget actions.

Despite these and other factors that enabled state and local governments to put off the day of reckoning on federal aid cuts in late 1981, the business of doing this was not without its costs and consequences. A mood of confusion and heightened uncertainty was created.

In Newark:
The extent of the cuts is still unknown, which in many ways has heightened the anxiety and inhibited any positive planning. . . . The most common reaction to the cutbacks is both fear and uncertainty.

In Illinois:
There is widespread frustration and uncertainty about federal aid. Major programs are still funded on a temporary basis up through three-fourths of the state fiscal year. Knowledgeable state officials know that Congress can cut or replace funds when they review appropriations or that the president may rescind funds already appropriated. Even for those programs that are not beset with uncertainty, regulations and allocation formulas are, or appear to be to state actors, still up in the air.

In his January 5, 1982, budget message, Oklahoma Gov. George Nigh referred to the uncertainty of the federal budget to justify ratifying federal aid cuts:

I am recommending that the state consider at a later time the possible make up of the loss in federal aid due to the confusion and uncertainty that currently surround the area of reduced federal funds.

MAJOR PROGRAM CHANGES

This section examines the effects of the federal spending cuts and related domestic policy changes for fiscal year 1982 in five selected program areas: AFDC and food stamps, the CETA public service jobs program and grants for the U.S. Employment Service, medicaid, block grants, and capital grants.

We focus on these program areas because they encompass the most important effects of the Reagan domestic program. Changes in the AFDC and food stamp programs, along with related program cuts and changes in the housing and child nutrition programs, primarily affect the poor and especially the working poor—the groups most affected by the fiscal year 1982 changes. The working poor are also the group most strongly affected by the elimination of the CETA public service employment (PSE) program. We include the medicaid program in this section of our report because it is the largest federal aid program, although it was not cut as much as were AFDC, food stamps, and PSE. Effects that are likely to stem from the establishment of new block grants and the expansion of existing ones is an important topic, though it needs to be treated in this early stage of the research in a preliminary and tentative way. The same is true of the final subject treated in this section, capital grants.

AFDC, Food Stamps, and Other Entitlement Programs

As governor of California, Ronald Reagan successfully pursued a policy of increasing welfare benefits for the very poor and decreasing them for the working poor. The term "working poor" refers to persons with income other than welfare (usually earnings from employment) who are close to the poverty line but do not depend entirely on public aid. The rationale generally given for reducing welfare benefits to the working poor is that dependence on government is debilitating, and that the best way to provide incentives for employable persons to be self-supporting is not to support them unless it is absolutely necessary to do so.[6] In 1981, the Reagan administration was very successful in achieving a set of interlocking reductions and changes in welfare programs to remove the working poor from welfare programs or to cut their benefits.

---

6. For a statement of this position, see chapters 10 and 11 of George Gilder, *Wealth and Poverty* (New York: Basic Books, 1981).

Two points need to be made about evaluating changes in entitlement programs such as AFDC and food stamps. First, their effects take hold over time. This is true of the 1981 changes, some of which were implemented on a delayed or phased basis. Second, the effects of changes in these programs are extremely hard to measure. Data for state and locally administered welfare programs vary widely from one jurisdiction to another in format and quality, and in timing of publication. Even when good data are available, it is difficult to sort out the effects of the Reagan policy from other factors, particularly economic, that influence the size of the welfare rolls.

In this section, we analyze changes made in entitlement programs under two main topics:

1. changes in program characteristics that reduce benefits to poor individuals and families with other outside income, i.e., the working poor; and

2. interactions among programs that (a) cause changes in one entitlement program to reduce benefits in others and (b) cause changes in entitlement programs to be compounded by reductions in service programs that affect the poor.

After discussing these topics, we describe how these changes took effect initially at the state and local levels.

Changes in Program Characteristics

In several programs, including AFDC, housing assistance, and school lunches, the reconciliation act changed the important "benefit-reduction rate." This is the rate at which a recipient's benefits are reduced as a result of his or her earnings. For example, a 100 percent benefit-reduction rate means that benefits are reduced by one dollar for each additional dollar in earnings. Changes in the rules for the AFDC program made in 1981 raised the program's benefit-reduction ratio to close to 100 percent for most working recipients.[7]

Entitlement benefits to the working poor were also reduced in the 1981 Omnibus Budget Reconciliation Act by lowering the amounts that a state can deduct from a recipient's earnings before applying the benefit-reduction rate. In the case of AFDC, for example, the reconciliation act limited the allowable standard deduction for work expenses to a fixed amount ($75 per month).

---

7. The increase in the benefit-reduction rate under AFDC had a delayed impact. The main reason for this increase was the elimination of the provision allowing recipients to deduct $30 each month plus one-third of their monthly earnings in calculating income for purposes of computing their AFDC benefit. The reconciliation act eliminated this deduction after four months, effective October 1, 1981 in most states. The result for purposes of this report is that, while this change was anticipated in the early observations, it was not in effect in this period.

Previously, states had discretion and some allowed higher deductions. A similar cap was placed on child-care deductions.

A third change that reduced welfare benefits to the working poor was the setting of an income ceiling for eligibility. This was done under both the AFDC and food stamp programs in the 1981 reconciliation act. Such ceilings create a "notch" at which a person or family is cut off of welfare. When their income reaches this notch, they lose all welfare benefits.[8]

A recent legislative analysis of the way work incentives are affected by the 1981 changes in state and locally administered and federally aided entitlement programs states the following:

> The proposals enacted in the Omnibus Budget Reconciliation Act of 1981 have reduced the financial gain from wages by about 50 percent for an AFDC recipient who also receives food stamps and public housing benefits. For example, an AFDC mother with children who took a half-time job at the minimum wage in July 1981, before the 1981 act, was able to increase her income (counting after-tax cash, food stamps, and housing benefits) by $111, 38 percent of her $290 wages. However, under the new rules this gain declined to $97 during the first four months of a job, and then shrank to $52, 18 percent of earnings.[9]

Program Interactions

In some cases, changes such as those just discussed interact with other programs. A family that receives AFDC benefits, no matter what the amount, is "categorically eligible" for medicaid benefits. As a result, the biggest loss to a working poor family that is removed from the AFDC rolls is likely to be the loss of medicaid coverage.

Two other factors that do not directly involve entitlements need to be discussed to show how the changes made in 1981 can come together to affect the working poor. One is "workfare." The Reagan administration favors the application of the "work-for-your-welfare" concept, whereby employable welfare recipients are assigned to jobs at the minimum wage for as many hours as needed to earn their welfare benefit. The interlocking nature of the changes in welfare programs can be seen if one recalls that other changes in AFDC, indicated above, have the effect of raising the benefit-reduction rate. The essential rationale of workfare in this setting is that if the benefit-reduction rate is very high (as it is under AFDC) then work incentives presumably are reduced and other approaches to the employment of welfare recipients are

---

8. The ceiling for AFDC was set at 150 percent of the state's standard of need, and for food stamps at 130 percent of the official poverty line. Other changes were made in AFDC that eliminated several narrowly defined classes of recipients—for example, women between three and six months pregnant with their first child.

9. Vee Burke, "Budget Cuts and Financial Work Incentives for Welfare Recipients" (Washington, D.C.: The Library of Congress, Congressional Research Service, March 26, 1982).

needed—i.e., workfare. The 1981 reconciliation act permits states to adopt various forms of "voluntary" workfare programs.

Another way in which the Reagan administration's policy changes can affect the working poor on a cumulative basis concerns social service programs. Reductions made in the social services block grant can produce cuts in day care programs or increases in the fees charged. Both kinds of changes can translate into a loss of care for children in working poor families, which might lead working mothers to leave their jobs. Similarly, reductions made in public health programs can affect the working poor at a time when people in this group who lose medicaid coverage may turn to local health clinics.

Field Assessments of Impact

The reports from field associates bear out this analysis. The associates reported that the effects of the domestic budget cuts and related policy changes made in 1981 were concentrated on the poor, and that within this group the most affected subgroup was the working poor. The following sections describe these effects.

Effects on the Poor. In Massachusetts, the associates reported, "Changes in programs targeted upon the poor seem to have been implemented far faster than other programs." The Ohio associates noted, "Low-income individuals have been the most significantly and adversely affected by changes brought about by the Reagan program." In Los Angeles, "The population groups most affected are the poor, of course, and especially the minority poor."

The associates emphasized that the poor have been primarily affected by cutbacks in the major entitlements—AFDC, food stamps, child nutrition, and medicaid. In Mississippi, "The most significant impacts of Reagan's domestic program are found in the reduced number of persons participating in assistance programs under the new eligibility rules." The New York associate observed, "The impact on people and programs has been greatest in those areas where the federal government makes payments directly to local governments or to individuals."

Further evidence that the Reagan domestic program is affecting the poor as a group is found in reports from many jurisdictions of cutbacks in new construction of housing for low-income families and individuals. The Seattle associate's comments were typical of observations made about the initial effects on the poor of the reconciliation act cuts in the section 8 housing program:

> While the program reductions in this category do not affect the city budget directly, they erode the city's efforts to provide affordable housing for those in need. The drastic cut in funding for housing assistance programs has almost eliminated the main subsidy for low-income housing in Seattle.

The Missouri associates stated that, as a result of the Reagan domestic program and related policy changes, "housing activities across the state are at a virtual standstill."

Data from preliminary reports showed that the Reagan domestic program in the first quarter affected a large number of people, although for many people the loss in benefits from any one program was relatively small.

Several associates indicated that practically all people receiving food stamps in their jurisdictions experienced a benefit reduction. In California, food stamp benefits were eliminated for 16,500 households and reduced for 360,000 households. In Massachusetts, "All 24,000 food stamp households that have earned income will have their benefits reduced." New York State, with a total caseload of 724,000 households, expects more than 9,000 households to become ineligible because eligibility is now restricted to those with gross incomes of no more than 130 percent of the poverty level; almost all food stamp recipients are expected to have their benefits cut.

The Working Poor. Most associates indicated that among the poor, it is the working poor who will be most affected by the Reagan program. Two programs—school lunches and section 8 housing subsidies—are examples of how cuts in entitlement programs hit the working poor hardest.

Several associates pointed out that it is in the reduced-price category that the school lunch cuts have had the widest and most significant effects. This is the part of the program for which the working poor qualify. Most jurisdictions in the sample increased the price of meals to students in the school lunch program to make up for cutbacks in federal subsidies. This resulted in a notable decrease in the number of students participating in the program in some jurisdictions.

In Florida, where there was a twenty-cent increase in the price of "reduced-price" lunches, a drop in participation was reported in forty-four school districts. In Illinois, where meal prices were increased by twenty cents, a 25 percent decrease in participation statewide was expected. For the Rochester City School District, the associate stated, "Fifteen percent fewer children received free lunches during the first quarter. In the reduced-price category, participation among students decreased by almost 18 percent."

For New York State, the associate reported, "The group hit hardest are those above the poverty line who qualify for reduced-price meals. An estimated 60 percent of these children have dropped out of the program." In Sioux Falls, the associate reported: "Most affected are those obtaining reduced-price meals—moderate- to higher-income children."

The section 8 housing program provides another form of income security to the working poor that will be affected by the cuts made in 1981. Although not technically an entitlement, section 8 is an important form of assistance to the poor and near-poor, providing tenants in existing, private-market rental housing with subsidies to help pay their rent. Prior to the reconciliation act, a tenant expected to contribute a maximum of 25 percent of his income toward rent. The reconciliation act raises this contribution by one percentage point per year, to 30 percent. This same increase applies to tenants of public housing, which is subsidized under another federal program. This change will affect large numbers of the poor, especially the near-poor.

On the basis of the effects of changes in these programs and others, associates generally agreed that the working poor were the group of federal aid beneficiaries that was most heavily affected. In Mississippi, "In the first-quarter of fiscal year 1982, there is no question that the low-income population was the most affected, and that the working poor within that group were particularly affected." In Arizona, "From the preliminary evidence, it appears that Arizona is an example of major effects being on the so-called working poor." Likewise, it was reported from Rochester that "the first-quarter effects fell on those with earned income, the working poor."

In Florida, the associates reported that state officials characterized the reconciliation act changes as "the type of changes that affect most the marginally poor, those persons getting by with minimal public assistance who might otherwise drop into the 'truly needy' category."

In contrast, the poor who are eligible for welfare and are not working are said to have felt little impact so far from the changes in entitlement programs. In St. Louis, the associates noted that "since most of these cuts reduce income eligibility thresholds, St. Louis, with its large number of low-income residents, was only slightly affected." In Tulsa, the associate emphasized that "the neediest of local residents will continue to receive benefits." For New York State, officials predicted that the impact of the reconciliation act provisions related to AFDC work expense and earned income deductions would be limited, because only 8 percent of the AFDC population has earned income.

It was too early in the first quarter of fiscal year 1982 to observe much effect of the workfare provision in the reconciliation act cited earlier. However, the capsule below summarizes emerging developments in one jurisdiction.

Massachusetts Workfare Experience
In Massachusetts, Gov. Edward J. King was in strong ideological agreement with the Reagan administration on welfare issues, and had begun planning a workfare program even before the federal statute was in place. According to the associate, however, "Governor King found that despite the increased state discretion implied by the Reagan program, an ideologically

sympathetic governor may well have to share program design decisions with others in the state who are much less favorably inclined to the Reagan approach.''

When the earliest versions of Governor King's workfare proposals became public in mid-November, they immediately aroused opposition from various interest groups and institutions across the state. Welfare recipients, advocates, and service providers strongly opposed a reqiirement in the plan that would force mothers of two-year-olds to either take a minimum-wage job or lose all AFDC benefits. The legislature, too, was opposed to the plan, but primarily because it saw the governor's attempt to make substantive changes in a public benefit program as an executive exercise of what was properly a legislative function. In the face of public protest over the requirements of the workfare proposal and the institutional challenge to legislative authority, the legislature passed a bill requiring that the executive branch submit for legislative approval any state-initiated public benefit eligibility change.

The governor asked the state Supreme Judicial Court to rule on the constitutionality of this new legislation. The court agreed with him that the bill was an ''unconstitutional abrogation of the governor's veto power.'' At this point, opponents of workfare shifted their focus away from the legislature and concentrated instead on the media, and on lobbying nongovernmental organizations and localities. The Catholic archdiocese, a powerful political force in Massachusetts, came out in opposition to the plan, labeling it ''antifamily.'' Gradually, a growing number of city and town councils announced that they would refuse to participate. State employee unions, fearing that the state would replace union workers with workfare participants, announced their opposition.

In February, the King administration entered into a written agreement with representatives from the legislature, public employee unions, and welfare organizations, which shifted the workfare program from a mandatory to voluntary basis and provided more job training opportunities. The final plan is still under negotiation.

The evidence to date indicates that reductions in individual entitlement programs have had a widespread effect, and that it is the cumulative effect of multiple cuts that has done the most harm to the working poor. The working poor as a group have been affected both by changes in such entitlement programs as AFDC, food stamps, medicaid, and child nutrition, and by cutbacks in social services. The Cleveland associate reported:

> About 4,000 adults in Cuyahoga County have been taken off the welfare rolls; in some cases, so have their children. Virtually no job training or placement exists to assist them in a transition to work. Their food stamp allotment will most likely

be cut in coming months, their children will have even lower chances than before of getting special attention in the Cleveland public schools; their public transportation costs have already gone up 50 percent and will rise again during 1982. Many of them may lose some medicaid benefits.

Future observations of this study will gather more detailed information on the effects of cuts in entitlement programs.

Employment Programs

The largest single cut in grants to state and local governments for fiscal 1982 was the reduction in the CETA program. Most state and local governments, however, were prepared for the demise of the public service employment (PSE) component, which was by far the biggest cut in the overall CETA program. They had expected it and planned for it. However, thousands of people lost their PSE jobs as a result of this action. They were the main victims. Such local public services as parks and recreation were especially affected, as were nonprofit organizations.

Effects on Governments

The reactions of state and local government officials to the end of PSE varied little. From Houston: "Elimination of jobs in the PSE programs has had no significant impact on public employment in Houston." From Rochester: "The immediate service and fiscal effects on Rochester of the elimination of CETA-PSE jobs were minimal." And from Chicago: "CETA-PSE was one of the few straightforward cases where one knew exactly what was going to happen and when."

Even if they were forewarned, why didn't local governments protest the demise of the PSE program? The answer, we believe, lies in the 1978 amendments to CETA, which tightened eligibility requirements under PSE to focus on a more disadvantaged group and reduced the wage ceiling for PSE workers. The Brookings Institution and the Princeton Urban and Regional Research Center conducted a field network evaluation study of the PSE program. Observations were made in a representative sample of recipient jurisdictions both before and after the 1978 amendments took effect: in July and December 1977, December 1979, and December 1980.[10]

This research showed that after the 1978 amendments took effect the average wages of PSE workers dropped; their jobs became less desirable entry-level or specially created low-level trainee positions; and the work they performed became more distant from the central functions of state and local

---

10. Richard P. Nathan, Robert F. Cook, and V. Lane Rawlins, *Public Service Employment: A Field Evaluation* (Washington, D.C.: The Brookings Institution, 1981).

governments and therefore less valuable to those governments.[11] To local governments, PSE became a much less effective instrument for providing basic public services or securing fiscal relief. Starting in 1979, many state and local jurisdictions began to assign smaller proportions of PSE participants to their own government agencies and subcontracted larger proportions to nonprofit organizations outside of government.

It is not surprising in this setting that, when the PSE program ended in 1981, government officials did not become involved on a widespread basis in public protests against its termination. The field reports provide examples of local actions to decrease PSE employment.

From Jackson, Miss., which was under moderate fiscal pressure, the associate reported, "PSE workers were not utilized in large numbers for two years prior to PSE's termination. The reasons were wage limitations and a reluctance to become dependent on PSE workers."

From Houston (with little fiscal pressure): "Governments had long before become disenchanted with PSE workers, whom they viewed as low-skilled, undependable, and more trouble than they were worth." In Boston (with extreme fiscal pressure): "Officials had long known that the PSE program was doomed and that training cuts were likely."

Cities and states that had retained PSE positions in government departments used them primarily in parks and recreation and maintenance functions. In the words of the New Jersey associate, "Most positions were supplemental and not direct service positions." Because this situation was widespread, most jurisdictions ratified the cuts in PSE by terminating all their PSE workers between March and September 1981, although some (such as Sioux Falls, Phoenix, and Chicago) were able to place PSE employees in unsubsidized jobs.

According to most associates, local officials regarded PSE in its final stage as temporary make-work for the very poor and unskilled, with little potential for helping workers make the transition to unsubsidized jobs. This pattern is not universal, however. For example, the field associate for Newark stated, "Administrators believed that CETA workers were productive and performing needed community services. . . . The program came to a screeching halt. The cutbacks came swiftly and suddenly with no notice and no opportunity to plan."

The St. Louis associate noted mixed feelings on the part of city officials about the 1981 loss of PSE workers: "On the one hand, PSE workers were erratic, with low productivity; on the other, they were 'free,' so any work they performed was a bonus for a financially strapped city."

---

11. *Ibid.*, pp. 118-119.

Of the several kinds of jurisdictions, cities terminated the largest numbers of workers when PSE ended. Los Angeles lost 5,600 PSE workers; Newark laid off 1,500 PSE employees. In Cleveland, 594 PSE workers were terminated. Also in Cleveland, a number of nonprofit organizations that were subcontractors under the PSE program and heavily dependent on these employees went out of existence.

As a general rule, nonprofit organizations were especially hard hit by the elimination of the PSE jobs program. Many community-based groups in such fields as neighborhood development, social services, and the arts had become dependent on this aid, because state and local governments after 1978 had increased the numbers and proportions of PSE workers subcontracted to these organizations.

Though in general the associates reported little organized opposition to the termination of PSE, an exception was reported in Chicago. Neighborhood organizations attacked the budget cuts in the PSE program, the Economic Development Administration, and the Small Business Administration. A statewide coalition of these groups called "I-CARE" (Illinois Coalition Against Reagan Economics) was formed to protest these and other reductions.

Laid-off PSE workers, as noted, were most directly affected by the cutbacks, and in some cases they made their feelings heard. The Phoenix associate reported that there was "substantial bitterness" among individual PSE workers, "particularly those who were being trained in areas of the construction industry, which had come upon hard times by that time." The associate continued:

> City CETA officials, as well as some members of the mayor's reemployment task force, received substantial complaints from an angry group of nonplaced CETA workers. Then, after seeing evidence of their frustrations, they heard little from them again.

PSE-related unemployment was not limited to participants in the program. In several of the sample jurisdictions, the associates pointed out, non-CETA government workers who had administered the PSE program also lost their jobs.

The Employment Service

The U.S. Employment Service is federally funded and administered by state governments. The story of the cut in this program is interesting, because of the depth of the original cut and the fact that it was in substantial measure restored in the face of protests.

It is especially interesting to compare what happened with this program with what happened to PSE. In the case of the Employment Service program, although the amount of money involved was relatively small, protests by state officials, employees, and others resulted in a large restoration. In the case of the PSE program, where the constituency consisted primarily of poor workers and nonprofit organizations, relatively little protest and no restoration occurred.

President Carter's proposed budget for fiscal year 1982 recommended an employment level of 30,000 employees for the Employment Service. Reagan's revised budget of February 1981 reduced the budget authority from $879 million to $729 million, and the number of employees from 30,000 to 24,814. The continuing resolution passed in December 1981 made a further cut to $524.5 million, with a staff level of 17,900, which would have been a little more than half of what Carter had recommended. When Congress reconvened in February 1982, it restored $210.5 million and 6,914 positions to the Employment Service in a supplemental appropriations bill.

Most of the sampled state governments had to lay off significant numbers of Employment Service workers as a result of the initial federal cuts. In Illinois, 500 Employment Service workers were laid off. New Jersey dropped 364 people, but managed to keep all of its branch offices open. Mississippi closed sixteen local offices and eliminated 422 employees. New York State planned to lay off about 650 out of 4,000 employees. Florida closed sixteen local Employment Service branches, laying off 317 employees, and Missouri reduced its Employment Service staffing by more than 25 percent (127 workers) when it closed twelve branch offices.

Some states reacted strongly and vocally to these cuts. In New York, for example, the associate wrote: "The commissioner of the state Department of Labor is contemplating legal action, since federal law mandates job placement services by the states." New Jersey Employment Service workers demonstrated at the capitol in January to protest the cuts; however, the state's primary response to the funding cut was to ratify the layoffs and raise productivity standards. The Houston associate reported that labor, minority, and state employee groups held large public protests and threatened litigation.

Congress restored Employment Service positions after the observation period covered in this report, so the field associates did not report extensively on the effects of the restoration. However, some effects of the restoration are reported in the field data. For example, the Texas Employment Commission reopened most of the fifty-nine local offices that had been closed, and the state rehired most of the 900 laid-off workers after Congress restored the funds.

Medicaid

Even before President Reagan took office and began his budget-cutting program, many states had been seeking ways to reduce the costs of the fast-growing medicaid program, now the largest of all federal grants-in-aid to state governments. Costs of the program are shared between the federal and state (and some local) governments. The federal government's share averages 56 percent of total costs, though it varies from state to state depending on the state's per-capita income relative to the national average.

The reconciliation act affected medicaid costs in several ways. First, tightened eligibility rules for the AFDC program reduced the number of people who are "categorically" eligible for medicaid. Second, states were allowed to offer smaller and less generous programs for the "medically needy"—that is, persons whose earnings are just above the cutoff for AFDC or supplemental security income (SSI). Third, states were given the authority to exclude high-cost providers from the program. Many such hospitals and clinics had been eligible under "freedom of choice" regulations, but new provisions allow states to limit medicaid recipients' use of these facilities. The restrictions also allow states to limit the use of facilities that provide services that are of poor quality or are medically unnecessary. Fourth, states were allowed to reduce reimbursement rates by paying on the basis of "reasonable charges" rather than providers' costs. States were also allowed to purchase supplies on the basis of competitive bidding.

In addition to these actual and potential savings to both state and federal governments, the federal government saved money by simply lowering the percentage of a state's expenses that it will reimburse. This reduction amounts to one, two, or three percentage points depending on the state's unemployment rate, the stringency of cost control measures enacted by the state, and the success rate of the state's quality control system.

Several states have offset some of the effects of the reduction in the percentage of federal reimbursement. South Dakota used savings from the AFDC program to replace medicaid funds lost as a result of the changes in the cost-sharing formula. By contrast, some fiscally stressed states such as Washington, Ohio, and California moved swiftly to take advantage of the new ways to cut medicaid costs. Because California faced a $61 million reduction in federal medicaid reimbursement, the state froze the rate of increase in payment rates for providers, reduced the scope of benefits, and reduced some provider reimbursement rates. Other state responses to these changes will take some time to appear.

A consistent theme in the field reports is the significant impact of the cuts in AFDC on medicaid eligibility. For example, 27,500 people lost medicaid eligibility in Mississippi as a result of changes in AFDC, as did 26,000 people in Massachusetts.

The number of eligible people will also be reduced if states use their new flexibility to eliminate all services for certain groups of the medically needy, although none of the thirty-four states that have a medically needy program was reported to have made sweeping changes in the first quarter of fiscal 1982.

Though states have not yet eliminated the free or low-cost optional services for the medically needy, some may reduce the extent of such services. Most states have not yet done so, but fiscally stressed Washington State has more than doubled copayments—from two dollars to five dollars—for emergency room and certain outpatient visits for the medically needy. Ohio, also fiscally stressed, has moved to impose copayments for certain optional medicaid services.

Recipients may also be affected if states limit patients' freedom to choose providers, as permitted by the medicaid revisions enacted in 1981. Although several states have expressed interest in taking advantage of this provision, none had moved to do so in the first quarter of 1982.

Some states are moving to limit reimbursement payments to health care providers instead of, or in addition to, reducing benefits to recipients. For example, Washington State has declared its intention to limit the growth rate of provider reimbursements in the future, and California has set a ceiling on inflation increases for providers. In Ohio, nursing home reimbursement rates have been reduced, for an expected saving of $2 million. In New York, indications are that the hospital rate-setting process will become increasingly acrimonious. Gov. Hugh Carey's 1982-83 budget indicates a $70 million shortfall in medicaid "if legislation passing the impact of federal budgetary reductions on to providers is not approved." Although action against providers is not widespread yet, the early signs are that a number of states will use the new authority to limit reimbursements.

Block Grants

Block grants became a major issue of domestic policy during the Nixon administration. President Nixon proposed them as a way to simplify categorical grant programs for specific purposes and to place more responsibility for deciding how to use aid money in the hands of state and local government officials. To help secure broad support for the proposed new block grants—which included programs for community development, social services, and employment and training—the Nixon administration agreed to "sweeten the pot" by increasing funding levels and by channeling the bulk of block grant funds to local rather than state governments.

In 1981, the Reagan administration proposed consolidating eighty-five existing programs into seven new block grant programs. As was the case with Nixon administration proposals, the main purpose of these proposals was to shift the responsibility for making many decisions from the federal government to lower levels of government.

The Reagan proposals, however, differed radically from earlier block grants in several ways. First, all money was to be allocated to states, none directly to local governments. Second, states were to have broad discretion over the use of these funds; federal requirements were to be all but abolished. Third, funding for the block grants was to be, on average, about 25 percent less than the total of the existing programs that were to be replaced with the block grant programs.

Congress gave President Reagan only part of what he asked for. The reconciliation act passed in 1981 created nine "block grants" that affected fifty-four existing programs with total budget authority for fiscal year 1982 of $7.2 billion (see table 3.2). Besides the lower dollar amounts, the result was more modest than Reagan's proposal in other ways: Four of the "block grants" contained only one previously "categorical" program. Two programs approved by Congress were already block grants—social services (formerly title XX of the Social Security Act) and community development. These two programs were simply modified versions of earlier block grants.

The reconciliation act required states to accept funding under three of the nine programs. States had to take over administration of the social services and low-income energy assistance grants by October 1, 1981, and the elementary and secondary education grant by October 1, 1982. States had the choice of whether or not to accept the other six block grants. If a state declined to accept responsibility for any of the six, the federal government would continue to provide funds under the old categorical programs.

In the first quarter of fiscal year 1982, twelve of the fourteen states in sample for this study accepted or announced their intention to accept seven or more of the nine block grants. Of the other two states, Florida was undecided about three of the grants, and New York delayed a decision on five. Outright rejections were few: Three states were not planning to accept the primary health care block grant, two the small cities community development grant, and one the community services grant.

State Decisions on Accepting Block Grants

In almost all states, the governor took the lead in deciding whether to accept the new block grants. State legislators were largely on the sidelines. In Mississippi, for example, the associate reported that Gov. William Winter took the lead in the block grant planning process from the beginning.

> Because of the swift action by the governor in taking the initiative, the legislature has not been involved in the block grant process, although the legislators have been apprised of the process and its progress.

Similarly, in Arizona the associate reported:

TABLE 3.2
New or Changed Block Grants in the 1981 Reconciliation Act

Grant	Number of programs consolidated	Final FY 1982 budget authority (millions of dollars)
Social services	3	2,400
Home energy assistance	1	1,875
Small-city community development	1	1,037
Elementary and secondary education	29	470
Alcohol, drug abuse, and mental health	3	432
Maternal and child health	7	348
Community services	1	348
Primary health care	1	248
Preventive health and health services	8	82
Total for nine block grants	54	7,240

Source: Based on data from National Governors' Association and other sources.

Gov. Bruce Babbitt took the initiative to accept the block grants and to direct the process for determining the regulations, allocations, policies, and so forth; in doing so, he co-opted legislative action.

In several states, however, legislators are seeking a greater role in future decisions related to block grants, especially decisions related to allocating the funds. In Massachusetts, for example, the legislature passed a law requiring block grant funds to go through the appropriations process for state fiscal year 1983. The Illinois legislature set up a joint committee to hold hearings on the block grants. The committee drafted a bill calling for the legislature to play an active role in allocating block grant funds; although Gov. James R. Thompson opposed the idea, the legislature seems likely to increase its influence. Similar trends can be seen in some of the other states, including Missouri and Florida.

For some block grants, a major reason for accepting the grant was the prospect of a financial windfall. Such a windfall occurred in some cases because the state fiscal year or operating cycle for one of the "folded-in" categorical grants overlapped the federal fiscal year. As a result, agencies were able to draw upon grant funds allocated in federal fiscal year 1981 while simultaneously benefiting from the fiscal 1982 block grants. The capsule below illustrates this point.

Double-Funding in South Dakota

In South Dakota, the previous-year funding level for the programs consolidated into the alcohol, drug abuse, and mental health block grant was $4.0 million. The estimated funding level for these programs under the new block grant is $2.7 million. Nonetheless, the immediate effects from this large reduction have been inconsequential. The alcohol and drug abuse agencies had previously contracted with the federal government to provide services from May 1981 through April 1982. For the first seven months of federal fiscal year 1982 (that is, October 1981 through April 1982), the state was able to receive both these previously committed funds and new funding under the alcohol, drug abuse, and mental health block grant. Accordingly, the effects of reduced funding levels under the block grant have been temporarily delayed.

Decisions on Allocating Funds

An important question related to the allocation of block grant funds is whether states will reverse the previous federal policy of "targeting" funds to the neediest jurisdictions—usually large, distressed cities—and instead "spread" money more evenly among all jurisdictions.

Evidence from decisions made in the first three months of federal fiscal year 1982 is inconclusive on this issue. In this early stage of implementing the newly enacted block grants, most states simply followed the allocation patterns for the previous grants. (For some block grants, the reconciliation act required states to continue funding for existing agencies or programs.)

"Status quo" was the term several field associates used to describe allocational patterns in this initial period. The Ohio associate reported as follows:

> In general, even where state discretion was permitted, the state has taken a passive, status quo attitude with respect to the allocation of the block grants. Reductions in funding have been distributed across places and services on a pro-rata basis.

Despite this "status quo" response so far, several associates reported developments that may foreshadow future conflict. Of the new block grants, the elementary and secondary education block grant is likely to lead to the most controversy over allocations. This block grant consolidated twenty-nine relatively small programs that had total budget authority in fiscal 1981 of $561 million. Many of these categorical programs were targeted to distressed large cities and urban counties. Among them were programs to support "magnet schools" and other efforts to encourage or accommodate to school desegregation; the follow-through program, designed to provide compensatory educational opportunities for children from poor families; and the teacher corps program, designed to develop skills needed to teach inner-city students.

If the allocation formula for the education block grant spreads money evenly around all school districts, school systems in large cities will lose substantial amounts. In Mississippi, federal aid money to the Jackson school district is expected to drop from $2 million under the previous categorical grants to an estimated $150,000 under the block grant.

Even more importantly, the choice of an allocation formula for the education block grant could set a precedent for the distribution of basic school aid, usually called "foundation aid." Because of this possibility, heated debates are likely to occur on the formula for education block grant funds. Associates in Ohio and New York reported that urban officials fear the block grant formulas will be too generous to suburban and rural districts. The New York State associate noted, "The allocation of state school aid among districts was already one of the hottest political issues facing policy makers. The new federal law provides fuel for the coming debate."

A tendency to spread federal grant money has been reported for other block grants. In Washington State, the agency administering the community services block grant has decided to eliminate the "urban bias" of the previous categorical programs, many of which stem from the "war on poverty" of the 1960s; the aim now is for a "more equitable" geographic distribution of funds. In Massachusetts, the associate reported that Boston has already lost an estimated $1 million from the community services block grant as the state has spread funds more broadly. Moreover, local governments are fearful because they will be competing for block grant funds not only against each other but also against state operating agencies.

The reconciliation act changed the community development block grant (CDBG) by allowing the states to administer the small cities nonentitlement portion of the grant. This is a substantial shift, which may turn out to be one of the most important aspects of the 1981 block grant legislation. Under the small cities portion of CDBG, states can decide which communities receive funds and what factors are to be used in the allocation of these grants. Prior to the reconciliation act, the U.S. Department of Housing and Urban Development was responsible for making these small cities grants; it placed relatively great weight on such activities as housing rehabilitation, and particularly on the amount of benefits provided to low-income persons.

There is already some indication that the states that have accepted administration of the small cities CDBG grant will "spread" benefits to a greater number of communities than had previously received grants under HUD administration. In Ohio, for example, where the state chose to change the allocation process from a competitive one to an entitlement-based process, about 220 communities will receive aid, compared with 39 communities prior to the change. While spreading might be one effect of the conversion of the small cities grant to state administration, however, several jurisdictions appear to be retaining the federal government's emphasis on benefiting low-income individuals.

In Arizona, it was noted:

> The state is stressing "low and moderate" income objectives and is requiring local jurisdictions to demonstrate that 60 percent of the funds expended will benefit low- and moderate-income households.

In New Jersey, state officials are planning a review of the entire HUD selection process, and are likely to pay even greater attention than HUD to need as a factor in distributing small cities funds.

A few associates noted that their states will attempt to rectify what the states see as HUD's bias in favor of housing rehabilitation at the expense of economic development projects. Officials in Illinois and Massachusetts have plans to encourage localities to pursue goals other than housing revitalization. The Arizona associate noted that despite safeguards to continue to focus CDBG funds on low-income individuals, there will be greater and greater pressure to use funds for infrastructure needs such as streets and sewers because of the fiscal pressures on local governments.

The Illinois associate commented on the change in roles involved in the conversion to state administration of the small cities CDBG grant:

> There is some awkwardness within the agency at making the transition from broker and advocate for small communities with HUD, which previously made the final grant awards, to serving as both helper and arbiter of final grant decisions.

Block grants have provoked jurisdictional disputes and organizational changes in several states. Traditional rivalries among mental health, alcoholism, and drug abuse treatment agencies have come to the surface in disputes over the issue of who would be in charge of administering the block grant that combines the programs in these areas. The primary health care block grant has also caused contention. In Mississippi, uncertainty over who would administer this program has contributed to the state's reluctance to accept the grant.

Effects on Nonprofit Organizations

Nonprofit organizations, as a group, were in many cases adversely affected by the new block grants. The cuts in funding for these groups under the block grants is compounded by the loss of CETA jobs, already discussed.

For a few jurisdictions, associates said that private and philanthropic groups played a role during the initial stages of the Reagan domestic program. The Houston associate said:

Much of the pain initially suffered by individuals and agencies is being soothed by the private sector, composed of the United Way, various foundations, wealthy individuals, and churches. The local United Way agency experienced the greatest rate of growth of any United Way agency in its 1981 drive. At least in the short term, privatism and volunteerism appear to be Houston's way of responding to social service cutbacks—right in line with the Reagan philosophy.

In Tulsa, the local United Way added $300,000 in its annual fund drive for the specific purpose of aiding local social service agencies hard hit by federal aid cuts. Similarly, the United Way of Rochester departed from its normal budget practices to establish a special reserve fund of $200,000 "to be used to aid agency programs that risk losing government funding." Several associates also noted that nonprofit organizations have joined coalitions during the initial period of the Reagan domestic program to trace the flow of federal funds and to plan responses to the cuts.

Community action agencies dependent on the community services block grant will undoubtedly bear the brunt of the reductions in funding in this grant. In Missouri, it was observed:

A major casualty of the changeover to block grants has been the community service agencies, formerly community action programs of the Office of Economic Opportunity. The Human Development Corporation in St. Louis encountered a two-month funding gap. With creditors demanding payment, the agency terminated 180 full-time employees, leaving only a skeleton operation.

The associates in Tulsa and Orlando noted a shift in government support away from general advocacy organizations. In Florida, Orange County plans to shift services to emphasize client counseling and day care as opposed to general advocacy. Many issues in this area are as yet unresolved. In Ohio, the developing issue in regard to nonprofit organizations is not the character of the services they provide, but whether the state will continue to operate through community action agencies or instead will shift federal aid for community services to county welfare departments.

Summary of Block Grants

Even though most of the new block grants brought with them an average reduction in funding of 25 percent from the level of previous categorical grants, state and local governments had not yet felt much fiscal impact during the first three months of federal fiscal year 1982. Fiscal "windfalls" described earlier are part of the reason. Some states have been able to carry over unused balances from previous years. As a result, these governments have not yet experienced pressure to introduce greater efficiency in the programs supported by the new block grants, which is one of the benefits the Reagan administration claimed for the budget cuts that accompanied these block grants. Several associates reported plans to consolidate some services, and in some cases plans to eliminate duplication, but further observations will be needed to assess gains in efficiency as a result of the new block grants.

These block grants, more than any of the changes in federal domestic programs made in 1981, forced states to make decisions under the pressure of deadlines. These actions drew a great deal of attention to the block grant programs, though the actual effects on the activities of state governments have so far been limited. As the field associate from South Dakota noted, "The political hoopla over the block grants has diverted the attention of the legislature from the greater and potentially more significant reductions in the entitlement programs."

Capital Programs

Federal aid for capital programs assists state and local governments in funding mass transit, sewer, airport, housing, highway, and other construction projects. The major effect of the reconciliation act on these programs is to reduce federal contributions to future capital construction. The cuts do not affect current capital outlays, which depend upon past federal appropriations. For example, the reconciliation act and the congressional appropriations process reduced fiscal year 1982 budget authority for mass transit and assisted housing grants by 31 and 43 percent respectively, yet outlays for these activities were cut by only 7 and 2 percent respectively.

A number of associates confirmed that capital projects in process were unaffected by the fiscal year 1982 changes. In Newark, for example, "The Newark Economic Development Corporation is currently kept busy with projects which are already in the pipeline." In Tulsa, "Two new assisted housing units are already in the local pipeline, and no immediate effects are anticipated." Likewise, in New York State, "a large number of wastewater treatment projects are underway, and these federal funds continue to be paid to municipalities. Ten years from the planning phase to completion of such a project is common. About $1.5 billion has been allocated but not spent." In Chicago, "The impacts of the cuts on the city will be delayed because of a lag in highway expenditures obligated in previous years."

Public officials interviewed by the field associates confirmed our expectation that the heaviest impact of the cuts in capital programs would fall on future construction. The associates, however, noted widespread concern about future capital improvements.

In Orlando, according to the associates, the city's housing authority "is in the process of spending $13 million in new construction. The director expects that this will be the last new construction for many years." A similar concern was expressed by officials of the Orlando airport authority:

Federal cuts are not expected to significantly affect the airport because no major expansion is expected until 1988 or 1990. However, the authority did express considerable concern about being able to plan for the future.

Aware of the future impacts of these federal cuts, some state and local governments considered or took steps to adjust to them. The field reports noted several instances of changes that may emerge due to federal cuts in capital programs. In New York, "The state may well assume a greater role in assisting the state's various mass transit agencies to compensate for the federal cutbacks."

Some state and local governments were already starting to seek alternative funding sources to replace federal cuts. Special tax assessments and bond issues provide possible sources. In Sioux Falls:

The city will have to seek new funding sources or raise taxes to meet the consequences of the Reagan domestic program and will probably increase the use of bonds for street and neighborhood improvements.

In New York State:

A creative response being contemplated in view of highway funding cutbacks would permit the state to issue bonds in anticipation of federal highway construction funds to maintain the pace of construction.

Some jurisdictions are relying on user fees in anticipation of the federal aid reductions. In Orlando:

Sewer connection fees have increased from $400 to $1,000 and surely will be raised to $1,500 to meet future capital needs that will not be met by federal funding. Monthly water charges will probably be increased as will other user fees.

In Cleveland, "Federal capital cuts in airport funds of approximately $1.5 million per year are being made up by airlines through contractual fees." Arizona is considering replacing federal cuts in highway construction by raising the state tax on gasoline. These and other longer-term responses to federal cuts will be examined in the future.

One area in which some changes in capital spending may soon occur as a result of federal action involves the CDBG program. Local governments in past years have used CDBG funds to support a variety of both capital and public service activities. Under the reconciliation act, local governments are now required to use 90 percent of their CDBG funds for capital purposes and no more than 10 percent for social services. This requirement had not yet been implemented by HUD in the period of these initial field observations; hence, several jurisdictions have so far delayed required cuts in social programs. In Chicago:

The 10 percent limit on public services could be troublesome. The city currently budgets about 23 percent for public services, over half of which goes to the Department of Human Services. . . . It is unclear to the city what HUD will require with respect to getting down to the 10 percent limit.

In Cleveland:

The amount of CDBG funds allocated to social services has been maintained to offset expected losses in other social service programs and to maintain political harmony.

A number of associates reported increased use of CDBG funds to replace cuts in capital funding allocations by the federal government. In Rochester, the city is considering combining CDBG and urban development action grant (UDAG) funds to maintain neighborhood improvement projects threatened by federal reductions in housing rehabilitation funds. St. Louis has started using CDBG money to offset part of the cuts in its allocation of section 8 housing.

Associates in several growing jurisdictions predicted that the use of CDBG money for capital programs may redirect funds away from social service activities and economic development projects benefiting lower-income neighborhoods. In Arizona, despite state efforts to set targeting regulations for the small cities portion of CDBG, "concerns remain regarding use of funds for general infrastructure needs (streets and sewers) and less attention to needs of low-income citizens." In Tulsa, city officials have already limited the use of CDBG funds for social services. The agency responsible for administering CDBG money in Tulsa—the City Development Department—has reduced its role in social programs.

> The current climate ratified in the Reagan proposal has long been dominant in Tulsa and has resulted in reduced funding for social service agencies, enabling the City Development Department to devote more attention to physical development projects.

In Florida:

> Though city officials indicated a commitment to use CDBG funds for poor and minority areas, there is concern that without federal or state mandates these funds will come under greater pressure to be used in other areas.

CONCLUDING COMMENTS

The findings and program analyses presented in this report are from a very early stage in the research. It takes time for the effects of major changes in policy to materialize. For example, there was a decided delay—about two years—before important effects were manifest from California's tax-cutting initiative in 1978, Proposition 13. Firm and final conclusions about the effects of the Reagan domestic program cannot be based on the initial observations presented in this report.

In the next stage of this research, we plan to give substantially more attention to the institutional effects of the Reagan program, which are discussed in a limited way in this report, mostly in reference to block grants. In addition, we will, as noted above, have detailed information for the full year on the federal policy changes that have had a major effect in all fifty-four state and local jurisdictions in the sample for this study. These data will permit us to combine both quantitative and descriptive information for all of the sample units and to compare the effects of the fiscal year 1982 domestic policy changes on different classes of jurisdictions, with the sample units grouped by such measures as type, size, and fiscal condition. These two efforts are critical parts of the research plan.

As in previous field network evaluation studies, we have taken the position in preparing this report that it is our task to identify and analyze the effects of national policy changes, not to judge. What one thinks of the dramatic fiscal year 1982 changes in federal domestic policies is a function of the values that the individual brings to the subject matter.

Appendix A
Field Associates

Arizona and Phoenix

John S. Hall
Associate Professor of Public Affairs
Director, Center for Public Affairs
Arizona State University

Joseph Cayer
Associate Professor of Public Affairs
Arizona State University

Richard A. Eribes
Associate Professor of Public Affairs
Arizona State University

California and Los Angeles

John J. Kirlin
Professor of Public Administration
Sacramento Public Affairs Center
University of Southern California

Cristy A. Jensen
Associate Director for Academic Affairs
Sacramento Public Affairs Center
University of Southern California

Catherine H. Lovell
Professor of Administration
University of California at Riverside

Dale Rogers Marshall
Professor of Political Science

University of California at Davis

Ruth Ross
Assistant Professor
Center for Public Policy and Administration
California State University, Long Beach

Florida and Orlando

John M. DeGrove
Professor of Political Science
Director, Joint Center for Environmental and Urban Problems
Florida Atlantic University

Nancy E. Stroud
Senior Research Associate
Joint Center for Environmental and Urban Problems
Florida Atlantic University

Robert Bradley
Chief Analyst
Florida Advisory Council on Intergovernmental Relations

Karen Fausone
Analyst
Florida Advisory Council on Intergovernmental Relations

Edward Montanaro
Executive Director
Florida Advisory Council on Intergovernmental Relations

Illinois and Chicago

Charles J. Orlebeke
Professor of Urban Planning and Policy
University of Illinois at Chicago Circle

John N. Collins
Associate Professor of Public Administration
Director, Center for Policy Studies and Program Evaluation
Sangamon State University

Massachusetts and Boston

Frederick Doolittle
Associate Professor
John F. Kennedy School of Government
Harvard University

Neil Gordon
Cambridge, Massachusetts

Kathryn Haslanger
Boston, Massachusetts

Eve Sternberg
Cambridge, Massachusetts
Mississippi and Jackson
Lewis H. Smith
Professor of Economics
Director, Center for Manpower Studies
University of Mississippi
Stanley Herren
Associate Professor of Economics
University of Mississippi
Missouri and St. Louis
George D. Wendel
Professor of Political Science
Director, Center for Urban Programs
St. Louis University
George Otte
Assistant Professor of Urban Studies
St. Louis University
E. Allan Tomey
Instructor of Urban Economics
St. Louis University
New Jersey and Newark
Richard W. Roper
Director
Program for New Jersey Affairs
Princeton University
Nancy Beer
Senior Research Assistant
Program for New Jersey Affairs
Princeton University
Martin Bierbaum
Assistant Professor of Urban Studies
Rutgers University, Newark
New York and Rochester
Sarah F. Liebschutz
Professor of Political Science
State University of New York at Brockport
Irene Lurie
Associate Professor of Public Administration
State University of New York at Albany

Ohio and Cleveland

Charles F. Adams, Jr.
Assistant Professor of Public Administration
Ohio State University

Joseph M. Davis
Associate Executive Director
Federation for Community Planning
Cleveland, Ohio

Patricia Barry
Research Associate
Federation for Community Planning
Cleveland, Ohio

Frederick D. Stocker
Professor of Economics
Ohio State University

Oklahoma and Tulsa

R. Lynn Rittenoure
Associate Professor of Economics
University of Tulsa

Steve B. Steib
Associate Professor of Economics
University of Tulsa

Larkin Warner
Interim Director
Office of Business and Economic Research
Oklahoma State University

South Dakota and Sioux Falls

William O. Farber
Professor Emeritus of Political Science
University of South Dakota

Sue Brown
Sioux Falls, South Dakota

Rich Sagen
Physical and Transportation Planner
Sixth District Council of Local Governments
Rapid City, South Dakota

Texas and Houston

Susan A. MacManus
Associate Professor of Political Science
University of Houston, Central Campus

Robert M. Stein
Assistant Professor of Political Science
Rice University

Vernon H. Savage
Associate Professor of Finance and Economics
Southwest Texas State University

Robert D. Wrinkle
Associate Professor of Political Science
Pan American University

Washington and Seattle

V. Lane Rawlins
Professor and Chairman of Economics Department
Washington State University

Betty Jane Narver
Research Consultant
Institute for Public Policy and Management
University of Washington

Lawrence Wohl
Instructor of Economics
Washington State University

Appendix B
Conference of Field Associates

Following are excerpts from a conference of field associates, held March 15 and 16, 1982. The portion of the conference presented here consists of statements by field associates in four states, summarizing the major effects of the Reagan domestic policy on each state. The comments are based on the initial round of observations, made between October 1 and December 31, 1981.

Following are the members of the panel:

Washington: *V. Lane Rawlins, professor and chairman of the Department of Economics, Washington State University*

New York: *Irene Lurie, associate professor of public administration, State University of New York at Albany*

South Dakota: *William O. Farber, professor emeritus of political science, University of South Dakota*

New Jersey: *Richard W. Roper, director, Program for New Jersey Affairs, Princeton University*

Chair: *Clifford A. Goldman, former treasurer, state of New Jersey*

STATE OF WASHINGTON

Lane Rawlins: One of the difficulties in determining the impact of federal budget cuts in the state of Washington is that we are so plagued by internal fiscal problems and revenue shortages that the reduction in federal funds has become a relatively minor problem. The state's own fiscal problems are so difficult that the federal impact has received relatively little attention. Nevertheless, it is possible to see some definite effects.

357

The first and most direct effect is the employment impact. My best estimate is that five to six hundred people in the state government have been laid off as a result of the federal budget cuts. Most of these people were in health and social services. This estimate does not count the CETA workers, the temporary cuts in the Employment Service, unemployment insurance, or in education. It's really difficult to say what the long-term impact will be in education because the educational year and the fiscal year don't coincide, but education officials expect to have many layoffs.

Second, there seems to have been some increase in efficiency as a result of budget cuts, particularly in health and social services. Because Washington has very strong state agencies, they did most of the planning and implemented a program for handling the federal cuts. Priorities were set and followed quite carefully. If we assume that the agencies know which are the most effective and most important services, we can conclude that the least important are the ones that are being cut. For some services this is clearly the case. However, the reduction process is also partly a trial balloon. When knowledge is less than perfect, they cut things to find out where the pubic reaction will be the greatest, knowing that some services will need to be restored.

There is a process for political feedback at the planning stage. It consists largely of seeking the reaction of state councils that respond not only to the plans for handling federal cuts but also to state revenue shortfall. I think this process has been incomplete and that the full public response has not yet been heard. They haven't really touched bases with all of the interest groups. I expect that by summer we will see a lot more political reaction.

The clients affected largely are the working poor and those who are served by preventive programs, especially those for prevention of alcohol and drug abuse. Also, only those who have acute needs are now eligible for mental health services. Services for the aged and for children (particularly adoption services) have sustained very visible cuts. Again, it is too early to say what the political response is going to be.

In education, Washington has adopted the strategy of retaining all the basic education services and cutting out some of the frills. "Frills" often include special programs for the learning impaired or for gifted children.

One of the most interesting developments is the initiation of many user fees and new licenses to try to cover some of the cost of services by charging clients for them. Often this requires state legislation, changes in administrative codes, and even changes in federal regulations. The progress toward implementing these changes has been quite rapid. Fees have been imposed on a wide range of state services that were previously free, ranging from the Xeroxing costs for state records to the cost of staying in hospitals or mental treatment facilities.

The eligiblity requirements have also been tightened for many programs. You can no longer get services just because you're aged or just because you're handicapped or just because you're a child; you also need to meet income criteria to get the services.

Finally, there have been some effects in transportation, particularly on planning for capital expenditures in the future. There is a great deal of uncertainty. Some plans are being stopped, and regardless of what happens to the actual budget, this will affect construction and repair five or six years down the road.

NEW YORK STATE

Irene Lurie: In New York State the programs that seem to be affected most strongly are those where the federal government makes payments either directly to people or directly to a local jurisdiction. So, for example, CETA was cut drastically; significant cuts were made in trade adjustment assistance, which is a federal program administered by the state, and food stamps were cut significantly. Cuts in the Employment Service were also very large.

When the federal government makes payments to the state and the state then uses these funds to support its own programs, we saw effects that were significantly smaller. We were, in general, quite surprised that the magnitudes of the effects were as small as they are. So we began looking around for reasons to explain why the cuts were not as devastating as we had thought they would be.

One reason is that some funds were already in the pipeline and continue even though current appropriations are cut. Examples of this are wastewater treatment plant grants, highway trust funds, and section 8 housing.

Another reason for the relatively small impacts in the state was that New York State only assumed three block grants, unlike many other states. Two, of course, were assumed because they were required. The one that was assumed voluntarily was the alchohol, drug abuse, and mental health block. In that case New York accepted it because it actually provided a benefit to the state. Some of the funds under the categorical programs continued into the new fiscal year at the same time that the block began, so that there was a doubling up of the cash flow in that block.

Another factor was that the commissioners and others actively tried to temper the effect of the cuts, to cushion the effects. For example, money from the low-income energy block grant was transferred to the social services block grant, and that helped in the social services programs.

Another very important factor is that New York State did not alter its public assistance laws until the fall and the changes in AFDC didn't become effective until January 1, so that there were no reductions at all in the AFDC program during the first quarter of the federal fiscal year.

Also, in the medicaid program, New York benefited from a reduction in its personal income relative to the rest of the states, and that in turn increased the matching share for medicaid funding. That tended to compensate for any reduction, so New York up until this point has not done anything to reduce medicaid eligibility.

The one area of social services that does seem to have been affected is day care, under title XX and under the work incentive (WIN) program.

To summarize, we were surprised that the cuts were not as big as we thought they would be. They did seem to be focused in the areas where the federal government could directly get its hands on the programs; where it had to go through the state government, the effects seemed to be more muted.

SOUTH DAKOTA

William Farber: South Dakota is one of the more conservative states in the union, with over two-thirds of both houses of the legislature Republican. What has happened nationally has only confirmed South Dakotan conventional wisdom that government is too big, too costly, and too inefficient. A cardinal conservative principle is to avoid tax increases. The South Dakota legislature has already met and adjourned and silently approved the Reagan approach in general. There were no tax increases and total appropriations were decreased.

One of the things that perhaps has not been sufficiently considered in our studies so far is the extent to which a state has not taken advantage of federal programs. Since South Dakota has made use of some federal programs only minimally, the cuts will be relatively less significant. This is true, for instance, under supplemental security income, where we have not matched beyond what the minimum is for the federal program, and so at least for the present not much impact is expected. In the case of the school lunch program, 65 percent of the students that are entitled to subsidized lunches in South Dakota pay something for them.

I was interested in how similar we are in some ways to New York. The major impact of the Reagan program is on the direct payments and not in terms of what has gone to state government. Thus, South Dakotans are far more dependent upon what happens in the agricultural support programs in general then we are in other types of cuts. The Farmers Home Administration disaster aid program in South Dakota, for instance, is being cut from $225 million a year in 1978 to $40 million in 1982, and this is of much greater concern than programs administered through the state government.

As now projected for fiscal 1983, $300 million of a $700 million total state budget is federal money. For fiscal year 1983, the state anticipates about a $31 million cut in the amount of the federal funds from 1982. The greatest cut is in transportation. But because of the nature of highway planning and the way construction money is spent, there will be no impact this year and probably not much next. The cuts, if continued, will have a great deal of effect on future highway construction, and this will be very serious in a rural state like South Dakota.

The second greatest impact as now contemplated will be in the Department of Labor. The cuts in the Employment Service are severe and some have already taken place. I believe Congress may have already restored some funds, but some sixty job eliminations in the Employment Service have been announced.

The third largest reduction was in health, in the alcohol, drug abuse, and mental health aras. There was a considerable amount of concern about these particular programs. It appears that an attempt will be made to have some some cuts restored at the local level.

The wastewater treatment cut is also considered to be very serious, with a drop to less than half of the amount that had been received previously.

A local problem of considerable significance is impact aid to schools. Federal impact aid is classified in two types: (1) aid for school districts where the federal workers both live and work on federal installations or Indian reservations, and (2) aid for districts where federal employees work *or* live. The second type was cut more drastically, which will result in the closing of some schools. The state's senators and congressmen have been alerted and apparently have been successful in getting some funds restored.

Finally, there is the special problem in connection with Indian reservations. The initial cuts were to be very substantial, particularly in the labor surplus areas, but it appears these cuts will be reduced.

These, then, are the critical areas for South Dakota. The federal cuts in transportation, labor, and health constitute almost 90 percent of the total of $31 million that would be cut from the state budget this coming year. The total spending for the state will be less than it was this year as a consequence of this federal cut, and there will be no increase in taxes.

NEW JERSEY

Richard Roper: I'm going to tell you briefly about New Jersey's overall reactions to the Reagan domestic program.

Our conclusion is that the Reagan domestic program's effect on state government was relatively mild. Gov. Brendan Byrne, the former governor of New Jersey (recently replaced by Thomas Kean), in the spring of 1981 estimated that New Jersey would lose about $1.2 billion of federal financial assistance during 1982. In January 1982 that figure was revised downward to about $917 million. Of that amount, only about $110 million is money that would normally go to the state, that is, would be handled at the state level by the state legislature and the governor's office. The remainder affects local governments and individuals.

New Jersey officials are still unsure as to whether or not all of that is a loss. For example, we talked a bit about the wastewater treatment fund, and it's now unclear whether Congress will restore an additional $85 million, making the actual loss not $90 million in the state but $5 million.

It has already been said that the most dramatic effect in the state has been on entitlements—federal dollars that directly aid individuals. New Jersey's AFDC rolls were reduced by about 9,800 families as of October 1, 1981. An additional 1,900 families were dropped as of February 1, 1982. The milk and nutritional program lost about $30 million. Officials at the Department of Human Services estimate a loss from anticipated food stamp assistance of $60 million. In New Jersey the symbolic effect of the Reagan program has been greater than the actual dollar loss to the state government. New Jersey citizens perceive that a trend has been established at the federal level to cut back on the amount of government spending on a variety of programs. New Jerseyans seem to support this policy shift, as evidenced by the lack of organized public outcry against it.

New Jersey's response at the state government level to these program cutbacks has not been uniform. New Jersey ratified some cuts by simple program elimination. In other instances state money was immediately substituted for federal cuts. In other cases the loss of federal money has served as an argument to increase state spending in the coming state fiscal year. The state also was able to apply "savings" drawn from AFDC to make up for a cut in title XX funds, which resulted in only a slight disruption in service delivery.

Cliff Goldman asked me if I would say something about the difference between the Kean administration, which is currently in office, and the Brendan Byrne administration, which left office in January. The Democratic governor of the state, Brendan Byrne, attempted as much as possible to give the impression that the cuts by the federal government would have severe and lasting repercussions in the state, primarily affecting social welfare services. The governor was able to sustain this view throughout his tenure.

Tom Kean, on the other hand, campaigned with a lot of supply-side rhetoric, i.e. cutting taxes and government spending. However once in office and facing a $400 million shortfall in his fiscal year 1983 budget, he changed his message and his programs. He has spoken out sharply against the Reagan cuts and program, has cut certain taxes but raised others, and supported a 10 percent increase in state spending.

APPENDIX C

Report Form for Evaluation Study

Report Form, Part 1: Baseline

1. THE FISCAL SETTING

The fiscal pressure question is limited to the sample jurisdictions. Please assess the fiscal pressure on this jurisdiction as of September 30, 1981. In making your assessment, you should use the terms and criteria developed for the field evaluation study of the CETA public service employment program:

- *Extreme Fiscal Pressure*. The current level of service has been cut to essential services. (We distinguish between "existing" and "essential" services.) This means that own-source local revenue and anticipated external sources of revenue may be insufficient to meet the demands for even essential services, and there is no apparent and generally used revenue source to increase local own-raised revenue in the relative near term—that is, looking ahead one year.

- *Moderate Fiscal Pressure*. Anticipated own-source local revenue and external sources will be insufficient to support the existing level of services. Therefore, the maintenance of the current level of services in the jurisdiction requires difficult positive action, i.e. use of a new tax source, a significant increase in nominal tax rates, or the reduction of service levels.

- *Little Fiscal Pressure*. Anticipated internal and external revenues (using existing sources with possible small nominal rate increases) are expected to cover anticipated expenditure increases and even meet some, but limited, new service demands.

• *No Fiscal Pressure*. The jurisdiction is experiencing increases in existing surpluses or adopting tax reduction measures. There is no difficulty in meeting expected demands for public services (both essential services and desired existing and new services) with existing internal and external revenue sources and tax rates.

We would like you to consider two kinds of information in reaching your conclusion. The first is financial data for the preceding five years, which would include: end-of-year cash balances and unrestricted fund surpluses; rate of growth of taxes and expenditures; the presence or absence of fund deficits; the use of short-term borrowing; increases or decreases in the tax base; the bond rating or any recent changes in the bond rating; and increases or decreases in nominal tax rates. Please take into account any recent public referenda on bonding or spending. A second kind of information we would like you to consider is assessments by local officials of this jurisdiction's capacity to expand activities or add new programs or services.

2. LOCAL TAX OR EXPENDITURE LIMITATIONS

What is the recent history of budget and/or tax limitation measures in this jurisdiction? Were major fiscal constraints legislated prior to Proposition 13 (June 1978)? Have Proposition 13-type tax or budget limitations been the subject of recent elections? If so, who initiated this action? What was the outcome (percent for and against)? Discuss in general terms existing state and local limitations that have affected spending and programs in this jurisdiction.

3. PUBLIC EMPLOYMENT

Please discuss the condition of public employment in this jurisdiction. Have there been recent layoffs (not counting CETA; see next question), hiring freezes, reductions or decreases in force? If there have been layoffs, freezes, or limitations of force recently, please discuss the reasons for them. Are they the result of federal program reductions (real or anticipated), state and local politics, voter-mandated ceilings, the weakening of economic conditions, management efforts to improve productivity, or some combination of these and other factors? As emphasized in the introduction to this report form, we would like your answer to this question for local jurisdictions in the sample to take into account major overlying governments where important changes in public employment levels and policies have taken place.

4. CETA-PUBLIC SERVICE EMPLOYMENT

Please discuss the way the elimination of CETA-PSE jobs has affected the condition of public employment in this jurisdiction and major overlying governments. How was the elimination of PSE accomplished? What were the major effects on public employment and the provision of public services in this jurisdiction?

5. THE GOVERNMENTAL SETTING

We ask you to write a statement on the main actors in policy and budgetary decision processes and their relationships to each other for the sample jurisdictions and, where appropriate, to refer to overlying local governmental units. We are interested in knowing who are the most influential persons in policy making and finance in relation to federal grants-in-aid. We ask that you subdivide your statement to discuss the following:

a.   *The Executive.*

b.   *The State or Local Legislative Body.*

c.   *Agencies and the Bureaucracy.* We are most interested in agencies that administer federally assisted programs. Which ones are they? How are they organized? Which political actors within the agency and outside of it are especially influential?

d.   *Interest Groups.* Again, what we are interested in is the groups most involved in decisions about federally aided programs.

e.   *Other Groups and Individuals.* This part of the question has two purposes. One is to elicit information about other groups, for example political parties and churches, that do not get treated in sections a-d. The second purpose is to ask you which external actors are especially important in the decision process, especially with respect to federally-aided activities. It is here that we expect you to treat federal agencies and officials and, for localities, state agencies and officials who have been especially important in local decision processes with respect to federal grants.

6. THE BUDGET PROCESS

Next, we ask you to write a statement about the budget process for the sample jurisdiction, where appropriate referring to overlying local jurisdictions. In your statement please indicate:

a.   The fiscal-year period.

b.   Key dates and documents.

c.   How federal aid is treated in the budget process, and who is responsible for allocation of this aid. Does the legislature (council) appropriate federal money or approve federally funded positions? Or are federal funds and federally funded positions kept separate, with federal funds automatically passed through to designated agencies?

d.   How and when revenue estimates are made and revised.

e.   How capital funds and accounts are treated.

f.   We would also appreciate having information about the organization and quality of budget documents.

7. INITIAL RESPONSE TO REAGAN PROGRAM

Section 7 asks you to discuss the way in which the jurisdictions in the study responded to the Reagan program as it unfolded. We would like you to cover:

a.   The point of view of key public officials and interest group representatives. Please discuss their predictions and expectations in the weeks and months immediately after the Reagan budget reduction proposals were announced.

b.   Whether key public officials and interest group representatives were well informed, and the nature of any planning done to prepare for these federal policy changes. How much and what kind of publicity was given to the changes and their likely impacts on local programs?

c.   Preparatory or anticipatory steps taken. (This is likely to be a very important subject in your analysis.)

d.   Also please include any changes made to current-year revenue estimates and projections for future years resulting from provisions of the Economic Recovery Tax Act of 1981.

Please be sure to describe executive or legislative planning committees, new legislation (including tax changes made to offset provisions of the Economic Recovery Tax Act which affect state and local revenues), executive orders related to the Reagan policies, and new political coalitions which developed in response to the Reagan program. State-local relations are of particular interest to us.

8. INITIAL EFFECTS

Section 8 is the most important part of the report form for the preliminary report.

For the first quarter of the federal fiscal year, we ask that you discuss the effects on this jurisdiction of the Reagan domestic program. Of course, we do not expect the information for the February submission to be provided in as much detail as what will be submitted in Part II of the report form at the end of the fiscal year.

We ask that you organize your analysis of the initial effects of the Reagan program to discuss the following functional areas in the following order:

a. Income Security

b. Health

c. Education, Training, and Social Services

d. Community and Regional Development

e. Transportation

f. Energy

g. Other Major Changes

Under each heading, please *number and separately discuss* each of the major federal policy changes that have had what you consider to be an important effect, or are likely to have one, in the jurisdiction(s) you are studying.

We make the assumption that if you do not discuss a program change at the federal level, this change has not had, and is not at the moment expected to have, an important effect in the jurisdiction(s) you are studying.

We want you to include in your analysis federal program changes where federal funds have been cut, but services have not been affected, due to the substitution of state or local funds for federal aid.

If you can at this stage, we would like your narrative to include two other subjects: (1) the population groups in the community most affected by the changes you discuss; and (2) emerging institutional effects that you can flag now and which you plan to consider further in part II of your full first-round report.

9. BLOCK GRANTS

Section 9 asks you to discuss the way block grants have been treated by the jurisdictions in the sample. We would like you to take a *different approach* for state and local jurisdictions as described below.

1. *States:* We ask that you provide information on:

    a. When the state "picked up" the block grants (most have)—and, if not, why not, and whether they expect or plan to do so at a later time.

    b. The nature of the planning process, including the debates (if any) relating to the allocation and use of block grant funds. Who was involved—the legislature, recipient groups, task forces etc?

    c. For each of the block grants, please discuss the approach to be used for:

        * the allocations among programs, places, and recipients;
        * policies for the services provided;
        * administrative structures and systems;
        * the regulatory process;
        * transfers within the blocks; and
        * the way matching requirements are being met.

2. *Localities:* We ask that you write a short statemnt about the actions, attitudes, and perceptions of local officials in relation to the state's handling of block grant funds. Have there been local reactions to state actions on block grants? Your statement should cover (a) attitudes towards state policy, (b) expectations about changes that the states may yet make in the affected programs, and (c) political activity designed to influence the distribution and use of the block grant funds.

10.   EXPECTED LONGER-RANGE EFFECTS

Looking ahead, and based on the information provided in sections 8 and 9, what do you think are likely to be the most important *generalized effects* of the Reagan domestic program—fiscal, programmatic, incidence, and institutional—in fiscal year 1982?

Report Form, Part 2: Changes

Note: In reporting their findings for the full fiscal year 1982, associates complete a "major program change form" (see figure 1) for each change that had important effects in their jurisdictions. Following is the portion of the report form for the full fiscal year that provides instructions on completing the change forms.

INSTRUCTIONS FOR MAJOR PROGRAM CHANGE FORMS

You should prepare a separate program change form for each major program change. As in part 1, you will define what constitutes a major program change. However, we expect that you will include both local and state programs in which there has been a big change in either dollar amount or the percentage of total federal aid received, plus programs in which the dollar change was relatively small, but the local or state impact was great.

We make the assumption that if you do not discuss a program change that has occurred at the federal level, this change has not had, and is not at the moment expected to have, an important effect in the jurisdiction(s) you are studying.

Major program change forms should be completed for the level of government that directly administers a program, as well as for a government that provides substantial financing for it. Thus, you may find it necessary for AFDC to have both a state program change form and a county change form, if the county administers the program. In such instances, it will be helpful for the state associate and the local associate to coordinate their work.

At the state level, a separate program change form should be completed for each block grant. Block grants at the local level will require a program change form if you determine that the impact of the reduction in funding or

Major Program Change Form, FY 1982

Jurisdiction _____   Associate _____

Program Change Number _____   Service Provider _____

Program, & where appropriate, components	FY '82 Change in Federal Aid		Change in Other Revenue	
	dollars	percent	dollars	percent
_____	_____	_____	_____	_____
_____	_____	_____	_____	_____

Fiscal Effects
Pattern: Ratify _____ Compound _____ Replace _____ Augment _____

Employment Effects

Programmatic Effects

Incidence Effects

Institutional Effects

Regulatory & Administrative Changes

change in policy was of major consequence in fiscal year 1982.

Function or Program Areas

We ask that you submit the major program change forms grouped by function or program area, with a cover page for each function or program area. The purpose of the cover page is to have you point out interrelations of the changes made in a broader functional or program area and to discuss any explicit or implicit strategy in this area.

Following are suggested groupings.   You may vary these groupings.

1. Income security
2. Social services
3. Health
4. Education
5. Employment and training
6. Community and economic development
7. Transportation

Our purpose here is to organize our analysis at three levels: major program changes; functional or program areas of logically grouped major program changes; and the overall changes for the sample jurisdiction.

Some program changes will not fit into logical categories, and you should just submit them individually.

The next sections discuss the purpose of each part of the major program change form.

Organization of the Major Program Change Form

The form first provides for basic identifying information about the program change being reported.

Funding Information

The form then asks for the change in funding that has occurred in the program being reported. In some instances, involving major regulatory or administrative changes, there may not be a change in funding. You should also assess whether there has been a change in other funding, either to mitigate federal reductions or to add to them. The two types of reported dollar and percentage changes should combine to give a net change to the program. While the changes for operating and entitlement programs should be estimated on an expenditure basis, unless some other basis seems easier or more appropriate, capital grant changes will have to be on a contract authorization basis.

Because of differences in fiscal years, governmental account practices, and sources of program funding, it will be necessary for you to estimate the change in funding for each program reported. Our purpose is to compare the change in funding in the 1982 federal fiscal year (October 1, 1981 to September 30, 1982) to what would have occurred in the absence of the Reagan domestic program. We want to focus on changes that occurred as a result of changes in the economy. Since the federal fiscal year does not align with most state and local fiscal years, you will have to make the best approximation you can of the magnitude of the effect of the changes in the domestic policy of the federal government in fiscal year 1982. Your estimate will often involve a prorating from two different fiscal years. We know this type of quanitification can be difficult, but we ask that you estimate changes as accurately as possible. In particularly difficult cases, you may want to attach a separate explanation of how you arrived at your estimates or to call us to consult about decision rules. We believe it is important to report dollar changes by program so that the change in program can be related to the jurisdiction's budget.

Fund Changes By Type of Grant

Your estimates of changes and the analysis of effects will be different for different types of grants. Generally speaking, we will probably want to distinguish among operating, capital, and entitlement grants. Within operating grants, the analysis will often vary for formula and project grants. We will also need to take into account the special situation involving newly created (and genuine) block grants.

When several previously separate categorical grant activities have been combined into a block grant, we would like your estimate of the reduction in each of the previous categorical grant areas, after the state allocation of the grant.

Entitlement program dollar changes require that you estimate what amount would have been received but for the changes. In many cases the actual amount received may be higher because of the recession, but you should try to determine how much higher it would have been if there had not been specific actions taken to reduce spending under the entitlement.

Capital grants require you to estimate future reductions in program plans. These reductions will generally not be on an annualized basis, but instead will be on a project or program planning period basis. Just let us know the basis on which you show the reduction if it is not annualized.

For formula and continuing grants, you should be able to estimate changes in amounts from what would have been received but for the changes. However, for intermittent categoricals, such as UDAG, you may have to evaluate whether there was a reasonable expectation of receiving a grant if federal policy had not changed.

Analysis of Effects

The next part of the program change form asks for information about the effect of the change in the "traditional" (for us) categories: fiscal, employment, programmatic, incidence, institutional, and regulatory and administrative.

Under *fiscal effects,* we want to know how the government has responded financially. We use a framework here of four fiscal effect categories. Has the jurisdiction *ratified* the federal cut by reducing total spending accordingly; *replaced* it by increasing its own spending, to maintain total spending; *compounded* it by decreasing its own spending, as well as the federal portion; or *augmented* the program by increasing its spending beyond the previous combined federal and state and local spending? If you check off more than one of these four fiscal effect categories, please indicate in approximate terms (e.g., ten-percentage-point brackets) the proportion you would attribute to each. This point would apply, for example, where part, say half, of a federal budget cut is ratified and half is replaced.

We are also interested in how federal policy changes have affected the overall finances of the government. In many cases the fiscal effects may involve a rearrangement of funds so as to ratify some cuts while using state and local savings to replace other losses. If so, please try to describe the whole series of changes and the strategy—explicit or implicit. This may be done most appropriately on the cover pages for the groupings of change forms as described above.

We also ask in the fiscal effects area, and in the other areas as well, that you point out any differences that you ascertain between the initial effects and what occurs later in the budget process. We are already aware, on the basis of your part 1 reports and our field visits, of cases in which decisions you reported on in question 8 of part 1 have been changed later in the jurisdiction's budget process.

Under *employment effects,* please discuss changes in state and local public employment that result from changes in the Reagan domestic program. Please indiciate if any of the government reductions were offset by nongovernmental hirings (primarily the nonprofit sector), or if governmental hirings were caused by nongovernmental reductions.

Programmatic effects should include changes (or the lack thereof) in the *nature* of the service provided. For example, these may be categorized as follows:

1. No change was made in the program.
2. There were decreases in the quantity or quality of the service.
3. The price of the service was increased, for example, through the use of user fees or sliding scales for service costs.
4. Access to the service was restricted through tightened eligibility rules, etc.
5. The administrative processes or systems were changed in a way that reduced costs, but not the service level.

Incidence effects refers to the effects of the changes in services that occur in terms of who or what groups are most affected by the changes. We especially would like information about the numbers of people affected, and their characteristics. We would like you to classify people by income groups, racial or ethnic characteristics, or geographic area.

Under *institutional effects,* you should provide information on the way the provision of the affected programs and services is organized and which organizations and decisionmakers are responsible for their delivery. For example, a particular change may bring about an expanded role for governments (state and local); the greater involvement of elected officials or of some subset, like legislators; a reduced or increased role for program officials; less involvement of nonprofit organizations and community groups, etc. This section may include, for example, information about changes in the structure and procedures of the organizations that provide services, shifts of clients to different service providers, or changes in the groups that make allocation decisions. We are especially interested here in the ways in which you believe, or it is alleged, that federal policy changes made in fiscal year 1982 have increased or decreased the efficiency or productivity of state and local governments.

Regulatory and administrative should include effects on programs that were caused by either program or procedural changes resulting from federal actions. These can be changes resulting from the reconciliation act, regulations, or administrative action. At the local level, the effect may result from state changes caused by federal action.

RATING OF MAJOR PROGRAM EFFECTS

For each major program change, please rate the overall, fiscal, employment, programmatic, incidence, institutional, and regulatory effects on a scale of one to five as follows:

1. No effect
2. Low effect
3. Moderate effect
4. Strong effect
5. Greatest effect